Clw ☑ S0-EAQ-096

Catching Up

Catching Up

by
Charles
Veley

M. Evans and Company, Inc.   New York, New York 10017

The lines from T. S. Eliot's *The Waste Land* that appear on page 194 are reprinted by permission of Harcourt Brace Jovanovich and Faber and Faber Ltd.

Ezra Pound's poem "In a Station of the Metro," which appears on page 194, is reprinted from *Personae* by Ezra Pound. Copyright 1926 by Ezra Pound. Reprinted by permission of New Directions Publishing Corporation.

The two lines from "The Circus Animals Desertion" and eight lines from "The Second Coming" by William Butler Yeats that appear on page 195 are reprinted from *The Collected Poems of William Butler Yeats* with the permission of Macmillan Publishing Company, Inc., and the Macmillan Company of London and Basingstoke. "The Circus Animals Desertion": copyright 1940 by Georgie Yeats, renewed in 1968 by Bertha Georgie Yeats, Michael Butler Yeats, and Anne Yeats. "The Second Coming": copyright 1924 by Macmillan Publishing Company, Inc., renewed 1952 by Bertha Georgie Yeats.

M. Evans and Company titles are distributed in the United States by the J. B. Lippincott Company, East Washington Square, Philadelphia, Pa. 19105; and in Canada by McClelland & Stewart Ltd., 25 Hollinger Road, Toronto M4B 3G2, Ontario.

LIBRARY OF CONGRESS CATALOGING IN PUBLICATION DATA

Veley, Charles, 1943–
    Catching up.

    Includes index.
    1. Encyclopedias and dictionaries.   I. Title.
AG5.V44   001.3   77-24948
ISBN 0-87131-239-5

Copyright © 1977 by Charles Veley

All rights reserved, including the right to reproduce this book or portions thereof in any form without the written permission of the publisher.

Design by Al Cetta

Manufactured in the United States of America

9 8 7 6 5 4 3 2 1

CONTENTS

[5]

FOREWORD:
ON CATCHING UP

"You see," said Holmes, "I consider that a man's brain originally is like a little empty attic, and you have to stock it with such furniture as you choose. A fool takes in all the lumber of every sort that he comes across, so that the knowledge which might be useful to him gets crowded out. . . ."

If you had money back in Sherlock Holmes's day, you *knew* about the Great Things of our civilization. Your tutor would tell you about music and elocution, and probably French. Your boarding school would drill you in Latin, history, and sometimes Greek. At college, you'd compare the day's theatrical productions with triumphs from Sheridan or Molière, and scorn the day's politicians with barbs from Aristophanes and Juvenal. Then away you'd go for a romp on the Con-

tinent to see the great cathedrals and the fashionable museums and galleries, when you weren't too much otherwise
occupied. Culture was a part of growing up, if you had the
money. If you didn't you read Horatio Alger, and dreamed.

Once you'd been "cultivated," you were ready to take
your place in society. You were one of the Educated. You
knew the names and events and standards that one talked
about. You knew the Right Things, just as you knew the
Right People, and you had a peace of mind in this Rightness
that nowadays in America is found only in one or two political
columnists.

But today, knowing the Right Things is not simple. We
now have such an abundance of culture that it's hard to know
what to make of it all. There are public museums, libraries,
and universities. Traveling repertory companies make theater
more accessible, and better and better films are produced every
year. And of course there's ETV, on 365 nights a year with
something Worthwhile. How can anyone keep track of what's
important? It's no wonder we forget the right names, or how
to pronounce them.

We feel the need to catch up on what's important, but
we don't know where. It would be nice if local colleges had
a course in Today's Essentials. Then we could get the best
of all those courses we had to skip because we were too busy
with math requirements. But colleges, unfortunately, don't
operate that way. In the academic world, there's no such
thing as a General Practitioner. For alternatives, the *Britan-
nica* and the *Great Books* are both too big, and neither will
tell you what you can afford to leave out. Someone could go
to the library for two or three hundred Masterpieces of This
and Mainstreams of That, but would he ever get to the
bottom of the stack? And if he did, would he know what to
remember?

The point is that matters don't have to be this complicated.
There's no need to sift through thousands of pages of reference works, unless one wants to get really immersed in a

subject. For the comparisons and analogies that we all like to make in our everyday talk, a knowledge of a few basic best things in each field, from art to opera to philosophy, will be enough.

Catching Up has been written to provide that knowledge for the reader who's gone too fast, dropped out, or specialized too soon. My aim is to tell him what's best to know, what to say about it, and what not to waste time with. *Catching Up* will tell him what he should know about Atlantis, and why he needn't remember more than a line or two about Giotto or Locke. It will tell him why it's worth knowing about Mozart and why Tennyson is camp. It will also include many of those stories about the classics that make them more memorable.

Catching Up, in short, explains the few essentials in each area that can be most useful to today's civilized mind. It also looks at the phrases and opinions of contemporary critics, along with those classics to which they most frequently refer. But *Catching Up* is brief rather than encyclopedic, in keeping both with the impatient spirit of our times and with the Law of Brevity set down in the last century by the Sage of Baker Street:

. . . depend upon it, there comes a time when for every addition of knowledge you forget something that you knew before. It is of the highest importance, therefore, not to have useless facts elbowing out the useful ones.

—*A Study in Scarlet*

Catching
Up

I

THE ANCIENT WORLD

The One Ancient Idea You Need to Know

The Ancient World goes back from the Fall of Rome (A.D. 476) to the civilizations of Egypt, Greece, India, and China, and even further back than that according to believers in flying saucers and other prehistoric visitations. Naturally there's quite a collection of memorabilia left over from so many centuries of ancient productions.

When it comes to ideas, though, the one most important about the Ancient World is a pattern of mathematical harmony, discovered by the Greeks, that brings Classical Order into the creations of both nature and art. Knowing just this single formula could separate the civilized from the barbarian back then, and today will let you add to practically any discussion of ancient art, architecture, drama, music, or philosophy—in style.

The Golden Mean

There's a bit of geometry and math involved here, so we'll start off slowly, with something basic:

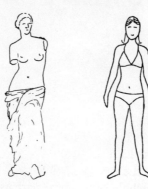

Which body looks more beautiful? If you have classical taste you'll take the Venus on the left, because her body's built in classical proportions—not human proportions, but those that would be appropriate for a goddess.

Question two: what's so goddesslike about her proportions? We'll look at the most obvious first. The Venus on the left has longer legs. As you notice, even though she's the same height as her human counterpart, her navel's quite a bit higher. Venus's lower half, from navel down, is longer (in proportion to the rest of her) than our human model's lower half is (in proportion to the rest of *her*).

Why not a bit longer still, or just a bit shorter? A question of taste, right? Wrong. The Greeks had figured out mathematically just where the best point to divide a line was—and they built their statues of gods and goddesses so that the navel, the central point of human growth, divided the length of the body exactly at that best point.

Here's how EUCLID (300 B.C.) described the formula for finding the best point:

> the proportion most pleasing for a divided line occurs when the ratio of the whole to the large part is equal to the ratio of the large part to the small part.

What Euclid calls the "large part" is the "mean" in the relationship between whole, large part, and small part, since it's in the middle with respect to size: the whole (a + b) is the greatest part; the small part (a) is the least in size; and the "large part" (b) ranks in size between the two.

And this particular "large part" (b) is a *GOLDEN* MEAN, because the whole is proportioned to the mean as the mean is proportioned to the least part.

Let's get back to the question, though. Why was this particular proportion—whole is to large part as large part is to small part—so beautiful? We could say that the Golden Mean, since it's mathematically like the part and like the whole, small and large, at the same time, sets up a kind of dynamic shimmering in our visions that our minds evidently find beautiful. But the Greeks had another explanation, coming out of the Pythagorean religion.

The Pythagoreans, followers of PYTHAGORAS, the first great Greek mathematician (pihTHAGuhruss, ca. 600 B.C.), taught that different numbers signified different things. The number one was unity, a point. Two was a line (two points) which meant female, since a line can be divided as a female divides when giving birth. Three was a male, which can't divide equally. And the union of male and female, 2 + 3, was 5, which therefore stood for the life-force, that power which brings about new life. The Pythagoreans found evidence that Nature agreed with their assessment of the number 5, since five-sided figures are found only in living things, like flowers and starfish—there aren't any five-sided crystals, rocks, snow-flakes, or other nonliving matter.

Now here's where the Golden Mean comes in. To make a five-sided figure, which was obviously a good thing to do, the first step for a Greek geometrician with his straightedge and pair of compasses was to make a square and then bisect it. Putting his compasses on the center of the bottom line and an upper corner, he measured out an extension of the bottom line that turned the bottom of the square into the "large part" of a Golden proportion.

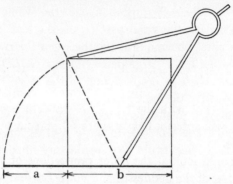

To make the rest of the five-sided figure he did some more work on this new line with his compasses, but we won't worry about that here. Even though pentagons are important (to the U.S. military and to baseball players touching home plate, at least), the Golden Mean is more important.

When the Greeks wanted to talk about this Golden ratio in mathematical terms, they were at a slight disadvantage because they didn't have decimals. When they wanted to write the ratio of the "whole" to the "large part," they said $\dfrac{1 + \sqrt{5}}{2}$ to 1. A few moments with a pocket calculator, however, and we can come up with a numerical equivalent. $\dfrac{1 + \sqrt{5}}{2} = 1.618034$. And 1.618034 is to 1 as 1 is to .618034.

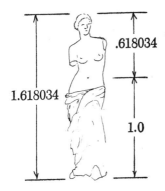

The small part is roughly 62 percent of the large part, and the large part is roughly 62 percent of the whole.

Now let's see a few other uses for this little proportion.

We could start with the PARTHENON, the Greek temple to Athena, which has a height that's 62 percent of the length at the base.

Or we could look at the other proportions of some of the Greek statues of the goddesses and gods. Loaded with Golden proportions. Besides the navel's being 62 percent of the way from feet to head, the width of the throat is 62 percent of the width of the head. The neck begins 62 percent of the way from navel to top. The eyes appear 62 percent of the way up the face. Thighs, at their narrowest, are 62 percent of the thighs at their widest. The ankle is 62 percent of the calf. The wrist 62 percent of the forearm. And so on.

According to the mean's unchanging, inexorable rigidity, Garbo's mouth, at 70 percent of her facial width at the point of her smile, is too big.

PLATO (which see) loved the mean. He used a mean-divided line to represent reality, and diagramed what he called the IDEAL WORLD (which see), the world of eternal constants, to be worth about 62 percent of the whole, leaving our changing visible world worth only 38 percent in proportion. Ideal Beauty, he said, was just one of the standards, or Forms, that existed in the realm of Ideals. He also said, "To join two things in a beautiful manner, the bond is best achieved by proportioning three magnitudes so that the greatest is to the mean as the mean is to the least."

When Plato's student ARISTOTLE (also which see) wrote up his standard of ethics, he called that the Golden Mean. And the ethical wisdom of Buddha, Confucius, and Christ has a familiar ring if we paraphrase their Golden Rule to make it sound like Plato: "As you would have the greatest act unto you, so act you unto the least."

The classic proportion also lurks within the dramatic arts. As every tragedian knows, the point where the hero's fortunes hit the skids (the falling action) comes just after the third act—about 62 percent of the way through the five-act play. And in comedy, after the third act we see forces start to work the hero out of his predicament, on his way to getting the girl in the end.

In music, there are 13 keys in an octave on the piano: 8 white keys and 5 black, making the proportion of major notes to the whole roughly the same as minor to major: 62 percent to 100 percent.

If we play around with the golden proportion a bit, we can even see places where it appears in the beauty of Mother Nature, aside from in starfish and five-petaled flowers.

First we make a classical golden rectangle, the two sides in classical proportions. (If this were the Parthenon, it would be the view from the front.) Then we make a square inside the rectangle, which leaves us with another classically proportioned rectangle left over. We make a square inside that one, and again there's a golden rectangle left over. We make another square, and then another.

And then we connect the centers of the squares with a curved line, forming a golden spiral, in which any line drawn from the center will intersect the spiral at the same angle.

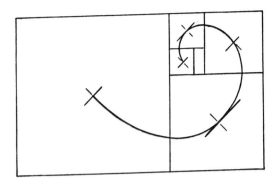

If anyone ever quotes that old Edna St. Vincent Millay poem "Euclid Alone Has Looked on Beauty Bare" at you, just show him these golden rectangles. If you think you can get away with it, tell him you've marked up a canvas by MONDRIAN (which see).

Knowing the golden spiral gives you a number of things to say about ancient art, or about nature, or both.

If someone starts bragging about the statues and paintings he saw on his trip to Pompeii, tell him how they're based on 1.618034, draw him the spiral, and point out that Nature's teeth and claws curl up along the same lines. And so do hoofs, snail shells, and elephants' tusks, not to mention mammoths'.

If someone starts praising the grace of the chambered nautilus, the curl of a wave, or the tail of a comet, you can tell him that it's because they all spiral up in the classic manner.

If he gets onto music, tell him that the inner organ of his ears, the cochlea, curls up in the classic spiral.

If he's a college student and needs a 2.5 out of 4.0 to graduate, tell him what proportion that is (62 percent).

Or suggest a game of cards, and show him the shape of the cards. Or look out the window, and tell him about the shape of the window. Or the panes in the window. The odds are that the proportions will be Golden.

Of course, we don't want to get carried away with the Golden Mean, or with the idea of having any absolute standard at all, these days. EINSTEIN (which see) has happened. Classical standards, requirements, and absolutes are ancient history. This is the age of relativity. Primitive passion has been O.K. since FREUD (also which see). Now is the point in time to go the hangout route and do, like, you know, one's own thing, man.

But you can use the notion of Golden, Classical Order for the times when you're pointing out that Einstein, even though he proved that time is a relative thing that depends on how fast you're going, also said that the speed of light is an unchanging constant. Or when you're noting that Freud wanted to control, as well as to uncover and accept, unconscious passions. The idea of order also comes in whenever you mention artistic form: the rational control for raw emotion in art, from music through film. When you're talking about almost any kind of rational control, for that matter, you can always refer to the Golden Mean, Nature's way of telling us that Order is beautiful.

Still, one can overdo this business of Classical Order. If there's too much reason and regulation, our art and our lives get too cold—a criticism that is often made of classical art, and dictatorships. ROMANTICISM, a little free play and inspiration from the passions (see THE NINETEENTH CENTURY), also fits into a liberated urbane scheme of things. APOLLO, the ancient god of light and reason, gives way to DIONYSUS, the god of wine and revelry (both of which see).

And maybe in our art we should opt for a bit more passion than reason. After all, our drama does come straight from the ancient Dionysian fertility frolics.

But in our everyday lives, as Kenneth Clark once remarked, "Classicism is health, Romanticism, disease."

We'll have to tip the balance the other way.

Somewhere around 62 percent Classical Order sounds about right.

The Ancient Names You Should Know

THE GREAT MYTHS AND HEROES

ATLANTIS

One of the ancient myths has been given a lot of publicity these days: the tale of ATLANTIS, the supercivilization. As PLATO (which see) tells it in two of his dialogues, there once was a continent out beyond the Mediterranean with enormous golden temples, stupendous stone-lined harbors, and men whose morals and intellects, once superb, began to take a turn for the hedonistic. According to the Egyptian priests from whom Plato, via another Greek, got the story, in 9400 B.C. ZEUS punished Atlantis by sinking it into the ocean, leaving only Atlantean colonists in what were then the hinterlands of what later became Egypt and South America, to build pyramids and carry on civilization.

Men have searched for Atlantis underwater ever since, unsuccessfully, but recent mapping of the Atlantic sea floor indicates that the geography of the sunken continent would have existed the way Plato described it, before the last Ice Age thaw caused the ocean waters to rise 150 feet. And recent carbon dating of undersea fossil shells laid down by that 150-foot rise indicates that Plato was very, very close on his timing of the Flood. The shells are dated at 9600 B.C.

Additionally, huge underwater monoliths were discovered in 1968 around Bimini in the Caribbean, apparently fitted together as a wall or road along the Bahama Bank, with some of the stones supported on columns. When fossilized mangrove roots growing over these walls were dated at 10,000 B.C., some thought the search for Atlantis was over. Publicity over the Bermuda Triangle, however, with some theorizing that leftover Atlantean lasers and energy refractors are what makes ships and planes disappear down there, has made the archeological establishment very, very cautious.

THE CREATION

Just about every culture has its own creation myth, but the only ones referred to nowadays come from GENESIS in the Judeo-Christian Bible and from THEOGENY and WORKS AND DAYS, by a Greek named HESIOD (HEEseeud, ca. 700 B.C.). Characters from both stories, especially the Greek, appear in much of our art, dance, music, and literature, and in everyday usage as grist for allusions.

Here is the Greek story in brief, along with some of our latter-day references to its various figures. Since most people are familiar with the Bible's six-days-and-then-rest version of creation, we tell it here only indirectly, as we go along.

It all began when URANUS, the starry heavens, bedded his mother, the earth. From this sordid union they begat the TITANS, titanic giants, among them the sun and the moon. Because yooRAYnuss would not let GAEA (as in Mother Earth, geology, geography) give birth to any of the children, however, conflict arose. JEEuh made a sickle and coaxed the bravest of her offspring, CRONUS, out of her womb to cut up his father. KROHnuss did. He hid under the bed, and when Uranus came to lie upon Gaea, Cronus reached up for his father's reproductive organs, grasped firmly, and sliced them off with the sickle.

After this traumatic separation of the heavens from the earth, Cronus, or SATURN, as the Romans called him, ruled the universe. He begat the gods, after whom we've named the rest of the planets, and ruled for what the Greeks, in a fit of nostalgia, called the GOLDEN AGE (not to be confused with their classical period of independence from Persian and other wars, which we call by the same name).

Cronus had a simple and direct method of keeping his god-children under control: he ate them. We personify a devouring "Father Time" partly because of Cronus's unfriendly association with his children, and partly because the Greek word for time was *chronos*. And at New Year's we show the old year with the equipment of a grim reaper.

As the story goes, Cronus threw his father's severed parts into the ocean, and from the bloody foam that they stirred up APHRODITE (afruhDYEtee), or VENUS to the Romans, was born. If you've seen the famous BOTTICELLI painting called *The Birth of Venus* (not to be confused with *September*

Morn or the White Rock nymphet, later imitations), you know how she rose up naked from the sea and walked onto the shore, where flowers grew in her footsteps. The story isn't quite clear on what she did while Cronus was still eating everyone in sight, but later, when ZEUS (ZOOSS) had conquered Cronus, she married the god of the forge, Hephaestus, whom the Romans called VULCAN. Then she took on Ares (the Romans called him MARS), god of war, and that good-looking mortal ADONIS (uhDOHnis) as her paramour.

But we get ahead of ourselves. Zeus, or JUPITER/JOVE to the Romans, was one of Cronus's children. Overlooked and smuggled away during infancy, he grew up to make his father regurgitate the other children and established himself as king of the gods, by Jove. He lived in the sky around Mount Olympus, the highest mountain in Greece, with the other gods, eating and drinking that which is fit for lofty Olympians to eat and drink: ambrosia and nectar. And to rule things, Zeus adopted a technique more refined than those his father or grandfather had used: when angry, he'd hurl lightning and Jovian thunderbolts.

Two of Zeus's companion-gods we've already mentioned: APOLLO and DIONYSUS. The god of light, uhPAHloh, was by temperament logical, contemplative: shedding light and bringing CLASSICAL order. On the other hand, dyeohNYE-suss was the god of wine and revelry, stirring men up to passionate suffering or ecstasy as they followed their instincts to ROMANtic adventure. Guess which one had blond hair?

Also of note on Olympus were two goddesses. Pallas ATHENA (uhTHEEnuh) had an unusual birth. She sprang from Zeus's head fully formed, armed with a spear and carrying a shield (an *aegis*). She was worshiped as the goddess of wisdom, and battle, and peace, and as the protector of Athens, which was under her shield (under her EEjiss). The Romans called her MINERVA. Another classic goddess revered for nonfeminine traits was ARTEMIS the huntress, or as the Romans called her, DIANA. She was Apollo's twin: he was the sun; she was the moon, and the goddess of hunts in the forest. A virgin, of course.

But Zeus wasn't. Though he was married to goddess Hera, JUNO to the Romans, Zeus was forever sleeping around with earth's women. He'd turn himself into a swan, a cloud, a bull, or once into a shower of gold, and away he'd go to earth, to impregnate some mortal maiden, ready or not. It's gods like Zeus who gave pagans a bad name. He was definitely not the sort of god one wants to take to Sunday school.

Speaking of earth's women, the first of them was made by Zeus, out of clay. She was like EVE, the gullible first woman of Judeo-Christian legend, who believed the sly promises of an upright serpent, ate the forbidden fruit, and so brought evil into the world by disobeying the deity. PANDORA didn't have a snake to tempt her, but she disobeyed, and became the scapegoat, all the same.

It seems there were these three Titan brothers, PROME-THEUS, EPIMETHEUS, and ATLAS. Zeus wasn't overly fond of them, since they were related to Father Cronus. He gave the brothers a large sealed jar, containing troubles, and told them to guard it. Then he offered Woman as a companion, not to prohMEEtheeuss, the clever one, whose name means "forethought," or to Atlas, the strong one. Pandora went to eppiMEEtheeuss, "afterthought," who was a slow learner. It wasn't long before he left Pandora alone with the jar, and in short order curious Pandora lifted the stopper and all Troubles broke loose. Hope stayed behind, caught in the lip of the jar (or under the lid of the box, in some versions), though it wasn't any help having her caught in PANDORA'S BOX. Hope had to be let out too, and she's been busy ever since.

Finally, after women and men and gods and Titans and troubles were populating the newly created Greek universe, there was still one thing missing: mortal intelligence. Men were still stupid. They didn't know about fire, or art, or science. It wasn't until Prometheus the Titan brought fire stolen from Olympus down to men that civilization, as the Greeks knew it, could get started.

Unfortunately for Prometheus, Zeus hadn't intended for man to taste, as it were, from the tree of knowledge. Prometheus's fire theft was roughly the equivalent of selling fire-water, or atomic weapons, to the natives. So as punishment, Zeus ordered Prometheus to be chained to a rocky mountain-top, where birds came flying around every day to feed on Prometheus's exposed liver.

And thus it was that the world came to be created, saith the mythmaker.

Many uses for the creation stories in everyday situations are fairly familiar, and others should be easy to imagine. Standard procedure for difficult problems is to say, "You really deserve an exception, but I don't want to open up Pandora's Box." Things, and people, are regularly excluded from everyday doings with talk about not starting trouble in Paradise or not letting a snake into the garden. Prometheus is often recalled to give credit for someone's inspiration. And remembering the birth of Venus has great potential for wise-sounding remarks on everything from the nature of love to woman's liberation—and can also be compared with Adam's rib for macabre effect.

And so on, through all the other myths.

THE OTHERS

The value of ancient names is well known by the United States Defense Department, many of whose weapons take on an inspiring cachet from the ancient gods and heroes. The more noble the name, the more worthwhile sounds the weapon. Consider the multi-billion-dollar guided missile "Nike-Zeus," named from the Greek word for victory (NYEkee). What kind of appropriation would the House Armed Services Committee and the Congress have voted for this weapon if they'd called it "Eddie Zeiss"? Nobility is necessary in weapons, and the classics lend nobility to all things. Other gods playing their part for national security are spread throughout the military-industrial complex, from POSEIDON (pohSYEdun, god of the sea—NEPTUNE to the Romans) missiles to TRIDENT (the three-pronged spear of Poseidon) nuclear submarines to ATLAS (the Titan who held up the world on his shoulders) rockets, and so on.

But the classics are useful for more than just glamorizing military hardware. Using classical labels can lend a certain dignity to everyday problems, making them appear either dragons to be slain or bottomless pitfalls to be avoided— depending on which myth one recalls. If you want a problem to appear vast, calling for a sweeping action, refer to the AUGEAN STABLES (ohJEEun) after the huge cattle barns that HERCULES had to clean out as one of his TWELVE

LABORS. Those stables were full of what hundreds and hundreds of cattle had been steadily producing in their stalls for many, many years. Hercules (HERAKLES to the Greeks) changed the course of two mighty rivers to cleanse these stables. The myth doesn't say what this did for the towns downstream.

If your problem is intricate, tangled, tedious to unravel, recall the GORDIAN KNOT. This huge tangle of rope bound a yoke of oxen to a pole, and the prize for undoing it was, in the myth, the empire of all Asia. Alexander the Great supposedly took the direct route to a solution, cutting through this ancient version of red tape with a blow of his sword.

Whatever your problem, it should be labelable by one or another classic. If troubles just keep cropping up, there's the HYDRA—a monster with nine heads that grew two more for every one that was cut off. If you've something that needs to be walled off or otherwise isolated, remember the MINO-TAUR (MIHnuhtawr), a man with a bull's head who ate maidens and had to have a LABYRINTH (maze) built around him. If your problem's a challenge, a prize ripe for the plucking, recollect the GOLDEN FLEECE—the prize snatched by JASON and the ARGONAUTS, voyagers on the ship ARGOS. The fleece was guarded by a fire-breathing dragon who slept under a tree at the end of the world—which was probably the eastern shore of the Black Sea, judging from landmarks mentioned in the story. Somewhere out there on the shores of what today is Turkey or Russia, Jason fleeced the dragon. He had help from MEDEA, the local king's daughter, but their love affair had an unhappy ending (see THE GREAT TRAGEDIANS).

Finally, if you think you can solve the problem if you just act cleverly and without emotion, call it after MEDUSA, the GORGON. She was a monster with a woman's head, boar's teeth, and snakes instead of hair; her face, if one looked at it, would turn a man to stone. PERSEUS escaped this hard fate and cut off her head by looking only at her reflection in his polished shield.

For those hopeless situations that you want to avoid, here are some other mythic equivalents. SISYPHUS (SIHsihfuss) was condemned to roll a huge stone up to the top of a hill, at which point it would roll back down. Then he'd push it back up, again . . . and again . . . (see also EXISTEN-TIALISM). Then there was TANTALUS, condemned to stand in waist-deep water beneath trees heavily laden with fruit. When he was thirsty and bent down to drink, the water would drain away from his parched lips. When he was hungry and tried for the fruit, it hung tantalizingly, just out of reach. If some disaster's impending, recall DAMOCLES' SWORD. To make DAHmuhkleez, a courtier, quit praising the king's happiness, the king sat him at a royal banquet with a sword hung over his head—suspended by a single hair. And finally, if trouble's weighing you down, remember Atlas the Titan, who had to support the world on his shoulders. If he let it drop, of course, it would crush him. He had to bear up until Perseus, wearing MERCURY's winged shoes, flew by, fresh from his triumph over Medusa. Perseus saw the Titan, popped Medusa's fresh head out of his carrying satchel, and discovered that she could turn Titans into stone too. Believe it or not, that's where the Atlas Mountains in North Africa come from.

If you still have a problem you can't label, see HOMER.

The ancients are also good references to dig up when talking about luxury or decadence. MIDAS, of course, we all know about. When speaking of wealth, better to say as rich as CROESUS (KREEsuss), who gave solid gold offerings to APOLLO'S ORACLE AT DELPHI. An interesting sidelight can be worked into this reference, if anyone asks, commenting on the annoying tendency of oracles to give ambiguous predictions. It seems that Croesus was not certain whether or not he ought to fight the king of Persia. He asked the Oracle: should he or shouldn't he? The answer:

"If Croesus fights the Persians he will bring down a mighty empire." After Croesus went ahead, and lost, he realized that the prophecy could apply not only to the Persians' empire but also to his own.

We've mentioned DIONYSIAN (dyeohNIHsheeun) revels, which are also called BACCHANALIAN (backaNAYleeun) revels, since the Roman god of wine was called BACCHUS (BACKus). These are the good-time orgies with nude maidens stuffing grape clusters into the greedy mouths of assorted ancient lechers reposed on couches. In the country, or ARCADIAN, versions, the revels were likely to include NYMPHS, amorous young maidens; and SATYRS (SATerz), men with goat's horns and hindquarters, who were infinitely lustful. Satyrs are not to be confused with CENTAURS (SENtorrs), who were also men above the waist but below were full-bodied horses with four legs.

The god associated with ARCADIAN, SYLVAN, PAS-TORAL, or country revels, aside from Bacchus, is PAN. Pan had goat's horns and ears, and sometimes legs. When not otherwise occupied, he played music for the revelers on his Pan-pipes, one-note whistles bound together, which later generations enlarged and bronzed into pipe organs. He also wooed both sexes, and could induce *panic* if he was disturbed.

Bacchanalian frolics are also comparable to street life in SODOM and GOMORRAH, decadent cities which in the Bible were punished by a rain of fire and brimstone. Another oft-recalled wicked city of old is BABYLON, where they had prostitutes in the temples.

As an individual example of decadence unbridled, we can use NERO, the Roman emperor who supposedly ordered a disastrous fire set in Rome (while he was out of town), because he wanted to rebuild the city. He also had his mother put to the sword; then, looking at her naked body, he said, "I did not know I had so beautiful a mother."

On the female side of decadence, there's MESSALINA

(messuhLYEnuh), who as empress of Rome slept with nearly everyone she could—once moonlighting in a brothel with twenty-five men in twenty-four hours. Also of note as being promiscuous on the Roman throne is CALIGULA (kah-LIGGyooluh), the mentally unbalanced emperor whose carryings-on have inspired contemporary novels by Albert CAMUS (which see), Robert Graves, and Gore Vidal. Caligula had the habit of taking other men's wives: he declared them to be legally divorced and then brought them home to bed in his palace. He also distinguished himself by taking baths in undiluted perfume, sawing his enemies in half, and giving a consulship to a horse.

Opposite such profligates we can set the example of SPARTAN discipline, after SPARTA, the city-state that defeated Athens in a war. The Spartans lived the simple life. Boys left home for the barracks at age seven, slept outdoors till age thirty, and were given one garment, a wool tunic, to wear—per year. The women went naked until marriage. Both sexes were so well disciplined to the idea of an army that they killed any children who didn't look healthy enough to be good fighters.

FAMOUS PAIRS
Lovers

Boy-meets-girl situations, bless them, are forever cropping up. Here are some from the classics which, besides appearing in ballet, drama, paintings, music, opera, poetry, and other works of art, may also work to label contemporary relationships you run across.

DAPHNE and APOLLO. She a nymph, he a god. She virgin, he lustful. Help! she cried, to Mother Earth, who obliged and turned her into a laurel tree. Apollo made a wreath out of what was left that he could get his hands on and wore it. LAURELS have been a prize ever since.

DAPHNIS and CHLOË. DAFFniss and KLOHee were rustic lovers of Greek pastoral romance. They've become a

symbol of innocent young couples, or those who're pretending to be.

CUPID and PSYCHE. The son of Venus and Vulcan,
Cupid came to Psyche at night. She could touch, but not
look, he said. But after the touching one night, when he was
asleep, she looked, and waked him with a drop from her
hot oil lamp. Miffed, Cupid split for parts unknown. Psyche
searched the world for him till the end of her days, whereupon Zeus obligingly made her immortal and reunited the
pair. A variation of this myth has each soul split up before
birth, so that on earth each half-psyche is looking for his
or her better half, or soul-mate, or EPIPSYCHE. The way
this myth had it, both marriages and divorces were made in
heaven.

PERSEUS and ANDROMEDA (anDRAHmuhduh). Like
Psyche's tale, another happy ending. She was chained to a
rock as a sacrifice to a sea-monster, but Perseus, still fresh
from his doings with Medusa and Atlas, saved her. The first
of the save-the-fair-damsel-in-distress tales.

PYGMALION and GALATEA (galuhTEEuh). The model
for *My Fair Lady's* Henry Higgins and all those who fall
in love with their own creations, pigMALEyun sculpted a
statue and was smitten. When Aphrodite turned the lovely
statue to life, Pygmalion called her Galatea. Presumably he
was too busy after that to sculpt again.

ORPHEUS and EURYDICE. Here frustration sets in.
When yooRIDihsee died, ORfeeus, son of chief muse CAL-
LIOPE (kalLYEohpee), used his musical talent to charm
PLUTO in HADES (HAYdeez), land of the dead. Orpheus
won permission to take Eurydice back out of the underworld,
providing he went first and didn't look back to see if she
was really following him. Well, you guessed it. Like LOT'S
WIFE at Sodom, Orpheus looked back. He didn't get turned
into a pillar of salt, but he did lose Eurydice. Many morals
to be drawn here, but not today, thanks.

PYRAMUS and THISBE. Lovers who met secretly, after

whispering the spot of the night's assignation through a crack in a wall. One night THIZbee was frightened off by a lion and dropped her cloak, which the lion chewed on awhile before he left. PIHruhmus arrived, saw the chewed-on cloak, and in a fit of mistaken grief stabbed himself. When Thisbe discovered him dead, she also took her life. Shakespeare used the plot for his ending of *Romeo and Juliet* and burlesqued it in *A Midsummer Night's Dream*.

ECHO and NARCISSUS. More unhappy love. A beautiful nymph, Echo, fell in love with Narcissus, but he let her pine away until nothing was left but—what else?—her voice. To punish Narcissus, NEMESIS, the goddess of retribution, caused him to fall in love with his own reflection in the water and then changed him into the waterside flower that bears his name. Be warned of the Narcissus Complex, said FREUD, to those vegetating in front of their mirrors.

HERO and LEANDER. Still another star-crossed pair. Her name was Hero and she was a priestess. leeANNder was her secret lover, who swam the sea at night to visit, guided in to shore by her lamp. Things were going swimmingly until one stormy night when the lamp blew out. Leander drowned, and Hero, suicidal with grief, did likewise.

CAESAR and CLEOPATRA. See *Cleopatra*, the movie with Rex and Elizabeth and the rug.

ANTONY and CLEOPATRA. See *Cleopatra*, the movie with Richard and Elizabeth and the asp.

ARTEMIS and ACTEON. Not lovers, exactly. She was the virgin goddess of the Moon (DIANA to the Romans), out for a bath in a stream. When akTEEon, the hunter, wandered by and ogled, she took it unkindly, changed him into a stag, and watched him get torn apart by his own hounds. Virgins and stag parties haven't mixed well ever since.

DIDO and AENEAS. She, queen of Carthage. He, Trojan survivor of war with Greece. eeNEEas loved Queen DYEdoe but had to push off on his way to found Rome. Their affair was fun while it lasted, but a man's gotta do what a man's gotta do. (See also VIRGIL, whose epic version of Aeneas is the AENEID.)

Other Pairs

ROMULUS and REMUS. Eight generations after ancestor Aeneas arrived from Troy via Carthage, these two were abandoned at birth, sent down the river Tiber, and nursed by THE CAPITOLINE WOLF, whose picture in ninth-grade Latin textbooks annually evokes gales of giggles. When the boys grew to manhood, they founded a city. Remus didn't like the height of the wall, though, and said, "This is how our enemies will jump over," and jumped over. ROMyoulus replied, "And this is how I will kill them," and killed him. That's why it's not called Reme.

CASTOR and POLLUX. Twin brothers who went along with Jason as Argonauts. Later turned into stars, the GEMINI (JEMMineye).

DAMON and PYTHIAS. Mortal friends to the death. Damon stood in as bail for Pythias, who had been sentenced to death. Pythias could have allowed him to be executed in his place but returned instead, so touching the heart of the governor that he granted a pardon.

DAEDALUS and ICARUS. Father and son. DEDalus made wings of feathers and wax, and they worked! But IKarus flew too close to the sun, melting the wax. Down came Icarus, feathers and all.

HELIOS and PHAËTHON. Another father and son story, with the same theme. HEELios drove the sun across the sky in his chariot. FAYehthon said, "Dad, can I drive?" often enough to make Helios give in, but when it came time to handle the horses Phaëthon wasn't strong enough. He would have burned up the earth if Zeus hadn't seen what was happening and stopped him with a thunderbolt.

OEDIPUS and THE SPHINX. Also, in its way, a father and son story. When told by an oracle that he would kill his father and marry his mother, EDihpus decided to thwart the prophecy; he left his parents, the king and queen of Corinth, and took to the open road. On the way he got into a fight with some travelers and killed four of them. He moved on to Thebes, a city besieged by a monster called the Sphinx. "What animal goes on four feet in the morning, on two feet at noonday, and three feet in the evening?" asked the Sphinx, who liked riddles. If someone got the answer right, the Sphinx promised, it would leave Thebes alone, but until then the Sphinx was eating Thebans who gave wrong answers, right and left.

Oedipus arrived and said "MAN!" This saved the city, because the Sphinx had to admit that man crawls, then walks, then uses a cane. As a reward, Oedipus was given the throne of Thebes, and the grateful Queen of Thebes to wed. (For the unhappy ending, see THE GREAT TRA-GEDIANS.)

THE AUTHORS

THE MUSE

There's a myth still surrounding poets and novelists that comes from the ancient Greeks: the myth of the MUSES. Muses were nine daughters of Zeus who lived around the top of a mountain called PARNASSUS and gave mortals a divine wind called inspiration. The theory the Greeks had about poets was simple: poets didn't write anything, really; they just wrote down or spoke whate'er the muse said. While the literary muse, whose name was EUTERPE if you were doing lyrics and CALLIOPE if you were doing epics, spoke, the mortal poet was in a trance: a humble unconscious mes-senger delivering the Word. If you were a poet, you would first invoke the muse with an invitation of sorts ("Sing! O muse . . ."), and then you would fall down in a frenzy. When you woke up, you would have written the ILIAD. Or rather the muse would have.

In universities, the idea of the goddess-muse persists in the way works on the syllabus are treated as Gospel (re-

ferred to in English departments as "reverence for the text"),
and in writings of critics like T. S. ELIOT (which see), who
compared poets to platinum wire, a catalyst that brings
about a reaction between chemicals but remains unchanged
itself.

In the world of publishing, the myth of the muse may
sometimes be revived full-blown, as Richard Bach did when
asked about his Jonathan Livingston Seagull. It was
5:00 A.M., you see, and he was walking alone on the beach,
and suddenly a still, small voice behind his ear started to
whisper to him, "Jonathan Livingston Seagull! Jonathan Livingston Seagull!" So he went home and sat at his typewriter
and wrote down what he heard the voice tell him, and by
noon or so he had half the book. Five years later the voice
came back; he found a typewriter and polished off the second
half. . . .

It's a good story. And the belief in the godlike status of
the muse, or the Creative Unconscious as it's sometimes
called, still gives authors a leader's charisma. We copy our
mannerisms and our dress from some: as Oscar Wilde put
it, "Life imitates Art." And we may think of others as
leaders in the political sense, inviting them to speak at an
inauguration, as Kennedy did Robert Frost, or even con-
sidering them as serious candidates for public office, as
thousands of New Yorkers did Norman Mailer and Jimmy
Breslin. In Shelley's words, "Poets are the unacknowledged
legislators of the world." A corollary of this part of the myth
might explain why John Lindsay and Spiro Agnew have
now turned to writing novels.

SAMUEL JOHNSON (which see), who in 1759 dashed
off the novel-length Rasselas during the evenings of one
week, had a more sensible view. "No man but a blockhead,"
said he, "ever wrote except for money."

THE GREAT TRAGEDIANS

If you were a Greek twenty-five hundred years ago, you'd
have gone to the amphitheater, sat on its stone seats with

eighteen thousand other Greeks, and watched tragedies
all day long, four plays in a row, during the five-day festival
of Dionysus. After the last three days, which featured dawn-
to-dusk tragedy, you'd wait for a time before you went home,
to learn which of the plays had won the tragedy contest for
that year's festival. You might even have had a bet on the
outcome.

Exactly what moved audiences to watch these tragedies,
and what moves some today to watch tragedy with the same
zeal others reserve for football at New Year's, is a question
that's occupied great philosophers and psychologists.
ARISTOTLE said that we purge pity and fear out of our
systems by empathizing with the suffering of others and so
feel better from this CATHARSIS (kaTHARsis). A more
prosaic theory says that the sufferings of tragic heroes, like
those on our soap operas, simply make our own troubles
seem small by comparison. Whatever the cause, when we've
followed the hero and feel his torment, his words of digni-
fied poetry can sometimes bring us close to our own deepest
fears and needs, and then let us rise through the pain to a
kind of nobility that's beyond speech.

What's more commonly associated with the Greek tragedies, though, is simply the names of the heroes and their
catastrophes. Most are based on the old myths. The most
famous is OEDIPUS REX, by SOPHOCLES (SOFfohkleez).
We watch Oedipus as he learns that he was abandoned, as
an infant, because of a prophecy that he would kill his
father and marry his mother. They'd pinned his feet together (*Oedi pus* means "swollen foot"), but a kindly shepherd found him on a hillside near Thebes and took him to
Corinth. The man he killed on the road from Corinth was
really his father, the king of Thebes. The queen of Thebes,
on whom he's fathered four children, is really his mother.
In the play, she hangs herself, backstage; he takes the
golden brooches from her robe and punctures both his eyes.

Other tragedies of note: MEDEA, by EURIPIDES (youRIPideez). Medea goes mad for revenge after Jason, her love from the days of the Golden Fleece, leaves her and the children to marry the king's daughter. She invites Jason to come for a family visit and then slaughters the children. Also still performed today is AGAMEMNON, by AESCHYLUS (ESSkillus). King AgaMEMnon is betrayed by his wife and her lover, caught in a net, and stabbed. Then there's his daughter ELECTRA, written about by all three of these tragedians, who gets her brother to kill both the lover and Mother. Also of note is PROMETHEUS BOUND by Aeschylus. Here we listen to the laments of the Titan who brought arts and sciences to men, as he lies chained to the rocky mountaintop with a spike driven through his breast.

And if you think these situations are tragic, imagine what the Greeks must have been watching back in 411 B.C. That was the year Sophocles entered *Oedipus Rex* in the annual tragedy contest and won second prize.

HOMER, ETC.

Homer was the first Western Poet. He wrote sometime between 850 and 700 B.C., and he was famous long before 1682, when the Duke of Buckingham said he was "all the books you need." Legend has it that he was blind, and that before writing was invented he wandered from Greek city to city singing these long adventure yarns he had memorized, in return for food. Later, Greece realized that Homer's songs were more than just entertainment; they were the ILIAD and the ODYSSEY. So then, too late for Homer, came the rise in Homer's reputation: "Seven cities claimed Great Homer dead, through which the living Homer begged his bread." And today, our synonym for primal greatness, à la Homer's heroes from the days when the world was new, is still HOMERIC.

Actually, the Homeric poems may have been written by several generations of ancient Greek poets, but that's a debate for Greek scholars.

What's to be known from the ILIAD? To know the opening line, "I sing of the wrath of Achilles," is really enough. But you might recall that Achilles, Greek champion, spears Troy's champion Hector through the neck. When the Trojan begs for an honorable death, Achilles replies, "I ought to cut you up and eat your flesh." Then for eleven days he has Hector's corpse dragged in the dirt behind a chariot. That's wrath.

The ODYSSEY, though, has places and characters in it that are frequently compared with today's troubles, so the story is worth repeating:

ODYSSEUS (ohDISeeyus or Ulysses to the Romans) had a long journey (odyssey) home after the Trojan war through many obstacles. First he had to drag his men out of opium addiction in the land of the LOTUS-EATERS. Then after a bout with a CYCLOPS and a bag of wind like Pandora's Box, and some cannibals, he washed up onto the island of CIRCE (SIRsee), the enchantress. She turned his men into pigs and kept Odysseus as her lover for a year. Then he sailed past the SIRENS, temptresses whose songs lure sailors onto rocks, by plugging the ears of his men with wax and lashing himself to the mast. His next obstacle is often compared with the horns of a dilemma: SCYLLA (SILLa), a monster, and CHARYBDIS (kaRIBdis), a whirlpool. Somehow Odysseus got between them, but alas, after that his ship was sunk and he alone swam ashore to the tropical paradise of the island nymph CALYPSO (as in the island dance). She held him as her playmate for seven years.

Eventually, though, Odysseus did land home on ITHACA and soon made it back to his house, where he killed the fifteen men who'd been wooing his faithful wife PENELOPE and set up the monarchy once again.

Odysseus has the line that's the best quotation from

Homer. Shipwrecked for the final time, after three days swimming alone on the sea, he finally gets a glimpse of the crashing waves and the rocks that mean there's land ahead. And he says: "There is no way to stand firm on both feet and escape trouble."

Another Greek poet who's evoked now and again is SAPPHO. SAFFoh wrote such beautiful passionate love lyrics that Plato called her the tenth muse. She also led a cult of women who worshiped Aphrodite on the island of Lesbos, from which we get the term "lesbian." Was Sappho? Women of both preferences have claimed her. Some of her lyrics are addresses to women, but some are also addressed to men. And she did marry and bear a daughter. Since she lived somewhere around 600 B.C., though, there's no conclusive accounting for Sappho's tastes.

Finally, it's sometimes useful to remember the names of HESIOD and OVID, the recorders of Greek and Roman myths. HEEsih-odd wrote down the Greek myths sometime around Homer's day, and AHvid wrote Roman versions until A.D. 7, when he wasn't too busy writing love poems or seduction manuals. His myths, stories of transformations like those of Daphne and Narcissus, were called the METAMORPHOSES. They were read by every generation after him, fulfilling the promise he makes at their closing lines: "I shall live forever."

THE PHILOSOPHERS

"TAKE IT PHILOSOPHICALLY"

If you believed in a universe where you never knew from one day to the next whether or not you would come home to find your wife making it with a shower of gold (see ZEUS), you needed philosophy. And if this sort of thing happened often, you probably needed STOIC (STOHick) philosophy. The Stoics, Greeks who met on a porch, or *stoa*, decided that man had nothing in this world to worry about except his own attitude, since he had no control over anything in this world except his own attitude. Rather than questioning the part fortune had given him, a man should play it out as best he could, and spend his time mastering his own emotions instead of complaining. The emotion for a Stoic to cultivate was a fine indifference called apathy, and the most famous example of Stoic apathy comes from the Roman EPICTE-TUS (eppickTEEtus). Though a philosopher, Epictetus was also the slave of a harsh Roman master in the first century A.D. When this Roman decided to torment Epictetus by cruelly twisting his leg, Epictetus said calmly, "If you go on twisting my leg, it will break." Then the leg broke. Epictetus remarked, "I told you that would happen."

Another famous Roman stoic was MARCUS AURELIUS (awREELyuss), emperor of Rome fifty years after Epictetus's time. One of his stoic MEDITATIONS is just dandy for quoting to appropriate people: "Begin the morning by saying to yourself, I shall meet today bores, stupid men, hypocrites, and liars. But I can still be reasonable and not be harmed by any of them."

A final example to stoics is CATO. A Roman who fought against Caesar and lost, Cato decided to kill himself rather than surrender. He used the Roman method of a sword in the stomach, but friends got a doctor and the doctor stitched the wound. As soon as Cato was alone again, however, he took off his bandage, unstitched himself, and removed his own intestines.

Then there were the EPICUREANS and the CYNICS, two other philosophical mind-sets that have embedded themselves in our language. It's wise to have them straight. The eppikyooREEanz taught that matter, composed of atoms, was the only reality a man ought to concern himself with, that there was no afterlife, and that therefore pleasure on earth was the only good. Because of this part of their doctrine, we describe a connoisseur of food or drink as an *epicure*. It's worth noting, however, that what the Epicureans meant by pleasure was simply the absence of pain, which came from mastering one's desires rather than indulging them. A good Epicurean learned how to be happy with bread and water, so that desire would never pain him.

The SINNicks had more than indifference to worldly fortunes: they had contempt. DIOGENES (dyeAHJeneez) is the famed example: he showed his contempt for possessions by living in a wooden tub, and his contempt for men by waving a lantern at them, to dramatize what he said was a fruitless search for an honest man. When Alexander the Great, the emperor, once was foolish enough to ask him whether he wanted anything, Diogenes had his chance to show contempt for royalty as well, and he took it. "Yes," he answered, "stand a little out of my sun."

THE EXAMINED LIFE

But the heavyweight Greek philosophers, those men whose writings are still taken seriously even though they've been dead twenty-three hundred years, are SOCRATES, PLATO, and ARISTOTLE. Everybody who's anybody has known at least something about these three for, well, twenty-three hundred years, and so should you.

First the basics. SOKrateez (469?–339 B.C.) taught in the streets of Athens during the Golden Age, the high point of Greek culture. PLAYtoe (427?–347? B.C.), his pupil, founded his own school, the Academy. Then ARRIStottle (384–322 B.C.), Plato's pupil, founded his own school, the Lyceum. Aristotle's pupil, Alexander the Great, founded the Macedonian Empire, but that's another story.

What people know about Socrates they got mainly from Plato, since Socrates never wrote anything. A stonemason by trade, he wandered the streets of Athens barefoot even in winter and didn't take fees for his teaching. He taught by asking embarrassing questions about justice and truth and other admittedly important things that most people would rather take for granted. It was Socrates who said that the unexamined life was not worth living, and that the man who was ignorant and asked questions was wiser than the man who knew much and was satisfied.

Unfortunately for Socrates, he had the bad habit of questioning prominent Athenians about their standards of right and wrong, and making them look stupid. You've probably heard the story about how in 399 B.C. they brought Socrates to trial and found him guilty of subversion and un-Athenian activities. The sentence was death by hemlock. Socrates drank this poison calmly, surrounded by friends, taking time to refute any suggestion of escape or civil disobedience. A good citizen ought to obey the law, he said, and besides, there might easily be a better world beyond this one. . . .

As Plato wrote up the story in PHAEDO, the tale of Socrates' death is achingly moving; so good, in fact, that Dr. Watson thought the last lines worth borrowing when he wrote up the death of Sherlock Holmes, "The best and wisest man that I have ever known."

THE IDEAL

PLATO developed Socrates' thought into the famous idea of THE TWO WORLDS. Somewhere, said Plato, invisible above or beyond this flux we perceive with our senses, there's a kind of heavenly fifth dimension called the IDEAL REALM, where qualities like Beauty and Truth live serene and pure as IDEALS, or PLATONIC FORMS. These forms are the essences of the qualities we see in earthly objects: we call some four-legged things "cats" and other four-legged things "chairs" only because we have learned to distinguish the forms of "cat-ness" and "chair-ness" in their earthly, material costumes. To learn to distinguish the forms of "Beauty" and "Truth" is a trickier business than just to tell a cat from a chair, because earthly substance imitates the forms of Beauty and Truth in many different ways. Just looking at things we think are beautiful and true won't be enough—to get to

know these higher forms, we'll need a great deal of philosophical discussion and reasoning. (See above, THE ONE
ANCIENT IDEA YOU NEED TO KNOW.)

Still, even though it's long and difficult, the way of the
philosopher is the only way to know. Just as you've got to
know the Dior original before you can tell whether the copy
at Korvette's is worth buying, so too you've got to have
reasoned your way to a knowledge of Ideal Beauty if you
want to judge what's on Earth with good taste. And since
Justice is an Ideal too, if you want to be a good king, you've
got to have reasoned your way to a knowledge of Ideal
Justice.

So it follows that we should be ruled by a PHILOSO-
PHER-KING. Right? Well, the Athenians didn't think so,
but Plato's plan to run a city-state that way, THE REPUB-
LIC, has its advantages. The Turks used it, in fact, to rule
the Ottoman Empire for two centuries. The idea was to test
all the kids from grade school on up, gradually selecting the
best and the brightest. Then when they were fifty years old
and their training was complete, and when there was a
vacancy in government, one of them would get the job auto-
matically. No primaries, no conventions, no campaign slush
funds. And no scandals either; Plato wanted these rulers to
have a different life-style. They'd be above wealth and pomp
and such mundane things, since they'd love Ideals more than
villas and jet planes. He envisioned their living in communes,
sharing children and sex-rights—an idea which does seem
to crop up now and again.

Another of Plato's ideas updated for our times is his view
of the unconscious. Your conscious power of reason, said
Plato, is like a chariot driver who has to control two horses,
a white one and a black one. The white horse is your conscience, and he tries to lead you back to the ideal realm
where your soul lives before and after your life on earth.
The black horse is your animal lust, and we all know where
he'll take you if you let him. When you have this pair

of horses both under control, said Plato, that's the Ideal of Justice: harmony of all the parts. (For the twentieth-century variation on this theme, see FREUD.)

Plato is also remembered for his description of ATLANTIS (which see) and for describing heaven and hell as after-life rewards and punishments: heaven being a paradise in the sky and hell being somewhere beneath a hole in the earth. The medieval Church explained this foreshadowing of its own dogma by saying that Plato was "Christian in spirit." (See THE MEDIEVAL MYSTIQUE.)

THE GOLDEN MEAN IN ETHICS

The most influential of these three philosophers is ARISTO-TLE. Even though he believed that the world was made of four elements (earth, air, fire, and water), Aristotle's remembered for his spirit of cool rationality, a scientific detachment not inappropriate for the son of a physician. He wasn't as cantankerous as Socrates or as visionary as Plato. No horses, no Ideals in cloud cuckooland, for Aristotle. Just LOGICAL ANALYSIS. In fact, it was Aristotle who gave us the basis of logical thought, the SYLLOGISM, which is a formalized way of saying that if you know something about all members of a group, you'll know that something about one of the group's individuals. Here's the classic example:

All men are mortal.   (major premise)
Socrates is a man.   (minor premise)
Therefore, Socrates is mortal.   (conclusion)

"Man" here is the middle term in the syllogism.

Two other ideas of Aristotle's that you're likely to run into, you've already run into: CATHARSIS and THE GOLDEN MEAN. Have a good cry at the theater and you'll feel better, said Aristotle—and in THE POETICS he outlined the way to write TRAGEDY to produce this effect. In his ETHICS, Aristotle saw moral questions as a matter of getting the right proportions in one's actions, with virtue as a kind of ideal middle ground, or Golden Mean. You don't want to be cowardly, with too little courage, but neither do you want to be foolhardy, with too much. The trick is to know how much of any quality (lust, anger, compassion, pleasure, courage, etc.) is required in a given situation and then to have enough (not too much) will power to act accordingly. Not easy, perhaps, but then Aristotle never promises to take us to an Ideal World for fast relief from this one. He just gives us the facts.

Or a reasonable facsimile thereof: the trouble with Aristotle was that he was better at reasoning with the facts than he was at experimenting with them, so by today's standards he wasn't much of a scientist. Besides his four-element theory, the classic example of his armchair mistakes is the story of the two cannonballs. If one's heavy and one's light, which will fall faster? Why, the heavy one, of course, says your reason, and so said Aristotle. But everybody knows that when GALILEO (which see) tried it nineteen hundred years later, the two balls fell at the same speed.

Aristotle still gets credit for bringing philosophy out of the clouds, and for having a more finely developed system for coping with the unenlightened than Socrates. When the Athenians charged Aristotle with the same crime they'd killed Socrates for, he left town and thus did them the good deed of, as he put it, "not letting them sin against philosophy twice."

SCULPTURE AND ARCHITECTURE
ANCIENT SCULPTURE

Though they're mostly of the same mythic gods and goddesses, Greek and Roman statues come styled in several different varieties. Each style has its own peculiar charm.

If the statue looks stiff-jointed, like an idol, and vaguely like African primitive, it's ARCHAIC (arKAYik), probably designed before the Greeks beat the Persians (ca. 500 B.C.) and started their own, non-Egyptian thing. The stepping-forward poses of these figures date back to Egyptian wood carvings from 2500 B.C.

If the statue's got a more graceful body than you do, with that universal serene face that's just ever-so-slightly plump, it's CLASSIC. That's the kind of sculpture the Greeks were doing during their Golden Age, full of classic .618034 proportions. The style lasted until Alexander the Great took over in 336 B.C.

If the statue's a bit fancier, with flowing robes or a face that shows some character or emotion, it's MANNERED, man, probably done after Alexander but before the Roman conquerors caused Greek art to really go commercial (146 B.C.).

If it's fancier still, with torso and limbs twisted into tortured, though classic, curves and spirals, it's GRECO-ROMAN, a style that later ages copied and called BAROQUE (see THE BAROQUE ERA). Art like this moved old-fashioned Romans like Cato to rail against Hellenistic decadence, and then, fifteen hundred years later, moved Italians to begin the RENAISSANCE (which see).

Aside from noticing these styles or the classic proportions of the limbs, there are a few other points worth looking for on ancient statuary. It's good to see how the posture's balanced to make the statue symmetrical on its own or bent in a curve to make it a dynamic part of a group. You can guess, too, what parts of the statue were painted, knowing that the Greeks used hot wax pigment to touch up highlights, like lips and eyes. After two millennia of weather and a few decades of pollution, though, the question of where those nude maidens really were painted remains a mystery.

On an emotional level, with ancient statues you'll either like the sleekly sensual surface of the smooth marble, or you'll hate the hard, unfeeling surface of the cold marble. But whether it's *amo* or *odi,* remember that the statue is probably only a Roman copy, and that the original Greek, judging from the surviving few, was much more expressive.

For historical interest, you can notice where the statue's been defaced, or disarmed, or beheaded, or otherwise mutilated by barbarian invasions and other disasters over the centuries. Statues of Aphrodite and other women lost their arms, mostly, broken away from poses in which they were arranging their hair. With the male statues, the noses and other protuberances (since they weren't wearing fig leaves) seem to have been the first thing the barbarians went for.

ANCIENT ARCHITECTURE

Here's where they put the statues on ancient buildings—or copies thereof.

THE PEDIMENT. That's the triangle that looks like the gabled end of a roof, only it's at the front end of the building. Statues carved under there are usually in HIGH RELIEF—less than half their bodies are attached to the wall.

THE FRIEZE (FREEZE) is the border running along under the roofline, sometimes all around the building. Statues on the frieze are usually in BAS (BAH) RELIEF. That means they're only raised up a bit from the surface of the wall, like the heads on coins. If the statues are only outlined, line drawings just carved into the wall like tracings in sand, that's HOLLOW RELIEF. The Egyptians did a lot of hollow relief design on their columns.

THE COLUMNS. If there are male statues actually holding up a beam, like Atlases, they're called ATLANTES (at-LANteez). If they're female, they're CARYATIDS (carry-ATtids), representing the burdened women of Caria, whom the Greeks enslaved for turning traitor during the Persian wars. The Carian men weren't enslaved; just killed.

THE REST OF ANCIENT ARCHITECTURE

Since our architects copied classical styles for nearly all important buildings up until World War I, there are still enough

Greek-temple imitations around to make one question worth answering:

Why do they all look so angular?

It's a short story. The ancients built out of rocks and trees, or rocks made to look like trees (columns—you can still see the trunk tapering at the top on most). Egyptian columns were huge and bulky, but the Greeks made theirs thinner and thinner as they went along. First came DORIC, with the plain tops; then IONIC (eyeONick), topped by rolled scrolls on each side; then finally CORINTHIAN, with tops of imitation leaves. Using the columns was what made the angular look necessary. Whenever you have columns and beams—or as the architects call it, posts and lintels—you've got right angles, or else you've got sagging beams and a potential new set of ruins.

Enter the Arch

The square-corners look was modified somewhat when the Roman engineers wedged stones in a half-circle to support their aqueducts, thus creating the ARCH.

Rome Makes Dome

When the Romans crisscrossed several arches and roofed them over, the two-dimensional curve became a DOME—an arch in 3-D. AVE! Temples no longer had to be filled with columns to hold up the roof. Their bottoms still had to be squared off at ground level, though. Otherwise the keystone drops out or pops out and one's faced with mint-condition ruins again.

If this sounds hopelessly antiquated, remember that ancient architecture was still enough to build most of official Washington, D.C.—including the Washington Monument. That's a column with four sides, tapered and topped off by a pyramid, a design the ancient Egyptians called an OBELISK (OBBehlisk).

What Not to Bother With

ANCIENT HISTORY

The phrase itself is synonymous with oblivion. If, however, you want to dazzle the company with a panorama of the past, you can do it with only three dates.

Ca. 2800 B.C. Egyptians were starting the pyramids, Indians were building great cities on the Indus River, and Chinese, evolved from Peking Man, were beginning the first of the legendary dynasties, the rule of Yu Hsia.

Ca. 1200 B.C. MOSES, after the original Passover, was leading the Israelites out of Egypt, and the Greeks, after a siege failed, were sneaking soldiers into Troy via wooden horse.

Ca. 500 B.C. BUDDHA was teaching the Indians that desire doesn't pay; CONFUCIUS was teaching the Chinese that friendship and generosity do pay; and the Greeks, at the battles of Marathon and Salamis, were teaching the Persians to leave them alone.

ANCIENT HISTORIANS

For tradition's sake, here are the names of the historians that every schoolboy used to know, plus one who's still worth reading.

HERODOTUS (heeRODohtuss)—the Persian wars. Greeks vs. Persians. Greeks win.

THUCYDIDES (thewSIHdideez)—the Peloponnesian (pelluhpuhNEEzhun) wars. Greeks vs. Greeks. Greeks lose.

XENOPHON (ZENohfun)—more Greek wars, with memories of his days as a student of Socrates.

TACITUS (TASSituss)—history of Rome from Augustus past Nero. Monstrous luxury, monstrous vice, and other stories.

PLINY (PLINNee) the younger. Eyewitness account of the eruption of Vesuvius. Dad (the elder) was a naturalist who died in the eruption, along with the rest of Herculaneum and Pompeii.

PLUTARCH (PLOOtark). Our ideals about the chivalric hero come largely from Plutarch's portraits of Alexander the Great, Caesar, Brutus, Pompey, *et alia* famous statesmen and generals of the day. He was all Shakespeare needed for *Julius Caesar, Antony and Cleopatra,* and his other Roman plays. If you want to catch the spirit of aristocracy and adventure, Plutarch's all you need to make you want to run out and begin a new empire.

GREEK AND ROMAN COMEDY

The only Greek comic playwright you're likely to hear of is ARISTOPHANES (arrisTOFFuhneez). They used to talk about THE CLOUDS, his satire of contemporaries Socrates and Plato, but nowadays the play of his that gets performed is LYSISTRATA. lissisTRAHta organizes the sisterhood of warring Peloponnesians in Athens and Sparta into a peace movement. Their platform: no sex for the men of both sides until a truce is declared. In the play this tactic works, since Greek comedies were part of the Dionysian fertility festival. The boys always had to get the girls in the end. (Greek comedy is full of this sort of bawdry.)

PLAUTUS (PLAWtuss) used the same sorts of coarse jests for his Roman comedies. He's remembered for his invention of stock comic figures like the boastful soldier (*miles gloriosus*), the lustful wife, and the brainy slave. Remember *A Funny Thing Happened on the Way to the Forum?*

The Romans, by the way, had each character in the play wear a mask, which they called a *persona,* as in *dramatis personae,* and narrative persona, and person.

ROMAN PHILOSOPHY

There are only two works to remember in Roman philosophy, and both of them are modeled on the Greeks. The first is DE RERUM NATURA (On the Nature of Things), a long poem by LUCRETIUS (looKREEshuss). In passionate rhymes, he takes the Epicurean philosophy of the world as atoms and gives it an atheistic twist. Gods, said Lucretius, are only the figments of our fears. A right understanding of the atomic nature of things would end both our belief in gods and our fear that they can punish us after death, for once our atoms are decayed and rearranged, we literally no longer exist to be punished.

If they believed Lucretius, Romans could therefore lean with confidence on their swords, knowing that suicide is painless. Lucretius seems to have taken his own advice, and his own life, in 55 B.C.

We get the opposite of this atheistic view from CICERO (SISeroh, though the Romans pronounced it KICKeroh). His work is THE REPUBLIC, like Plato's, only not just a Greek city-state. This republic is the Ideal Empire, where duty rules. Author Cicero was also a model senator, and his speeches are still studied for form by speech and English classes.

Philosophically, Cicero follows Plato in his assumption of an afterlife. As he foresaw it, souls who have indulged in bodily pleasures must flit about the earth for ages to atone for their weakness, à la Dickens's Jacob Marley, while souls of those who are dutiful to the Fatherland fly swiftly up to heaven. Presumably Cicero expected his own soul to rise in 43 B.C., when Antony had him beheaded.

ROMAN LITERATURE

Once *de rigueur* at the best and even the not-so-best schools. Now nobody reads it after graduation, but they still talk about it. So you might one day be glad to remember:

VIRGIL (or VERGIL, VURjil, 70–19 B.C.). His epic, the AENEID, tells of Aeneas, who rescues his father from burning Troy, loves Dido, the queen of Carthage, but must leave her for a higher duty: voyage across the sea to Italy and the founding of Rome.

HORACE wrote Horatian odes and satires. He's remembered as a model of urbanity and classical literary form. His advice to writers is often quoted: let the action tell the story, in one place and in a short time; start in the middle of things; cut *purpureus* (purple) prose; beware the praise of your friends; and don't take on too much, lest you labor to give birth to a mountain and produce a mouse.

Ovid, Virgil, and Horace are known as the "Golden" Roman poets, since they wrote during the AUGUSTAN AGE (27 B.C.–A.D. 14), the days of Caesar Augustus when the Roman spirit was relatively untarnished.

SENECA (bloody tragedies), PETRONIUS (orgy and satire), and LUCAN (epic) belong to the "Silver" age, when there was more corruption to satirize. See Fellini's film of Petronius's SATYRICON for proof in living color, or recall that between A.D. 65 and 66, all three of these poets were forced by Nero to commit suicide. They chose the method then fashionable, opening their veins.

The most useful Latin quotation however, is from none of the above. CATULLUS, who wrote just before Virgil, said it about his mistress, and you'll find it useful in any time of ambivalence: *"Odi et amo"* (I hate and I love).

ANCIENT SCIENCE

Here are some splendid ancient scientific theories. Too bad most went virtually ignored for more than a millennium and a half.

1. The earth revolves around a central fire, in regular mathematical harmony with other heavenly spheres. PYTHAGORAS said that in 530 B.C. or thereabouts. He was also the one to discover that a string, halved, vibrates an octave higher when plucked; the one who drew the golden rectangle; and the one whose $a^2 + b^2 = c^2$ theorem (recorded by EUCLID two hundred years later) has been used to measure right triangles ever since.

2. The earth is made up of atoms. DEMOCRITUS (de-MOCKrituss) thought that one up, in about 400 B.C. The

idea went well with another theory by HERACLITUS (hairaKLIGHTuss, ca. 500 B.C.) that all matter was in flux, everything changing, so that one could never step into the same river twice.

3. With a long enough lever and a place to stand, one could move the world, said ARCHIMEDES (ca. 250 B.C.) arkiMEEdeez is also the one who, when he discovered that the weight of liquid displaced by a body equals the exact amount of force that buoys it up, leaped from his bathtub. HEUREKA! (I've found it!), he cried and dashed naked into the streets of Syracuse, thus providing all future eccentric scientists with a role-model.

4. The Earth is round. To be exact it's 24,662 miles around (today we compute the circumference at 24,902). ERATOS-THENES (airuhTAHSthuhneez, ca. 200 B.C.) deduced this astonishingly accurate piece of information with simple arithmetic. He knew that at noon in Alexandria, on midsummer day, the sun was not quite directly overhead. By the shadow of an obelisk, it could be measured at about 7.5 degrees away from zenith. But about 500 miles south, at noon of the same day, the sun cast no shadow, even down a deep well, and was therefore at zenith. He concluded that about $\frac{7.5}{360}$ of the earth's surface was therefore about 500 miles, and that the whole circumference was then roughly $500 \times \frac{360}{7.5}$ miles, or about 24,000.

In his GEOGRAPHICA Eratosthenes also mentioned another little theory of his: that one might voyage by sea from Spain, across the Atlantic, to India.

Ignoring such stuff was what the Dark Ages were all about.

II

THE MEDIEVAL MYSTIQUE

The One Medieval Idea You Need to Know

Must you know how to play chess? Nay, verily. How to crusade? Not in the seventies. Ditto for protecting virgins from dragons, slaying infidels and heretics, and chasing grails: that's closer, but wrong again.

On grounds of universality and longevity, the most important medieval (A.D. 410–ca. 1500) idea of them all would have to be the one that helped ignite, so to speak, most of these medieval doings:

The Inferno

Though the idea wasn't new (see PLATO), Christian and Moslem theology gave eternal flame its first star billing.

The New Testament quotes Christ as mentioning outer darkness, and a furnace "where there shall be weeping and gnashing of teeth." Scriptures also record His remarks about vines that would be thrown into the fire and burned if they weren't connected to the main branch.

By A.D. 400, AUGUSTINE wrote of the City of God, a Platonic Form which, on the Day of Judgment, would become a real Heaven. Its counterpart, the Earthly City, would also materialize after Judgment to welcome Satan and worldly souls to perpetual torment.

Over in Byzantium, where Greco-Roman civilization grew Christian, fat, and prosperous as it mingled with the Orient, the Greek Orthodox bishops of Constantinople found the notion of Satan and Hell agreed well with the populace. Many Persians already believed in ZOROASTER (sometimes called ZARATHUSTRA)'s demonology, where a god of evil perpetually warred with the god of good.

From these modest beginnings, the idea caught fire.

In A.D. 600, MOHAMMED envisioned a judgment day when souls would have to walk a superfine tightrope over Hell, trying to get across to Paradise. Sinners and infidel dogs, of course, would fall off, plummeting down to one of seven levels appropriate to their offenses, there to drink boiling water and filth, wear shoes of fire, and take fire into their bellies.

Roman Catholic monks, by the twelfth century, were describing a burning gridiron where Satan, chained in red-hot shackles, crunched the damned between his teeth, while assistant devils boiled, sliced, pounded flat, stabbed, and hung up by the tongue other misbegotten souls. One version added sulfur to the flames to pollute the atmosphere, while another imaginatively envisioned diabolic cheesecloth, through which sinners could be eternally strained.

Toward the end of the thirteenth century, even the most rational of medieval theologians, THOMAS AQUINAS, located Hell in the lowest part of the earth.

And in the beginning of the fourteenth, DANTE, the most poetic, pictured the abyss at the end of a long tunnel to the earth's core. In his INFERNO, the first book of THE DIVINE COMEDY, he saw nine levels, each progressively less pleasant for those progressively more wicked. The eighth circle is for, among others, robbers, alchemists, and schismatics. The most famous of the latter is Mohammed, who must perpetually tear open his chest, throat to waist so that the entrails dangle, because in life his doctrines divided the faithful. The ninth circle is for traitors—buried in ice up to their chins—and the three most famous, Brutus, Cassius, and Judas, are perpetually chewed in the jaws of the frozen-in Lucifer.

Not until the disciples of FREUD would man's fear of the unknown be systematized with such brilliance.

WAR

Of course, though the basic sin now—pay later ideas is still very much with us and is even enjoying a revival in some quarters, the really devilishly clever variations on the theme, exploited so well by the medievals, have long gone.

Mohammed seems to have been the first to think of it. In the seventh century, with the simplicity of genius, he promised those who died fighting for him the reward of paradise—a paradise whose milk and honey were supplemented by seventy-two beautiful virgins, and eternal youth, for every man.

That was the idea that got all those swords of Islam out on the road from Mecca, heading west to conquer Spain with an offer the Spaniards couldn't refuse.

With equal inspiration, in 1095 Pope Urban promised absolution from all sins to all fallen crusaders—which amounted to the same paradise, minus the virgins. That got all those Christian lances on the road south to recover Jerusalem.

For those on both sides, the Holy Wars were a fail-safe proposition. As long as they were crusading, warriors no longer had the idea of the inferno kicking them around.

Defenders of the Faith were safe for eternity and could make war with a light heart.

They just don't make war like they used to.

MORALS

The inferno also had its everyday peacetime influence. In the tradition of both Zoroaster and the Bible's Book of Job, medieval theologians cast Satan as the tempter of men. To yield to temptation, from Eden and ever after, meant no paradise, yes inferno.

High on the list of temptations was lust. The Church underscored lust's sinfully pagan qualities by giving Satan the hoofs-and-horns image of those lusty Greek satyrs—inflated, reddened (scorched, no doubt), and in some versions, since he was a fallen angel, winged. Satan was everywhere. With his assistant demons, he flew up from the inferno to tempt presumably because, like the earthly sinful, he enjoyed spoiling things for the pure. If one wanted to give in to the whisperings of one of these devils, it was best to schedule the sinning so that one could get to a priest soon after; otherwise one might die unshriven and burn *in perpetuum.*

Virginity was in for both sexes. Saints (there were twenty-five thousand by the tenth century) got straight passes to heaven, as did the monks, priests, and nuns who stayed celibate. All others had to go to purgatory, if incontinent, where flames would gently singe them to atone for their impurities.

Through good deeds on earth—such as giving more than the required tithe or bequeathing one's estate to the Church —one might atone for sins and cut down on one's purgation time. By 1200 the Church, which had exclusive jurisdiction over the probate of wills, owned whole cities, thousands of serfs and slaves, and nearly a fourth of the land in Germany and England.

One might also earn time off by becoming a pilgrim. Jerusalem was the Mecca for the Christian, but there were other spots throughout Europe worth visiting. Most shrines had relics: bits of the True Cross, toenails of saints, and so on, which one might draw near to and cleanse not only one's soul for the future but also one's body for the present. Miraculous cures were wrought by relics, and the flocking of pilgrims to successful shrines soon brought on competition. Different bishoprics claimed skeletons of the same saints, and even complete corpses, so that one hardly knew which to believe. The rivalry reached its height in France, where five churches claimed to possess the one true relic from Christ's circumcision.

ARTS AND SCIENCES

Sins of the flesh were not to be encouraged, especially in the art of the Church, much of which had to substitute for scripture because the people couldn't read. The flesh portrayed in these illustrations is therefore appropriately bloodless. The idea was for the artist to deny the body and emphasize the soul, which was infinitely more worth illustrating because it would live for eternity. Hence the soulful expressions and portrayals which give medieval art its uniquely ethereal charm.

As might be expected, morbid fear of the inferno put a damper on science and learning. Reason was something the Greeks had advocated and was therefore suspiciously pagan. Relics were better than experiment. Since only a few outside the Church could read, and since the churches held most of the manuscripts, clergy didn't get much argument from budding young scientists. Arguments were reserved for theological issues and taken very seriously. If a careless scholar botched a point of doctrine, that could mean heresy —and an automatic ticket to the flames of Dante's Circle Number Eight.

JUSTICE

The belief in the inferno helped sanctify the pagan custom of trial by ordeal. Hot irons to hold, boiling water to dunk in, fire to walk on barefoot helped separate the guilty from the innocent. In another variation, a river was exorcised to reject sinners and the accused, bound hand and foot, was thrown in. If he was rejected (i.e., floated), he was guilty. If he sank, he was declared innocent, which must have been cold comfort.

The inferno, though, was worse than any of these temporal torments. The body didn't really matter, and, if the man was innocent, he would be saved later, when it counted.

Also sanctified by infernal flames were the Inquisitions. Since heretics led those who followed them to damnation, they were endangering men's souls—the worst possible crime, for which they were to receive the worst possible death. By doctrine the Church wasn't allowed to spill blood, so she had the secular authorities preside while the *auto-da-fé*, the act of faith, was performed. To further avoid bloodshed, the favored mode of execution was burning at the stake.

If these Gothic ways seem barbaric, remember that at this time (ca. 1300) the Goths had only recently stopped being barbarians. Europe was a frontier during the Middle Ages, and the harsh laws and threats, like automatic hanging for horse thieves, helped tame some most uncivilized souls. The Celts, for example, when they overthrew their queen, tied her feet, hands, and hair to the tail of a horse, and then galloped the horse till the queen was dead.

One might likewise remember that an enormous number of medieval lives were saved by that other innovation of the Church, Christian charity.

POETIC JUSTICE

Still, it's somehow appropriate that the Holy Wars (A.D. 1095–1291) instigated by Pope Urban helped to bring the medieval era of feudalism and Church dominance to an end. After two hundred years of wholesale slaughter on both sides—Richard the Lion-Hearted had fifteen hundred prisoners beheaded one afternoon, for example, to show his impatience with a city that was slow to surrender—Christendom emerged the loser. Not only was Jerusalem still in infidel hands after the Fourth Crusade, but the Christian city of Byzantium, Constantinople, had been sacked by invaders—Christian invaders, hungry for some victory, any victory.

With this inglorious finale the seeds of doubt were planted; and with the harems and spices and luxuries of the Mediterranean, they were fertilized. The power of the Church's stern authority was beginning to wane.

And while the ruling class was off crusading, the tradesmen and middle classes were rebelling, ending the feudal system by setting up town governments. At least one bishop reluctant to yield his rule and give a town its charter was hacked to pieces with sword and battle-ax. The Church's power to strike mortals numb with terror was diminished greatly. Perhaps to show that their thoughts were now on heaven rather than hell, the new communities each tried to outdo the other with the height and airy grandeur of their cathedrals, the most beautiful and permanent achievement of the Gothic mind.

The idea of the inferno, though, was still smoldering. When a new continent needed civilizing, Mother Church would bring it out again. A primitive belief, true, but when faced with a primitive world, she fought fire with fire.

The Medieval Names You Should Know

MYTHS AND LEGENDS

ROMANCE

If it weren't for the romances—the medieval's Disney version of knight life—our operas and theater companies would be in deep trouble, to say nothing about Prince Valiant comics, TV late shows, and 25 percent of Disneyland. Ever since the twelfth century, when early French writers—whose language was called *roman* and whose stories *romans*—started playing up the sentiments of knightly honor and courtly love, all the world has loved a good romancer. In fact, it loved the stories long before it knew what name to call them, so the label *romans* stuck.

Stories of KING ARTHUR and CAMELOT are probably the most famous of the romantic tales. By now everyone knows how Arthur pulled the sword from the stone, got another from a lady under the lake, diplomatically invented the Round Table, hired a wizard of an advisor named MERLIN, worked overtime, neglected his marital bed, and lost face when LANCELOT filled in for him. We all cheered when he sent Queen GUINEVERE packing to a nunnery, but we wept when, wounded in the winter mists by wicked Modred, he sailed away over the great deep on a mystical barge with three-maidens, and disappeared into the horizon just as the sun rose bringing the new year.

Still, we know that one of these years, in the spring, he's going to come back.

Besides Lancelot's indoor sport, the knights of the Round Table had their share of adventures. The most famous of these is that of THE GRAIL—the chalice Our Lord drank from at the Last Supper and which Joseph of Arimathea later used to catch a few drops of Christ's blood as He hung on the cross. To recover so sacred an object was a quest worth undertaking, and the tale was worth telling in several languages. In English the quester is GALAHAD; in French he's PERCEVAL, and in German he's PARZIVAL. All three succeed: the first two are borne up to heaven with the grail; but Parzival marries and settles down instead, fathering LOHENGRIN and, hundreds of years later, two WAGNERIAN operas (see THE NINETEENTH CENTURY).

A good story too, and in better poetry, is SIR GAWAIN AND THE GREEN KNIGHT, a tale of seduction and chivalry with the most spectacular opening in English letters. It's New Year's Day. Arthur and his knights are New Year's dining when a Green Knight rides into the Camelot dining hall, horse and all. He dismounts and offers a knightly version of the old "trading hits" game: he'll let one of Arthur's crew take an ax to his neck today, if in a year he can return the blow. GAWAIN accepts the challenge, and the knight's razor-sharp ax, and with one stroke cuts off the green head. Then the knight walks over to where his head has rolled, picks it up, and still spouting blood, climbs back up on his horse. The head, which the Green Knight holds up by the hair, faces Arthur's table and says the Middle English courtier's equivalent of "See you next year, Gawain." Then, Lone Ranger–style, he gallops off, leaving the rest to ask, "Who was that Green Man?"

Tune in next year, and we learn that the Green Knight's game was to test Gawain's bravery (is he man enough to stand up to an ax?) and his knightly virtue (can he resist a lovely, seductive enchantress?). Gawain passes the test, but narrowly enough to keep the suspense humming.

Other nations besides England had their knightly heroes of romance. The French read about Charlemagne and ROLAND, who blew his horn for Charlemagne's reinforcements against the Spanish Moors, then held them off and died in God's knightly service, his gaze fixed on the fatherland. The Spanish sang of EL CID, another quester against infidels, and the Germans of SIEGFRIED, the Achilles-like invulnerable warrior who bathed in dragon's blood, but whose Achilles' heel was a spot on his back, where a leaf, fallen during the bath, kept the blood from working its magic. Aside from winning battlefield glory, Siegfried also distinguished himself in the bedroom with reluctant Queen BRUNHILD on her wedding night—in a painfully violent knock-down struggle. Having subdued her, Siegfried didn't claim his prize, because she wasn't his. He was just doing a favor for a less pugnacious friend, to whose attentions he left the exhausted Brunhild. (For a much more romantic version of these two, see WAGNER.)

It's worth noting two other tales from medieval history that have found their way to fame: the stories of MACBETH, one-time king of Scotland, and AMLETH (move the "h" to the front), Prince of Jutland, were recorded by medieval chroniclers before SHAKESPEARE brought them onto the stage.

THE KNIGHT

The knights we find in medieval journals and letters seem to have been a rapacious lot, rather like the Old West gunfighter or the Japanese samurai. Though sworn vassals of the feudal lord and hence arms of the local law, it appears they frequently put the arms on the local serfs' livestock, money, and women. On the Crusades they achieved notoriety enroute by more of the same, and when they finally reached the cities of the south, which had brothels, many simply refused to come out and fight.

The IDEAL KNIGHT, found in medieval romance, is sworn foe of these fellows. He's pro-chastity and pro-Church, in the mold of England's knightly ideal and patron saint, GEORGE. As the legend goes, a virgin damsel by a lake was about to be eaten as the local dragon's yearly pacifier. George happened by while she was awaiting, and weeping over, her fate. Fear nought, he said, in the name of Our Savior. Then as the dragon, a Loch Ness type, emerged hungrily from the water, George crossed himself, commended his soul to his Maker, lowered his lance, and charged.

What happens then varies with various storytellers. Some have George simply slaying the beastie, but the most knightly has George backing away from his initial thrust and commanding the damsel to throw her girdle around the dragon's neck. Thus charmed, the monster's instantly domesticated and follows the damsel home. Presumably papa, the local king, added it to his defense arsenal.

FAIR LADIES

Aside from your stock helpless-virgin figure, there are three other medieval ladies whose figures, albeit draped, were placed on medieval pedestals just as high as those of the Greek goddesses.

Uppermost, of course, was the VIRGIN MARY. Worship of her could be said to have begun at Egyptian shrines of ISIS, the ancient Egyptian Mother of God, who was shown suckling the infant HORUS in a stable during the Egyptian midwinter festival. Horus, according to Egyptian legend, slew death and so enabled the Nile-god to be resurrected (i.e., rise) in the spring. Early Christians converted Isis shrines. Medievals saw Mary as an intermediary between them and a harsh male deity rather than as a fertility symbol, but they kept the Madonna-and-child motif.

A secularized form of praying to the Blessed Virgin was a love lyric to one's fair lady—whose divine perfections one could not ever hope to win. Such exaggerated praise for the wives of manor lords was sung by knights and troubadours that one couldn't possibly take it seriously. Lives were pledged to defending and honoring various lovely eyes, smiles, and souls of women who were wed to others, and their inaccessibility seems only to have generated a more intense outpouring. Perhaps it was necessary to see the LADY OF THE CASTLE as holier than all because her spouse was away on various crusades for long stretches. Or perhaps it simply made good court entertainment for women who married for politics or property alone. Whatever the motive, the idea of the lady fair was at the heart of chivalry and romantic love, raising womanhood far above the status she had held among the Greeks, to love-object.

ECCLESIA, or MOTHER CHURCH, was also reverenced.

She, however, was much less photogenic, looking positively masculine in some renditions.

THE PAGAN SUPERNATURAL

Though hardly as grandiose a collection as the Greek and Roman pagan deities, a few of the Norse gods nonetheless managed to leave their mark before missionary Christians ended their rule (ca. A.D. 800). They lived in VALHALLA, a beer-drinker's version of Olympus, where warriors who died in battle were taken by VALKYRIES (maiden goddesses) to quaff nightly a bucket of mead or two with the immortals. Warriors who died elsewhere went to HELL, where, though there weren't flames, were neither excitement nor brewers. Incentive again.

Two Valhallans of note were TIW, a god of war, named phonetically from the same Indo-European root as was ZEUS, and ODIN, or WODEN, the head god. Odin ruled wisely because he'd drunk from the well of wisdom—after plucking out one eye as the price of a cupful. Also up there was Odin's enforcer, THOR, who threw his hammer to make thunderbolts and drove his chariot to make thunder. Finally there was FRIGGA, or FRIGG, Odin's blond-haired wife.

If you're not sure yet of the mark Tiw, Woden, Thor, and Frigga made, add the sun and the moon and Saturn, and tack on "sday" after each. If you want to see them all again, the place to go is Bayreuth (see WAGNER).

PHILOSOPHY

Contrary to popular belief, the major question debated by medieval philosophy was not how many angels could dance on the head of a pin, though the dispute was equally practical. Medievals reasoned over whether it was reasonable to use reason, posing this burning question: Is philosophy any use at all?

Their answer? Well, yes and no. Or, taking it chronologically, no and yes, and then back and forth.

In about A.D. 400, AUGUSTINE began the attack on reason. He convinced the Church of man's essentially sinful nature, helped by the famous anecdote of the PEAR TREE in his CONFESSIONS. In boyhood days, Augustine recalled, he and the gang would steal pears—unripe, and more than they could have eaten anyway—when they weren't even hungry. They stole just for the sheer hell of it—a clear proof of man's essentially damnable nature, which only a deity could save.

Philosophy classes liken Augustine to Plato because of the IDEAL cities he wrote about in THE CITY OF GOD. One was an ideal of good, the other of wickedness, in which all earthly cities participate to a greater or lesser degree. But come Judgment Day, said Augustine, these ideals become the real heaven and hell.

Putting the two ideas together, essential sin bars mortals from making it to the heavenly city on their own. One can only have faith and trust in supernatural help. So, reasoned Augustine, reason was out, faith in.

Next comes BOETHIUS (boEEtheeuss), who by A.D. 524 had written the CONSOLATION OF PHILOSOPHY while in jail. Reviving Stoicism, Boethius argued the pain-killing virtues of taking a reasoned look at things. If one sees the Big Picture—the favorite Stoic viewpoint—one sees that fortune's like a spinning wheel. What goes up must come down, and then up again. His painful present was compensated for by past glories, although having known happiness, he admittedly missed it the more. Yet he kept on writing. If Boethius knew that his jailers, for his plot against the emperor, were preparing to tie a cord around his head, tighten it until his eyes burst from their sockets, and beat him to death with clubs, then his philosophy was powerful consolation indeed.

Peter ABÉLARD, a Parisian theologian nearly eight centuries after Augustine, questioned the supremacy of faith. He tried to know, in order to believe, rather than believe first in order to know. Unfortunately he made the mistake of getting HÉLOÏSE, one of his students, pregnant, which hindered his theological career. Neither was he helped when her uncle, after Abélard put Héloïse into a nunnery so that he could remain a priest, avenged the family honor by, as Abélard put it, cutting off "those parts of my body whereby I had done that which was the cause of their sorrow." Héloïse wrote him letters from her nunnery afterward, though Abélard was in no condition to respond with similar passion.

Finally THOMAS AQUINAS, another Parisian in residence, adopted Aristotelian dialogue to prove the existence of God as the First Cause. His prodigious SUMMA THEOLOGICA tried to prove, by reason, both God's presence and the validity of Church doctrine. It took him twenty-one volumes and gave rise to the movement called SCHOLASTICISM.

The philosophizing became excessive, however. DUNS SCOTUS made such logic-chopping and hairsplitting out of doctrinal questions that the Church eventually laughed scholasticism away. A Duns man, or dunce, is now the name for a fool.

One of the men who helped give Duns his bad reputation was WILLIAM OF OCKHAM. He brought some sanity, or at least brevity, into late medieval philosophizing with the idea we call OCKHAM'S RAZOR. If two explanations sound equally reasonable, he reasoned, prefer the shorter. In other words, keep it simple and don't louse it up.

LITERATURE

In addition to the great romances, it's not a bad idea to be familiar with the oldest of England's poems. BEOWULF (BAYohwolf) was written sometime between A.D. 450 and 700, when the Christians were just starting and the Romans were just leaving. The Anglo-Saxon poet, whoever he was, tells a bloody adventure yarn about two monsters and a dragon, chanting Old English in a tone Howard Cosell would have used if he'd been a bard in one of primitive Britain's mead halls.

If you remember that the hero's name was Beowulf, that the first monster's name was Grendel, and that Grendel liked a Danish warrior or two for a midnight snack, you'll know more than most people. But the best part comes later, after Beowulf tears off Grendel's arm. Grendel runs home to his mother and dies, and his mother sneaks up to the Danes' mead hall in search of her son's arm. After she eats a warrior, Beowulf gets on her trail and chases her down to the bottom of her black lagoon. A fight. Warriors on the shore see the water churned into bloody froth. Despair. Then Beowulf swims up with Grendel's head, a trophy so big that it takes four strong men to drag it back to the mead hall.

The dragon? That battle comes after Beowulf's gone back to Sweden and been king there "fifty winters," and it's Beowulf's last fight. All but one of his men are too cowardly to face the dragon's fiery breath and poisoned claws. Beowulf's sword fails him, but he stabs the beast with his dagger. His reward for the kill is a mortal wound, a look at the dragon's treasure hoard, and then later a funeral pyre.

The one medieval poet to know, besides DANTE, is GEOFFREY CHAUCER (JEFFry CHAWsir, ca. 1340–1400). Not too many people read Chaucer nowadays, and for good reason: he wrote in another language, Middle English. His poetry, which he wrote as a sideline when he wasn't too busy as the king's agent, was copied out by scribes and read by the limited audience of the English nobility in the courts of King Edward III and Richard II. English poets have been using Chaucer's metrics ever since.

THE CANTERBURY TALES, Chaucer's masterpiece, had a respectable run on Broadway not long ago. Many of the tales are bawdy. Lovers perform Explicit Acts in strange situations: once in a tree, another time through an open window in the dark, as well as in more conventional positions. The WIFE OF BATH, Chaucer's most unforgettable character, is sometimes recalled these days as an archfeminist. On the pilgrimage to Canterbury that provides a frame for the tales, she gives the other pilgrims first a blow-by-blow account of how she's mastered five husbands, and then a tale in which the bridegroom wins all by giving his wife "maistrie." But when it came to "maistrie" between the sheets, the Wife was just a gal who can't say no. As she says, "I koude noght withdrawe / My chambre of Venus from a good felawe."

Another of Chaucer's pilgrims, the Prioress, put it more delicately. She said, "Love conquers all."

ARCHITECTURE

As every art history class learns, around A.D. 1000 man invented the pointed Gothic arch to let more light into the cathedrals and so, with one stroke of brilliant architectural innovation, ended the Dark Ages.

Here's how it happened. They built ROMANESQUE

cathedrals in a line of rectangular box-sections called BAYS. Holding up the roof of each bay were four round Roman arches, aqueduct style, which made the round ceiling of each bay look like the ceiling of an igloo. And naturally the ceiling came down lower on the short sides of each bay—the sides where the windows were—because the round arch on the short side couldn't be as tall as the round arch on the long side.

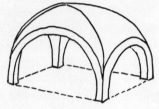

It made for small side windows and pockets of gloom in the ceiling.

But with the Gothic arch, the top of the window could go all the way up to the roofline, like so:

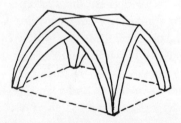

In the words (last words, in fact) of GOETHE (which see), "More Light!" Or as they say in today's A-frame building and real estate trade, "a cathedral ceiling!"

When they added the outside prop called the FLYING BUTTRESS, the walls didn't need to be so thick. Cathedrals could build up instead of out, higher and higher, a style which, art historians are also fond of pointing out, shows that man now had bold aspirations toward the Divinity, elevating himself to a more lofty position, or "flinging his passions against the sky." If that sounds like an overly poetic way to talk about tall buildings, it at least gives you something to say if the kids ask what those pointed arches are doing at the base of the World Trade Center.

A few other things to know about cathedrals, since today's are still built with many of the old parts. The medievals liked a floor plan in (what else?) the shape of a cross. You walked in at the bottom of the cross, under the big round window called the ROSE WINDOW. The top of the cross— the end of the cathedral where the priests stood—was called the CHOIR. The cross section, as it were, was called the TRANSEPT. This is the part that's missing from today's smaller churches. The central part of the cross, where the people stood, was called the NAVE, because its ceiling, with those pointed arches, looked like the inside hull of a ship turned upside down. The windows along the side, going up to the roofline, were called the CLERESTORY (KLEER-story), because that story of the cathedral was kept clear, above other roofs, so that light could come in.

FLYING
BUTTRESS

CLERESTORY

Incidentally the derivation of those spires, that aspire to such heights, comes from an Old French equivalent of "spear."

What Not to Bother With

HISTORY

1066, the year the Normans gave Harold an arrow in the eye at Hastings, and 1215, the year the Barons gave John his comeuppance at Runnymede, were important points in time. But they're too well known to be of much use in a conversation after, or even before, one's finished junior high social studies.

The Crusades are too embarrassing for all but Moslems to mention.

It was no doubt exemplary that Charlemagne kept wax tablets under his pillow to teach himself writing, and good for the Church that he stopped the Moslems at the Pyrenees, but does anyone care?

Like the battles of the Old West, the battles of the Older West tend to fade away. Only the romanticized tales of Camelot retain their life.

However, the one thing that does concern us about the past, to paraphrase Oswald Spengler (the German philosopher who in 1928 published *The Decline of the West*) is that we not be condemned to repeat it.

What interests us about the Middle Ages, historically speaking, isn't the Middle Ages. It's how they began. How did a sweaty pack of Vandals and Huns, whose idea of a hot lunch on the road was to gnaw at one of the raw meat hunks they kept under their saddles, manage to bring down an empire? Where did the Romans—and where might we—go wrong?

Well, some Romans blamed it on the Christians, maintaining that the old gods had punished the empire for turning away and that the new god wasn't warlike enough. Augustine, however, neatly turned the tables on these arguments, proclaiming that the new God was punishing the old Romans for their sins.

Theological explanations aside, hindsight shows some obvious Roman blunders. First of all, they lost control of their armies. After a century or two, most of the Roman soldiers weren't Romans but mercenary tribesmen from the invading tribes.

Second, ruling-class tastes were a bit self-indulgent. Pies made with parrots' tongues—parrots which had been trained to talk, naturally—were in. And tastes of the masses likewise ran to the decadent. At the Colosseum between the acts, they watched attendants dressed up in Charon (boatman to the underworld) costumes, who would wander among the dead bodies, prodding them with hot irons. If any bodies moved, their skulls were promptly smashed.

Third, and perhaps most indicative, Roman rulers simply lacked the energy to rule. In fourth-century Rome there were 175 holidays a year, supplemented with *ad hoc* celebrations which might run three months at a time. Pay for these binges, and for the daily welfare handouts of bread and corn, came from heavy taxes on the surrounding towns and farmers. As one might expect, patriotism in the outer regions was not bolstered by this practice.

Ten years into the fifth century, Alaric the Goth laid siege to Rome and cut off its food supply. Soon, instead of parrots' tongues, the Romans were eating each other—before they finally surrendered.

MUSIC

About all you need to know about medieval music is that, when the Gothic flowering came, it got fancier.

Until 1040, when an Italian monk named Guido invented musical notation, medievals all sang in unison. Today's folk purists and devotees of the Gregorian plain song—that chanting quasi-oriental church music derived from the Hebrew

cantors—still aren't sure that Guido made an improvement.
And whatever one's taste, it must be admitted that after a
few hours of Norman Luboff the medieval monophones do
sound refreshingly simple. When heard in solemn moments,
as in the great Christmas and Easter festivals, their weird
minor-key power borders on the hypnotic.

But by the twelfth century with nothing but unison parts
to sing, it's clear that the medievals were bored. They
rushed into polyphonic hymns just as soon as their local
monks, using Guido's system, could write out the parts
for them to learn. Soon they had the formula for two-part
harmony: when the main voice ascends on the scale, the ac-
companying voice descends. And from there it was on to
four parts, five parts, even six, with counterpoint so complicated that, in the fourteenth century, Pope John XXII
condemned the new style as a distraction to piety.

Soon, though, popular taste prevailed. Even the top-level
clergy had to admit that the ornate music went well with the
ornate Gothic cathedrals, and that written music was in
church to stay.

The same Guido, incidentally, named most notes of the
scale from a Latin hymn to "Sancte Joannes" the Baptist,
since the music went conveniently up one whole tone (except for between *mi* and *fa*, where it went up one half tone)
at each half-line of the hymn. The notes changed on these
now immortal syllables:

> *Ut* queant laxis *Re*sonare fibris,
> *Mi*ra gestorum *Fa*muli tuorum,
> *Sol*ve polluti *La*bii reatum,
> Sancte Joannes.

Si, or Ti, a half tone away from the next *do*, was added later,
perhaps from the last line, and all but the French preferred
to sing "do" instead of "ut." That's a *Major Scale*. A *minor
scale* puts the half step between *re* and *mi*, and between *sol*
and *la*.

Secular music was carried from town to town by the traveling minstrels, or troubadous, or, in Germany *Minnesingers*, of which the most famous was a man called Tannhäuser. In later Middle Ages, these German vocalists organized themselves into guilds, so that one might serve an apprenticeships and then become a *Meistersinger*. WAGNER carried both traditions into two of his operas centuries later.

DRAMA

Just remember that medieval drama evolved the same way Greek and Roman drama did—from religious ritual.

The Church abolished secular drama as obscene, which the old Greek and Roman phallus-wavers certainly were. Then over the centuries, out of choral responses and holiday pageants, drama grew up again. Soon productions were too big for the cathedral choirs and had to be moved out to the churchyard, and then down to the town square, or onto portable wagon-stages which performed, parade-float style, throughout the town.

Naturally the plays had religious themes. Those about Biblical figures were called MYSTERY PLAYS, and those about post-Biblical heroes MIRACLE PLAYS. Both had, as one might expect, happy endings.

Interestingly enough, the farther the plays got from the church grounds, the more folk humor and bawdry crept into the scripts, until they were soon being used as background entertainment for drinking bouts. It was at this point (ca. 1250) that church edicts gave actors a bad name, and a worse future in the inferno, by excommunicating all who trod the boards.

DANCE

Aside from recommending a jig or two before the image of child-martyr St. Vitus as a cure for nervous disorders, the Church frowned on dancing.

That didn't stop people, of course. Open-air folkdance frolics, with troubadours and minstrels, pretty girls, and maybe a maypole or two, were widespread. Indoors, though, there wasn't much room for the common folk to dance except at taverns, where dancing embellished its bad reputation. Court nobles, better housed, could move their tables aside and have dancing after dinner, supplemented by jugglers, tumblers, and perhaps an occasional belly dancer up from the Mediterranean.

UNIVERSITIES

Take away football, research labs, coeds, large classes, and fraternities, add everyday academic gowns and Latin, and you've pretty much got a medieval university. (Of course, some might argue that football, research labs, etc., are pretty much all there *is* to a modern university, but we'll have to let that pass.)

Point is, medieval students, exempt from the laws of the medieval town, were as spectacular a band of hell-raisers as their modern counterparts. Drinking was the everyday pastime. Students wined their masters after examinations and each other almost constantly, since the water was bad and the rooms were cold. Other popular ways to keep the circulation humming were hazing new students, debating, wenching (sometimes, in Paris, classes were held upstairs over a street-level brothel), and rioting in the time-honored town-versus-gown tradition. Cambridge, it's said, was founded by fugitive academics from Oxford, after three Oxford students, at the hands of irate Oxford residents, were hanged.

ART

Two schools of thought here. One sees medieval art as primitive. Figures are half-finished, inhuman, like a child's drawings, fit products of the Dark Ages, when painting and the rest of the civilized arts lay dormant in the barbarian freeze.

The other finds medieval art *intentionally* primitive, symbolic of the view of man as a fallen creature, low, inglorious, an earthly grub whose body was best forgotten.

Either way, it looks the same. Squatty, flat, cartoon-style figures without depth—yet haunting, otherworldly. Especially the ones in stained glass and tapestries. Most all of it, of course, is religious—saints and so on—except for the wood carvings under the hidden "misericord" seat braces (where tired clergy rested their backsides while pretending to stand).

In Byzantium, however, the figures were less gnomic, and the art of mosaic—creating figures out of little colored chips set in at uneven planes to make sparkles rather than a flat glare—gives the wide-eyed icons a mesmerizing quality.

Gothic artists, like Gothic builders, made their figures taller. Unicorns and princesses and knights and heralds come in by now, too—in the age of romance. But they were still flat.

By the end of the Gothic era, however, the Italian artist GIOTTO (JOTToh, 1266?–1337?) was making paintings with a sense of depth, or solid roundness, to the human figure, and man was ready to look at his body in public again.

That began THE RENAISSANCE.

III

THE RENAISSANCE

Italy, ca. 1350–1600
Rest of Europe, ca. 1500–1650

The One Renaissance Idea You Need to Know

Anybody or anything can have *a* renaissance; the term just means a rebirth (re-nascence), or as they say in show biz, a comeback. But when people say *the* Renaissance, they usually mean the wave of nostalgia that hit Italy not long after those English, French, and German upstarts from the north had shamed Christendom by bungling (see **THE MEDIEVAL MYSTIQUE**) the Crusades.

Of course, nostalgic old Rome was still around in Italy, waiting to be dug up and dusted off. When the Italians dug and dusted, they liked what they saw. They had festivals and paraded the ancient statues in the streets. These shapely pagan figures and spicy manuscripts did more than just make monasticism look like less fun than before: they stirred Italian blood in a number of new ways.

In art, Italian painters and sculptors brought back the nude.

In architecture, they brought back classic domes, arches, pillars, and pediments.

In literature, PETRARCH wrote sensual sonnets, and BOCCACCIO lusty tales, that would have pleased the ancient Greek spirit of the fertility fest.

In court life, the Italian elite flocked to formalized revels of costume, dance, and song called MASQUES—the predecessors of today's ballets and operas.

In politics, MACHIAVELLI (which see) took the pretense of Christian charity out of politics, codifying the art of dirty tricks and petty wars.

And in lifestyles, Renaissance individualism (what we used to call "hedonism" and now call "self-fulfillment") was in for Italians. Gentry were expected to learn and do all they could about everything (well, almost everything). Artists were allowed to be vain, well paid, to sign their works, and to become famous. Doges (local governors), bankers, and merchants were expected to spend as lavishly for old and new art as the churches did—which helped accelerate the trend toward the *glorioso* both for art and for Italian artists.

That was just in Italy.

The rest of Europe more or less followed this Italian lead a century or so later. Sensuous northerners were encouraged by gold from the New World and by the first printing presses, and discouraged by wars, puritans, and a vandals' renaissance in 1526, when German Lutherans sacked Rome a second time.

As one might expect, after three hundred years of this rebirth of individualism a large collection of individual names and ideas may be found in Renaissance history books.

Fortunately, there's only one Renaissance idea you need to know:

Ripeness

RIPE ART

You can see the difference between Renaissance and Gothic (as the Renaissance Italians labeled the art of their northern neighbors, whom they now considered barbarians) just by looking for ripeness in the bodies. Flesh wasn't always exposed, but when it was, it looked *good*. No longer did the bodies look sickly and misshapen, groveling mortal coils hoping only to earn spiritual rewards. As the Renaissance developed, so did the muscles, sensuous curves, and the healthy complexions. Gone was the yellowed, anemic, carved-ivory look. Tops and bottoms were rosy. Gone too were the cramped postures that might have been carved from a single elephant's tusk. Figures struck comfortable, even heroic, poses that would do credit to, and have inspired, many *corps de ballet*.

All this lush ripeness soon caught on and helped spread the Renaissance northward. In later generations, particularly the eighteenth century, the Renaissance nude, in statue or oil, became a necessary trapping for the properly prosperous home decor. Obligingly enough, latter-day Italian hacks turned out copies by the thousands and palmed them off on unsuspecting tourists, especially British. The British in turn did the same to wealthy unsuspecting Americans in following centuries, but that's neither here nor there any longer. What matters is that the Renaissance ideal of the splendid, well-fed flesh was considered to be what beauty was all about for centuries after it began.

Today this kind of beauty goes in and out of fashion. The most frequent objection to Renaissance art is that it's too familiar and too easily appreciated, both of which qualities, some maintain, pander to tastes that are hopelessly middlebrow. For those who demand art that's difficult and disturbing, many Renaissance Madonnas and nudes look too nice. Especially those cherubs. Some intellectuals are more prone to appreciate the austerity of the Gothic form, or, of course, the modern, both of which derive their beauty from subjects less akin to today's centerfolds.

Yet under the lush beauty of much of Renaissance art is something for intellectuals to figure out: another revival from the past called CLASSICAL PROPORTION. The Italians appreciated the measurements of the ancient statues and incorporated them into many of their own, long legs and all. Besides that, they gave proportion to their paintings and statuary with the use of PERSPECTIVE, SYMMETRY, and FOCAL POINTS, designing figure groupings with an underlying geometric, one might almost say Platonic, form.

PERSPECTIVE gave paintings the illusion of a third dimension. The artist looked (spective) through (per) a network of threads at his model and sketched the outline of his subject onto paper lined off into squares that corresponded with the strings. That way he'd be sure that the nearer figures, drawn larger than those farther away, were in proportion to the sizes they really appeared to have when seen from the artist's point of view. The perspective grid also made it easy to get the angles of the floor, the windows, the ceiling, and any items of furniture properly lined up. Some artists, of course, just squinted and measured with an outstretched arm, and a thumb.

FOCAL POINTS presented the events of a painting as if they had been posed to emphasize the most important thing. A good example is DA VINCI's (which see) *The Last Supper,* where the pointing arms of the disciples, their gazes, and their body angles are all directed to the figure of Christ in the center of the table and to His gesture of submission to Divine will, the outstretched hand, palm up.

We can use the same painting to illustrate SYMMETRY. Six disciples on the left, six on the right, each group in clusters of three, one cluster on each side raised higher than the other. Naturally the background windows and wall panels are also equal on each side.

Realists object to this posed, balanced "composition" as being artificial—here, for example, there's not room for all twelve disciples at the table—yet the Renaissance artists wouldn't have cared. They were doing art, not life. And since then they've had many to agree with them.

RIPE IMAGINATIONS

Even in Northern Europe the Renaissance mind wasn't afraid of the inferno any more. Boundaries to thinking were coming down. In England, SHAKESPEARE (1564–1616) could write a play called *The Tempest* in which a magician named Prospero calls down the gods to perform at a mortal's wedding. Also in England, MARLOWE (1564–93) could have his Faust sell his soul to the devil and spend the night with Helen of Troy as a reward. In Spain, CERVANTES (sir-

VAHNtease, 1547–1616) could portray medieval chivalry as a pastime taken up by the bungling, obsessional (though well-intentioned) Don Quixote. And RABELAIS (rahbeLAY, 1494–1553) could become France's best-selling author with his satiric tales of the lusty, gluttonous giants Gargantua and Pantagruel.

Renaissance audiences appreciated, in fact demanded, the rich and the strange. The idea was to be well-rounded by becoming familiar with everything there was around. One of the Italians at the northern city of Urbana, CASTIGLIONE (casteelYOHnay, 1478–1529), even wrote a book about it, *The Courtier*. Here was the model of the "Renaissance Man," accomplished in dance, verse, song, and witty conversation so as to be able to win the favor of the ruler and the other courtiers and yet also solidly grounded in the more practical arts, and in ethics, so as to give good and honest advice to his majesty. No doubt with ripeness in mind, Castiglione described the former graces as "the flower" of the courtier's calling. "The fruit," he said, was in those accomplishments which "enable the prince to govern well." People liked his advice on how to develop these courtly virtues well enough to make him the Emily Post for nobles and kings centuries after he died. The fact that RAPHAEL (which see) painted his portrait didn't hurt his reputation either.

The Italian school of thought that made these liberated, secular attitudes possible was known by the name of HUMANISM. Humanists, as the name implies, spread the belief that man was the master of his fate, his own source of divine inspiration. Moving from town to town, as traveling lecturers and tutors, collecting high fees and lovers and applause as they went, many humanists also spread a fondness for the old pagan traditions of revel and orgy. Some Italians refused to let their children come near them. Yet the humanists made a knowledge of classical art, architecture, and literature the mark of a gentleman or lady, and doubtless improved

Renaissance manners as much as the more libidinous among them degenerated Renaissance morals.

Because of the humanists, Italian artists painted or sculpted, and the wealthy bought, scenes from classical myth such as BOTTICELLI's *The Birth of Venus,* and RAPHAEL's *Parnassus.* If the humanists had not been so enthusiastic, doubtless generations of schoolchildren would not have been required to puzzle over and through Greek and Latin syntax and, after puberty, to join college societies with Greek names. Following in their tradition, the study of languages, philosophy, literature, and the fine arts is called "the Humanities," and practitioners of those disciplines are generally expected to behave with a touch more of the libertine than their colleagues in the more somber natural or social sciences. Also following humanistic tradition, later generations have made pilgrimages to Greece and Rome in the belief that they would acquire a cultural "finish," among other things.

SOME OVERRIPE IMAGINATIONS

First there's MACHIAVELLI (MACKeeahVELLee, 1469–1527), the Florentine philosopher who systematized the arts of broken promises, fraud, lying, cruelty, and crime and called them politics. His ideas, needless to say, have been followed by countless heads of state from Henry VIII to Idi Amin and have inspired misdeeds from purges through petty burglaries.

If we want to be exact about it, of course, Machiavellian ideas weren't something new when he wrote them; he was just the first to set down the rules of the game, as he'd seen it played during his years as a diplomat and courtier. When he fell from favor and was more or less exiled to a small farm out of the action, he decided to write up what he knew and send it off to the local duke, hoping it would get him back into those corridors of power. (It didn't.)

The advice in *The Prince* stays resolutely fixated on the unpleasant parts of people and politics. Men are beastly folk, he says; by nature they're utterly unprincipled. If you leave them alone, they'll be unafraid and unmanageable, and you won't be prince any more.

So a prince has to be ruthless to keep this lot of naked apes in line. They've got to be made afraid of him, and afraid of the gods. The prince, though, must recognize that religion is their opiate, not his. He can't take religion seriously. What comes out of his mouth should be only virtuous mouthings, but he can't act that way. He'll have to commit "honorable frauds" and "glorious crimes" for his own good, and for the national security, while he's reassuring the populace that he's not a crook.

Furthermore, princes must be bold, managing fortune as if she were a woman "who must be kept down by beating and pounding." The idea is to win by intimidation, which makes it extra important for the prince not to fall for Christian values. Glorifying generosity, humility, and unworldly things is for slaves. Princes are different.

What's a prince to do, then? Machiavelli had a number of helpful hints. First, he should make war. Too much peace leads to comfort but then degenerates to laziness, dissent, disorder, and ruin. A war primes the economy and keeps the rabble busy fighting, looting, and pillaging over in some other prince's territory. Second, he should disregard the law and rule by the rewards-and-punishments system—though with finesse. His punishments should be ruthless and swift, so as to be less offensive. If a city is conquered, for example, Machiavelli recommends brisk slaughter of the opposition leaders, so that later atrocities will have a precedent and may even appear merciful by comparison.

On the other hand, rewards should be doled out little by little so that their flavor will last longer. The prince should be known for his stinginess; then men will work harder for less. If he's fool enough to be liberal, his subjects will expect more, and they'll also grow more powerful. And then if the conquest business falls off and there's a shortage of foreign loot pouring into the treasury, the prince will be in trouble. He'll have to either increase taxes or cut down on his largesse, both moves that will cause him more problems than would a reputation as a skinflint.

For presenting the pornographic side of politics with such patient fidelity, Machiavelli has been read for generations —though not discussed too much in polite company.

The most overripe of the Renaissance families, at least according to Renaissance gossip, was the house of BORGIA. The Roman underground had it that both the father, Pope ALEXANDER VI (1431–1503), and son (CESARE BOREjah, 1476–1507) slept with daughter LUCREZIA (1480–1519). In the words of one wag, these attentions made looKREE-tseeah "the Pope's daughter, wife, and daughter-in-law." There are stories that these three amused themselves with night orgies at Cesare's palace watching naked courtesans chasing chestnuts. Rumor also had it that during the day, the family once watched Cesare take target practice with his bow and arrow on a courtyard of live prisoners. Two separate papal bulls had it that a young child (*infans Romanus*) that suddenly appeared with Lucrezia was the offspring of Cesare, or Alexander—though not necessarily of Lucrezia. Scandalmongers swore that the Borgias poisoned rich churchmen with arsenic in the communion wine, so that the pope could confiscate their estates. And historians agree that Cesare, after calling four enemies to a dinner meeting to discuss peace terms, had them all arrested and put to death within days.

Tactics like this led Machiavelli to model *The Prince* on Cesare Borgia. Emulation of Cesare's ethics may also have led to Cesare's death at age thirty-one, when his men abandoned him in a difficult battle. The lives of princes, as Machiavelli said, "are short."

A more successful dynasty was that of THE MEDICI, who ruled Florence for a nearly unbroken three hundred years and numbered among them popes and queens. The most famous Medici was LORENZO THE MAGNIFICENT, whose florins bankrolled an academy of neo-Platonist scholars and commissioned a stable of Renaissance artists including BOT-TICELLI and MICHELANGELO. Lorenzo's son, Pope LEO X, tried Michelangelo but preferred RAPHAEL and LEONARDO, while Lorenzo's illegitimate son, who became Pope CLEMENT VII, was able to get Michelangelo to do two of the Medici Tombs and *The Last Judgment*. Another Medici pope, PIUS IV, was able to keep Michelangelo working on the dome of St. Peter's Basilica.

The Medici family money came from banking, mostly at 100-percent-and-up interest rates that almost compare with the loansharking demands of certain Italian families today.

Like their modern counterparts, the Medici godfathers too had to endure their share of conspiracy and gossip, but it seems that in comparison with the morals of the time, most Medicis were relatively circumspect. Many Renaissance Italian women were easy, though not all of them were free; a 1490 census of Rome tallied the number of registered prostitutes at about 15 percent of the entire female population. Fashions called for lots of velvet, many women wearing below-the-breast necklines and accenting their figures with rouge. Men strutted about in robes and tights, sampling what they could when they weren't otherwise engaged. Poisonings and street murders were as common as duels—which even young boys fought, with knives—over women or honor.

So much loose living and so much money naturally drew the displeasure of the Lutherans to the north, who frowned on this sort of thing and called for Reform. LUTHER (1483–1546) himself said that if there was a hell, then Rome was built upon it, after he made a visit there in 1511. That was six years before he declared independence from the pope.

Ten years after that, in 1527, German armies were raping nuns in Roman convents in the name of the REFORMATION. After extracting as much ransom as they could, they also burned most of the city and murdered about ten thousand people.

Art historians are fond of pointing out that after this second sack of Rome, one sees a sombering, almost surrealistic effect in the work of Michelangelo, the greatest of Renaissance artists. A look at some of his later work—the altar wall of the Sistine Chapel, on which he painted *The Last Judgment,* for example, or the brooding face of his Moses on the tomb of Julius II—is convincing evidence. Nonetheless, Rome revived, once again to become the destination of northern tourists who wantd to lose their innocence. TITIAN painted nudes as lush and tempting as any that had gone before. And even Michelangelo remained astonishingly productive until age eighty-nine and designed the colossal dome of St. Peter's, the most imposing work of Renaissance architectural grandeur.

But by then the Renaissance was fading in Italy, its exuberance moving on to the northern countries to bloom again.

Incidently, reincarnation buffs are fond of pointing out that Michelangelo died in mid-February, 1564. Why? Because in mid-April, 1564, was born in Stratford, England, one William Shakespeare. That other titan of the ripe Renaissance spirit is today the world's most popular playwright, both at the box office ($3.5 million a year at one theater alone) and in book sales (more titles in print than any other dramatist).

One of Shakespeare's most famous lines, a typically Renaissance comment from *King Lear* on the inevitability of death, should by now also be one of his easiest to remember:

Men must endure
Their going hence even as their coming hither:
Ripeness is all.

The Renaissance Names You Should Know

ART

THE TOP THREE

It's easy to keep straight the three greatest Renaissance artists if you know something about their characters. LEONARDO DA VINCI (dahVEENchee, 1452–1519), was an aristocrat (born in Vinci), a homosexual, and a perfectionist. One pope thought him a dilettante and took back a commission. It's likely that Leonardo may just have been interested in something else at the time; he was interested in so many things —from making war machines for Cesare Borgia to drawing fetuses *in utero*—that he finished only a fraction of the projects, beautiful charcoal and pen sketches, that survive in his notebooks. His art is known for composition and for subtlety and enigma, as in that portrait of the Florentine banker's wife known today as Mona Lisa, where the *chiaroscuro* (keearuh-SKYOORoh: light and shadow) around the eyes and mouth makes her smile so impossible to read. Leonardo also did *The Last Supper*, the fresco we've already discussed.

MICHELANGELO (MYEkelANjeloh, 1475–1564), on the other hand, finished an astonishing amount of work, including the greatest fresco (Sistine Chapel ceiling), sculpture (*Pietà*) and architectural design (St. Peter's Basilica dome) of the Renaissance, and many say of all time. He slept with his manservant but seems to have been asexual—at least we are told that he slept in his clothes and boots and went for months without changing them so as not to lose work time. It's said that Michelangelo painted the whole seven hundred square yards of ceiling in the Sistine Chapel while complaining that he was a sculptor, not a painter, which may explain the lack of painterly ornament: his art scorns subtlety and background frills in favor of titanic figures and heroic postures.

Yet he could be delicate, exquisitely meticulous, and poignant in the *Pietà*, the only work he ever signed (in a band across Mary's chest). There both Mary and her Son are hauntingly serene, aching with youth and beauty. Michelangelo was about twenty-five when he completed the *Pietà*, the most admired work of Renaissance sculpture. One could hardly guess that this work had been done by a man who would say, at age thirty-three, that he had not known a moment's well-being in fifteen years.

Michelangelo's darker side comes out in the frightening distortions of his late works, like *The Last Judgment* or the upside-down *Crucifixion of St. Peter*. Both works contain self-portraits, both unattractive. In *St. Peter*, Michelangelo's a passive old man; in *The Last Judgment*, he's the skin of a soul that has just been flayed, mouth and eyes gaping emptily, horribly. These works weren't appreciated as much then (*St. Peter* was left to blacken on the wall until only recently) as now, which could hardly have improved Michelangelo's sense of well-being.

Still, he's stood unequaled in heroic sculpture and painting for four hundred years, and his distortions have inspired expressionists like RODIN (which see). By now the praise for him has become so unanimous that we might simply sum him up the way Mark Twain did in *The Innocents Abroad:* "Lump the whole thing! Say that the Creator made Italy from designs by Michel Angelo!"

RAPHAEL (RAFayel, 1483–1520) worked both Leonardo's techniques of composition and Michelangelo's heroically muscled figures into his paintings. His borrowing of Michelangelo's style for one of the foreground figures in his huge fresco *The School of Athens* may have prompted Michelangelo's judgment of him: he called Raphael an outstanding product of study and technique.

In some other ways, Raphael can also be compared with his two famous contemporaries. He has more finesse than Michelangelo but less torment. His figures don't have the inverted emotion that Leonardo's have, but Raphael was more productive. Some have called him a painter of classic Greek models in Hebraic settings, which gives an idea of the serene quality in his works. His figures manage to look both splendid and almost happy at the same time, or at least to give the impression that they're not carrying around a guilty secret. His Madonnas are especially famous for their sweetness of expression, a sweetness that has led some to criticize Raphael's art as being too soft, too lacking in "message" quality.

Unlike either Leonardo or Michelangelo, Raphael seems not to have worked out of a creative frenzy. In art, that is. He was known for his mistresses, and his relatively early death at thirty-seven was blamed by one contemporary on "an unusually wild debauch."

THE OTHERS, AND WHAT TO DO WITH THEM

Of course it's doubtless good for the soul to know who the three greatest artists of the Renaissance were, but that's not likely to come up in a conversation too often. What's more likely to happen is that someone will talk about tortured, heroic genius, whereupon someone else will mention the productivity of Michelangelo. Or subtlety and perfectionism, which leads to Leonardo. Or the issue of decoration vs. provocation, which calls for Raphael vs. his critics.

The same conversational use can be made of two other Renaissance Italian artists, BOTTICELLI (1444–1510) and TITIAN (1477–1576). BOTtihCHELlee is early Renaissance, so his figures are leaner, a bit more pale and delicate, and touched with just a shade of melancholy, as if they knew that this sort of sensual sport couldn't last. TISHun's sensual figures, on the other hand, show splendid, lush colors, and Venuses who seem to know they're immortal and still love every minute. Titian himself lived till age ninety-nine, doing many of his most nubile nudes in his eighties. He's also known as a portraitist of the Renaissance popes and nobility, but that's not as sexy a topic.

You shouldn't limit your Renaissance artists to Italy, though. There are others north of the Alps whose styles come in handy when referring to today's.

First, Flanders (today's Belgium), where the banking houses rubbed elbows with Medici agents, dabbled in wool and tulip futures, and bought paintings for their homes at a splendid rate. RUBENS (ROObenz, 1577–1640), the most famous, is known to have done at least twelve hundred paintings, many in a huge Antwerp studio beneath a balcony built for spectators. He's more Italian in style than most, since he lived in Venice and Rome for eight years and came back at a time (1609) when the local fashion called for Catholic taste and classical subjects.

Ruben's trademark is the plump, plump nude woman, with "Venetian" colors of red, brown, and bright gold sunlight. You can refer to him whenever the subject of commercial art comes up—Rubens had a stable of young artists working for him and died very, very wealthy, a titled lord complete with castle and estate. You can also think of Rubens as a Raphaelite in spirit, since his paintings show pleasure and avoid giving pain. In *The Rape of the Daughters of Lucrece,* for example, there's no visible suffering—not even in the face of the Roman soldier who's struggling to heft one of Lucrece's hefty daughters up onto his horse, without much success.

The counterpart to Rubens is of course REMBRANDT (REMbrant, 1606–69). He wasn't corrupted, some would say, with the Italian Renaissance influence because he never went to Italy. He wasn't aristocratic either and liked to paint some of the less attractive commoners in Amsterdam—an old man or woman, Christ healing the sick, a woman cutting her nails—not exactly fee-bearing commercial subjects.

Rembrandt's style is also different from Rubens's in the way the subjects of the paintings are lit. Rubens's figures appear to be washed with bright sunlight, but many of Rembrandt's look as though they're standing in the dark, each with a tiny candle hovering just above the face. This aura-in-the-darkness effect is highly valued today ($2.3 million for *Aristotle Contemplating a Bust of Homer*, and that was in 1961), but in 1642, the buying public wanted more light, not art. Many of Captain Cocq's Company of Harquebusiers, for example, who commissioned a group portrait, complained that the painting we know as *The Night Watch* put them too much in the shade, so their friends couldn't recognize them. The more they grumbled, the fewer commissions came Rembrandt's way. Fifteen years later he was bankrupt and evicted from his studio, living in the Amsterdam ghetto. But he rallied with another group portrait that was well lit enough to please the subjects, *The Syndics of the Drapers Guild*. We can wonder if Rembrandt would have done it had he known the portrait would adorn Dutch Masters cigar boxes three hundred years later.

All right, that's Rubens, the aristocrat, and Rembrandt, the people's artist. They're the greats of the northern Renaissance, but they're also straight. There were kinky artists back then, too, and what they did can be likened to some of the strange tastes of today.

You've seen surrealism, yes? The melted watch, the huge detached eyeball? Well, in Flanders HIERONYMUS BOSCH (BAHSS, ca. 1450–1516) was doing the same thing with a huge detached ear and a harp. In Bosch's vision of hell, hundreds of tiny nude figures leap around a demonic landscape, tormented by the evils of that devil's lure, music (symbolized by the ear and the harp). In another panel of the same work (*The Garden of Earthly Delights*), there are at least three hundred tiny nudes, sinful but oddly wholesome, frolicking with giant birds, bubbles, grapes, and of course with each other. Bosch has his surrealist imitators even today, artistic and otherwise.

Then there's the sixteenth-century psychedelic, MATTHIAS GRÜNEWALD (GREWnehvalt, ca. 1480–ca. 1530). He did religious art also, with a luminous, not quite eerie glow that the stage lights for *Jesus Christ Superstar* and *Godspell* couldn't come close to matching. His figure of Christ in *The Resurrection* looks as if he were pure phosphorus, lit at the top.

There are two other masters of the aberrant whose styles are often borrowed by those who dabble in artistic satire. PIETER BRUEGHEL (BREUgel, ca. 1520–69) showed the Netherlands peasants in all their loutishness, though his scenes were washed in a strangely tranquilizing fluorescence of color and nothern light. Many louts today look like something out of Brueghel and don't even know or care, alas.

But nobody looks like *The Four Horsemen of the Apocalypse,* except in cartoons. That one, done by ALBRECHT DÜRER (DEWrer, 1471–1528), has survived to inspire visions of Armageddon in many an antiwar op-ed frame. Dürer's paintings are also remembered; they have the lithe, half-Gothic outlines of Botticelli, perhaps as a result of Dürer's two trips to Italy.

Finally, consider the precursors of today's "superrealism" (images even sharper than those from a photograph) school, VAN EYCK and VERMEER. vanIKE (1370–1440) is the one whose portrait of *Giovanni Arnolfini and His Bride* had been used as an example of quality art in art-appreciation ads. If you consider the detail and the perspective planning that made him able to paint four recognizable figures reflected in a curved-glass convex mirror that's barely two inches in diameter, you'll see that Van Eyck's skill wasn't only in his ability to calculate proportions. VERMEER (verrMARE, 1632–75) is also known for his steady hand as a miniaturist in oils, painting a string of very round-looking pearls, for example, each of which is not much bigger than a grain of salt. Vermeer's real fame, though, comes from his skill with light and abstract form. PROUST (which see) raved about the clarity of Vermeer's sunlight, and others have praised the precision of color in the reflections and shadows that play on the objects in Vermeer's settings. The effect is so startlingly clear that some think Vermeer used mirrors, lenses, or pinhole projectors to trace out his figures—like those "you-too-can-draw" mirror-box gimmicks on the wire stands that they used to advertise in the comic books. Maybe so. But aside from the superrealism, the composition of the works is also hailed as masterly. Vermeer arranged quadrilateral shapes in his scenes—tables, pictures, maps, windows, boxes—so that these four-sided outlines would please the eye as abstract forms all by themselves, even if the rest of the painting were taken away. Three hundred years later another Dutchman, MONDRIAN (which see), was to do just that.

WRITERS

SHAKESPEARE

He's been chided for too much exuberance and too little Latin and Greek (classical learning), but of course he was the greatest. For images it's Michelangelo, for sounds it's Beethoven, and for words it's Shakespeare. He used more words (over twenty-one thousand different ones in the plays that survive) than any other (Johnson's dictionary, more than a century later, listed only forty thousand). He coined words (lonely, bump) and idioms (strange bedfellows, in the mind's eye). He has more familiar phrases ("heart upon my sleeve" from *Othello,* for example, or "white as driven snow" from *The Winter's Tale*) than any other. Also, as we've said, more plays in production and more in print.

Though there's still a certain status attached to a liking for Shakespeare, he wrote for everyone. If audiences of all sorts hadn't flocked to his theater, THE GLOBE, he wouldn't have grown rich. But they did come, and at a good rate, when you consider that the theater probably held about twenty-five hundred people and that Shakespeare's London was only two hundred thousand—about half the size of Canton, Ohio. The audiences sat, some of them, on the benches in the three galleries; the rest, the groundlings, stood on three sides around the platform that was the stage, mingling with strolling women who sold cakes, ale, and themselves. To hold an audience under these conditions took strong stuff, or as Prospero (the magician in *The Tempest* who's often compared to Shakespeare as playwright) put it, "Potent art."

The characters Shakespeare invented are still models for practically every emotion going: the grand madness of Lear, the pathos of Ophelia, the melancholy of Hamlet, the hatred of Iago, the jealousy of Othello, the guilt of Lady Macbeth, the avarice of Shylock, the sulky servitude of Caliban, the clever buffooneries of Falstaff and Bottom—and that's only eight out of thirty-seven plays.

Those characters live today outside the theater. Many former schoolboys are still showing off memorized soliloquys and sonnets, especially the more somber ones about life, "Tomorrow and tomorrow and tomorrow . . . ," and suicide, "To be or not to be . . . ," and true love, "Love is not love which alters when it alteration finds . . . ," and humanism, "What a piece of work is man . . . ," and death, "Alas, poor Yorick. . . ."

Whole libraries have been written about Shakespeare. Nearly every year there's a new volume about who "really" wrote the plays or about whether the mistress that Shakespeare wrote of in his sonnets was married, black (the "dark lady"), or male. Nobody's proved anything conclusively yet. From a contemporary story about him, though, it does seem evident that Shakespeare also had wit when he was away from his writing desk:

> Once upon a time, when Burbage played Richard III, there was a citizen gone so far in liking with him that before she went from the play she appointed him to come that night unto her by the name of Richard III. Shakespeare, overhearing their conclusion, went before, was entertained and at his game before Burbage came. Then, message being brought that Richard III was at the door, Shakespeare caused return to be made that William the Conqueror was before Richard III.

Along the same line, Shakespeare's will is remembered for leaving his wife his "second-best bed."

Literary folk also love to study the music of his lines: the poetic sound play, the images, the rhymes, and the way the pace speeds up with large Latinate words, only to slow down at the dramatic moment with short, Anglo-Saxon ones. Lit classes look for the announced themes "Fair is foul, and foul is fair" in *Macbeth*, "Foul deeds will rise" in *Hamlet*, "Reason and love keep little company nowadays" in *A Midsummer Night's Dream*. And all those patterns of symbols: blood throughout *Macbeth*, light and dark in *Romeo and Juliet*, space in *Antony and Cleopatra*, art in *The Tempest*. . . .

Something for everyone. As his publishers said to preface his first collected plays seven years after he died, "You will find enough, both to draw, and hold you: for his wit can no more lie hid, than it could be lost. Reade him therefore; and againe, and againe." "For all time," as rival playwright Ben Jonson put it.

Or as Cassius says in *Julius Caesar:*

> How many ages hence
> Shall this our lofty scene be acted o'er
> In states unborn and accents yet unknown!

THE CAVALIER POETS

These were the swashbuckling courtiers who fought for the Royalist (King Charles I) side during the English Revolution, writing, wooing, and dying like gentlemen. They didn't write much, but what they had time for was seductive, elegant, and romantic to the hilt: "Stone walls do not a prison make . . . ," "I could not love thee, dear, so much / loved I not honor more . . . ," "Why so pale and wan, fond lover?" And that one of MARVELL's (marVELL, 1621–78 who was a Puritan, not a Cavalier, but could write just as seductively) "To His Coy Mistress":

> Had we but world enough, and time,
> This coyness, Lady, were no crime. . . .

But at my back I always hear
Time's winged chariot hurrying near. . . .
The grave's a fine and private place,
But none, I think, do there embrace. . . . [so]
Let us roll all our strength and all
Our sweetness up into one ball, . . .
Thus, though, we cannot make our sun
Stand still, yet we will make him run.

Almost a title in every couplet.

PHILOSOPHY

Besides Machiavelli, there are only two other names to remember. Both also begin with M: MONTAIGNE, the French
skeptic (monTAYN, 1533–92), and SIR THOMAS MORE,
the Englishman for All Seasons (1478–1535). Each distinguished himself from Machiavelli by writing about an Ideal
Society. Montaigne's, *On the Cannibals,* spoke of the New
World, where NOBLE SAVAGES lived healthfully, with
natural foods, and peacefully, without laws. More's was no-
where (that's what UTOPIA, the name of his book, means in
Greek). Utopians weren't savages, but rather super-reasonable
communistic farmers and town dwellers. The town folks had
to switch jobs out to the country to avoid becoming too citified,
an idea later adopted and enforced by another communistic
philosopher named Mao. A second notable quality of
the Utopians was their attitude toward gold: they used
it for chamberpots. As many would say, strictly from no-
where.

Aside from his essays on the good natural life (borrowed
later by ROUSSEAU), Montaigne's remembered as the skeptic
whose ideas inspired Shakespeare and VOLTAIRE (which
see). Two samples: To show that he preferred experience to
philosophical theory, Montaigne writes, "If I show my servant a book on love he can't make head nor tail of it, but he
makes love and knows what he is doing." Not quite as well-
known as Shakespeare's "There are more things in heaven and

earth, Horatio, than are dreamt of in your philosophy," but it amounts to the same thing, practically speaking.

Second sample? Montaigne was also skeptical of the Catholic Church, as Voltaire was to be after him. "The Church must be divine," they both wrote, "to have survived so long in spite of the corruption of its administrators."

More, on the other hand, died defending the Catholic Church. But he died with more wit than most. On his way up the scaffold to be beheaded (for refusing to support Henry VIII's new Church of England) he accepted help. "See me safe up," he said; "for my coming down, I can shift for myself." Then as he placed his head on the block, he drew his beard away from where the ax would fall and said to it, "Thou hast not offended the king."

What Not to Bother With

TWO MORE PHILOSOPHERS

Descartes (dayKART, 1596–1650). Though he was born and died in France during the late Renaissance, Descartes's head wasn't in line with his Renaissance peer group, or with anyone else's for that matter. He began by doubting everything, except that he existed. Uttering that immortal *"Cogito ergo sum"* (I think, therefore I am), he then went on to prove by reason that things and God exist, that mind and body were separate (a doctrine known as DUALISM), that animals were unthinking automatons, and that the soul was located in the pineal gland.

Philosophers do credit Descartes for accepting nothing on faith, however, and for bringing mathematics into his reasoning.

SPINOZA (spihNOSEuh, 1632–77). Known as the first to start out with mathematics and end up with PANTHEISM, Spinoza saw God as a kind of cosmic Mother Nature, who worked in everything, including people, according to fixed and unchanging principles. He reasoned that all our desires and actions have been controlled and determined by prior causes (DETERMINISM), so the only thing to do about our fates is relax and enjoy—or philosophize and try to understand, which is harder. But better. As Spinoza said, "All thing excellent are as difficult as they are rare."

Spinoza's beliefs about a fixed-principled God were rare indeed, especially among churchmen. Spinoza was expelled from the synagogue of Amsterdam and had to grind lenses to make a living.

OTHER WRITERS

CERVANTES wrote a great book about a nostalgically addled knight (DON QUIXOTE, keeHOEtay) who tilted at windmills for lack of dragons. Cervantes also died the same date as Shakespeare. (But not the day—though both are listed as April 23, 1616, what was April 23 in Spain was May 3 in England, since the two countries were using different calendars.) That's all you really need to know, other than how to pronounce "quixotic," which is what you call someone who's foolishly idealistic: he's kwicksOTTick. Of course you could read the book, but it's long and nobody does these days outside of required lit courses. Sad state, but trying to change it would only be tilting at windmills.

JOHN DONNE (DUN, 1572–1631). He was first a rakehell, then a clergyman. Hemingway used a phrase of his for a title (*For Whom the Bell Tolls*) as did John Gunther (*Death Be Not Proud*). His metaphysical conceits (farfetched metaphors, such as comparing lovers with drawing-compass ends because they both remain linked while they move apart) are splendid puzzles. Coleridge called him "rhyme's sturdy cripple," because his poems are hard to scan, and "meaning's press and screw," because he's hard to understand. An unbeatable combination to be seen reading if you want to prove to someone that you can read. He also wrote some nifty seduction poems (before he turned clergyman and wrote "holy sonnets"), if you want to prove to someone special that you think she/he can read too.

PETRARCH (PEEtrark, 1304–74). Give him credit for helping start the trend to antiquarianism and for inventing one form of love sonnet: fourteen lines usually of ten syllables each, the first eight of which set up a situation that the last six answer. That's the Italian or Petrarchan sonnet, as distinguished from the English or Shakespearean sonnet, in which there are three stanzas of four lines each, and then an answering couplet.

But scorn him for being too sloppily sentimental in his view of his women, unless you can find yourself an old-fashioned maiden in a tower. Refer to him, as did WALLACE STEVENS (which see), as "Butch" Petrarch.

RABELAIS and BOCCACCIO (bowKAHcheeoh, 1313–75). One was French, the other Italian, but they both add up to the same thing: bawdy folk stories. Or stories of bawdy folk. Rabelaisian (rabbeLAYzian) is a good word to use when you run into something earthy (read: "ribald") and clever and like it.

MARLOWE (MARloh, 1564–93). Nobody reads Marlowe's version of *Faust* much any more, though Liz and Dick did film it. Remember him for his seduction poem ("Come live with me and be my love") and for his initiating the lifestyle of the pub-crawling, brawling writer. He died of knife wounds in a tavern brouhaha over the check.

MUSIC

If you're into cultural snobbery, some think that liking Renaissance music is highbrow. Perhaps that's because of the Renaissance instrumental pieces were written for aristocratic ears at court, prior to the days of the concert halls. Or perhaps it's because the melodies sound refreshingly simple played on recorders and lutes, clavichords and dulcimers, or because the melodies themselves are refreshingly different, since many Renaissance tunes aren't based on the chordal structure we're familiar with. It was only later Renaissance composers who exploited the movement from the *dominant chord* (based on the fifth note, *sol*, in the scale) to the *tonic chord* (based on the first note, *do*) to give a piece a satisfying sense of movement and climax.

You might compare instrumental music at this stage of development—prior to the CLASSICAL period (which see)—with art prior to the Italian inventions of perspective, symmetry, and focal point, the formulas for a painting's "composition." Then again, you might just relax and enjoy it.

Much of the secular instrumental music was written for court dances, but it wasn't until later that music to accompany the various dance "movements" like the *gavotte* or the *minuet*, would be put into the same musical key, gathered into a *suite*, and still later formalized into the symphony or the quartet of chamber music.

Renaissance vocal music, especially church music, is still performed by congregational choirs, though rarely on the booming scale of Renaissance years. Back then towns and countries vied for the most magnificent choirs as their medieval ancestors had vied for the most magnificent cathedral. Composers like GABRIELI (ca. 1555–1612) wrote festival music calling for choirs in all four corners of the church, for trombones, cornets, recorders, flutes, viols and violins to accompany the four choirs, and for two organs as well. With all that material, it's not surprising that Gabrieli was one of the first to also call for shadings of musical dynamics (loud = *forte;* soft = *piano*), in terms that are still used today.

Another Italian vocal innovation from the late Renaissance (about 1550) was the *castrati*—former boy sopranos who agreed to remain sopranos, even though considerable sacrifice was required. The pope's choirs had many of them, and they appeared in seventeenth- and eighteenth-century opera (to the horror of some audiences in France), but there are considerably fewer volunteers around today for this type of work.

A northern innovation in church vocal music was the *chorale,* or hymn, where the parishioners could sing along, often to tunes they already knew from outside the church. The hymn was especially popular in Germany. Luther himself orchestrated "A Mighty Fortress Is Our God," which resounds in the rousing chords of an earlier German secular melody. Luther wasn't concerned about the propriety of using folk tunes in church; supposedly he said that it wasn't fair for the devil to have all the fun.

OPERA

MONTEVERDI (montehVAIRdee, 1567–1643) was inventing opera in Italy about the same time that Shakespeare was writing plays, but the great operas came later. True to their origins, though, later operas were frequently set in Renaissance Italy (just as were many of Shakespeare's plays; he knew a sexy locale when he had one). Italians called these new productions "drama with music" or MELODRAMA, a word that still describes their Machiavellian or Borgian intrigues and bloodbaths.

BALLET

Ballet started with dances between the acts of plays in Renaissance Italy, which is why it still contains lots of the mannerisms of classical acting, or MIME. But it wasn't until Louix XIV in France got enthusiastic enough about ballet, in the mid-seventeenth century, to support a professional company, that this dancing really caught on as a main-billing entertainment for audiences other than the royal court.

That's why French is the language of classical ballet. Thanks to Louis, we say *"pas de deux"* (pah de deuh) to describe a duet between dancers (usually the male and female lead dancers), instead of whatever that would be in Italian.

SPANISH ART

EL GRECO (the Spanish name for Domenicos Theotocopoulos, 1548–1614, the emigrant Greek who studied under Titian) is famous in Spain, and in art history classes for figure distortion in the modern mode—the bodies are extra tall and thin, and the faces look as if they've been stretched to make pointed heads and chins, like Dracula's. Maybe elGRECKoh had an astigmatism, but he made the most of it.

ENGLISH ART

To get an idea of how far behind Italy the English artists were, look at an official portrait of Queen Elizabeth. She looks as though someone had mashed her flat with a flyswatter.

HISTORY

Every English schoolboy used to have to "know his kings" by heart, but you don't. Over here, that's not history; that's entertainment. So catch Shakespeare's *Richard II*, *Henry IV* (in two parts) and *Henry V* the next time they're performed, and *A Man for All Seasons* and *Elizabeth R* the next time they're rerun on TV, for all the English history you'll ever need.

But if you must memorize something English, make it the English kings who came after Elizabeth. Notice the symmetry of this list of letters now: J, C, (R, C, R), C, J. Got it? That's James I, Charles I (Revolution, Cromwell, Restoration), Charles II, James II. James I's rule (1603–1625) is known as the JACOBEAN AGE, while Charles I's (1625–49) is the CAROLINE. Both from the Latin versions of their names. CROMWELL'S Puritan supporters cut their hair short and so were called "roundheads." Cromwell was the one who wanted his portrait painted "warts and all."

One other politico you might want to have straight is RICHELIEU. The French "Iron Cardinal" REEshelyuh was Louis XIII's Machiavelli, Haldeman, Ehrlichman, and Kissinger in the king's battle to make a France out of separate and feuding feudal states. Called the "Eminence Rouge" because of his red cardinal's habit, he ruled by secrecy (*lettres de cachet*) and intimidation, executing nobles as well as underlings, taxing mercilessly to build forts and wage war with an

army he built up to ten times its original size. One of Richelieu's sayings survives to haunt us today: "Nothing so upholds
the laws as the punishment of persons whose rank is as great
as their crime."

SCIENCE

Heavy objects fall at the same rate as light ones, said GALI-
LEO (galuhLEEoh, 1564–1642), and dropped two cannonballs from a tower to prove it. Small boys and college students
carry on in the same experimental spirit today, with water
balloons. Other Renaissance discoveries, as everyone knows,
were the telescope, the microscope, and the Western Hemi-
sphere.

Back home in Europe, though, scientific methods were still
pretty medieval. Doctors employed bleeding as a cure-all,
using razors and leeches. Bathing was not fashionable; some
yeoman farm folk and their daughters in the English country-
side were sewn into their clothes for the winter and let out
in the spring—"the sweet of the year," as Shakespeare called
it. Doubtless this custom helped them follow the tradition
of the June wedding. Queen Elizabeth, too, was not overly
hygienic. She accumulated inch-thick layers of makeup on
her face, and her teeth were uniformly blackened. Yet she
did appreciate one triumph of Renaissance science enough
to write a letter of gratitude: to the inventor of the first
water closet.

Renaissance scientists and nearly everyone else believed in
the four HUMORS, which are fun to describe people with
even today. If you had abundant blood, you were SANGUINE
—happy, and good-natured, even amorous. If you had too
much yellow bile, you were fiery, or CHOLERIC—stubborn,
vengeful, testy. Too much phlegm made you PHLEGMATIC,
which meant you were a coward, a dullard, and probably
pale of complexion. Black bile made you MELANCHOLIC:
sentimental, affected, and probably an unenterprising glutton.

It was all caused by vapors, you see, which these humors sent up to the brain. . . .

One other experimenter you might want to remember: FRANCIS BACON (1561–1626), known as a Renaissance man for his philosophy and literature, which included *The New Atlantis,* a latter-day utopia. Many have suspected Bacon of being the author of Shakespeare's plays, but most consider it hardly likely. He was also suspected, and convicted, of taking bribes in office, which sank his political fortunes. In 1626, trying to prove that one could keep foods fresh by freezing them, he died—of a cold he contracted while outside stuffing a chicken with snow.

ARCHITECTURE

The Italian innovations are just combinations and reworkings of the classics. A round Roman arch, and a triangular roof, for example, make Italianate, or Tuscan.

A Spanish version of this style in California is called "mission."

Turn a triangular Greek pediment upside down, and slice off the point so it looks like a Renaissance-man's hat, along with an arch:

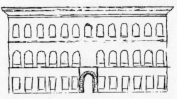

That's now called Renaissance Revival.

Or a Roman dome and Greek columns and pediments, like St. Peter's:

Up north, what we sometimes call Tudor or timber-framed houses were invented by the English, who patched up their walls with stones and plaster but let the oak frames show, outside and in.

Facing stiffer winds, early Americans soon learned to cover those plaster walls with English weatherboarding, or clapboard. By then, in Europe, the BAROQUE period was under way.

IV

THE BAROQUE ERA
1660-1789

The One Baroque Idea You Need to Know

The baroque was the era of ornamental extra, rendering the gentry of two hundred years ago as full of struts and affectations as their art was full of shells and curlicues. Whether it was in manners or in music, in philosophy or in poetry, the age was that of:

The Powdered Wig, or
The Well-Ordered Aristocrat

After Louis XIV began balding and took to wigs in 1670, the powdered wig became the mark of polite society. Everybody wore one; that is, everybody who was anybody. From

BACH (which see), the hefty German choirmaster who, as a devout Lutheran, faithfully turned out new cantatas by the dozens every year, to VOLTAIRE (which see), the slender French skeptic who satirized religion and nearly everything else except gardening, the eighteenth-century greats all appeared, in portraits at least, bewigged. Men even took to carrying their hats under their arms so as not to disturb the wig on top.

What was it all about? Well, it wasn't just imitation of Louis the Sun King. During the baroque age, the idea was to gild the lily and the head, as a badge of what academic humanists might call civilization, sociologists might call conspicuous consumption, and the boys in the corner tavern might call "class, man." If you were middle or above, by 1660 you had begun to use a fork instead of your fingers, and to wipe your hands on napkins instead of on the table-cloth. The general trend was to direct your attentions and your nose upward, away from the beastly rabble toward the finer things—ornaments. The wig was just a symbol of how the aristocrats of the period wanted to go Nature one better.

In France much of the refinement came from an innovation of aristocratic ladies: THE SALON. Salons were conscious-ness-raising gatherings for both sexes, where conversation on refined levels was held about various topics of the day. During the talks the men and women showed off their manners, intellects, and wits—just as they do on today's reincarnation of the salons: the talk shows (well, some of the talk shows).

Back then, of course, there weren't studio audiences. The finest people simply came to the receiving rooms of which-ever lady was holding the salon, where they might watch philosophers perform, and occasionally hear musicians such as the eight-year-old MOZART (which see). Naturally those of them who could, performed conversationally as well, sometimes on serious subjects but often just in fun.

A favorite salon game was called "Sentences," which required one person to make a one-sentence comment on human nature, and the rest to bandy it about to produce a topper or two. For example, "A man's whole life is but one continued exercise of self-love" might give rise to "We all have strength enough to endure the misfortunes of others." Or, "Everyone complains of his memory; no one complains of his judgment." Or, "True love is like ghosts, which everybody talks about but scarcely anyone has seen."

Those "sentences" came from the salon of one Madame de Sablé; they were written down by the man who said most of them first, LA ROCHEFOUCAULD (rohshfooKOH, 1613–80), and published with several hundred others in a favorite book of the age called *Maxims* (1665).

A bigger project of salon-goers was intended to be more of a serious influence: the first French encyclopedia. Its editor, DIDEROT (deedeROH, 1713–84), aimed to provide useful knowledge to everyone, and did, even to the point of including various trade secrets of the French guilds. In 1772, after twenty years of work and occasional hiding out from the authorities, Diderot finally brought out the opus in twenty-four folio (newspaper-size) volumes, with sections on politics, philosophy, music, and opera written by the likes of VOLTAIRE and ROUSSEAU (which see). The encyclopedia also included pages of illustrations depicting the varieties of then-available wigs.

One other far-reaching effect of the salons was to raise the status of the French woman in the eyes of the rest of Europe. Because of the deference and intellectual respect shown to the lady salon hostesses and their friends, what was French soon became what was *chic* for the rest of the West, whose women were not accorded such a high conversational station by intellectual leaders. Britisher SAMUEL JOHNSON (1709–84), for example, once remarked, "A woman preaching is like a dog's walking on his hind legs. It is not done well; but you are surprised to find it done at all."

Even in more liberated times, Parisians still hang on to their fashion-setting role—though whether this is still because of the *Parisienne*'s intellectual abilities remains in question.

In England, the intellectual gatherings were held in coffeehouses, especially during the Restoration and in the early part of the eighteenth century. Literary men like JONATHAN SWIFT, JOSEPH ADDISON, and JOHN GAY (which see) met to argue heatedly and wittily about those things that the French were discussing politely across the Channel. The English coffeehouses didn't have ladies present.

Later in the century, the English center of intellect moved to the Turk's Head Tavern in London, where the original Great One, Samuel Johnson, held forth about once a week far into the night with men like Oliver Goldsmith (*She Stoops to Conquer; The Vicar of Wakefield*), EDWARD GIBBON (*The Decline and Fall of the Roman Empire*, which see), Edmund Burke (the American colonists' speech-making friend in Parliament), Richard Brinsley Sheridan (*The School for Scandal*), painter Sir Joshua Reynolds, and actor David Garrick. What did Johnson do to deserve being at the head of such an illustrious group as this literary club? He wrote a weekly newspaper, book reviews, an edition of Shakespeare, ten volumes of biographies of poets, a prose romance (see VOLTAIRE), poetry, and the first comprehensive authoritative dictionary (though not the first; there had been two lesser attempts before his appeared in 1755) of the English language.

And he founded the club.

BACK TO CLASSICAL ORDER

As one would expect of a man who was moved to create an English dictionary, Dr. Johnson had a passion for preserving standards. The epigrams that dropped from his lips reeked of authority, classicism, and conservative politics, not to mention male chauvinism. Here are a few of the more famous, as recorded by his biographer James Boswell, often within a few hours of their utterance:

> Wickedness is always easier than virtue; for it takes the short cut to everything.

> Depend upon it, sir, when a man knows he is to be hanged in a fortnight, it concentrates his mind wonderfully.

> Whatever you have, spend less.

> There are people whom one should like very well to drop, but would not wish to be dropped by.

> Classical quotation is the *parole* [speech] of literary men all over the world.

And the famous line about dictionaries, written by Johnson:

> Dictionaries are like watches; the worst is better than none, and the best cannot be expected to go quite true.

What they believed in the eighteenth century was that there really *was* a truth in time that watches could aspire to—and that words had right meanings that a gentleman should adhere to. A right answer for most everything was around, somewhere. The eighteenth-century mind would brook none of this business of "relativity," "situation ethic," or even Renaissance individualism. At least the conservatives wouldn't. There was a Right Way to be found, almost like a PLATONIC IDEAL or a GOLDEN MEAN (see THE ANCIENT WORLD), and the job of the gentleman was to find that right answer and scorn anything less.

SCIENTIFIC ORDER

The search for the truth became almost a kind of *noblesse oblige,* a civic obligation for those of the upper strata who had brains. And their activity wasn't limited to making epigrams, dictionaries, and encyclopedias that would improve the mind of the general public; they began to dabble seriously in scientific experiment as well. Voltaire spent many of his evenings cutting up worms and weighing molten metal. British and French noblemen like Boyle and Lavoisier worked with bell jars and vacuum pumps, discovering that air conducts sound and contains oxygen. And some French *grandes dames* even devoted salon meetings to lectures on physics and chemistry for the benefit of their guests. Knowledge became so fashionable, in fact, that philosopher Immanuel KANT (which see) later described the baroque era as THE AGE OF ENLIGHTENMENT. We still use this term today, even while we condemn the aristocratic inhumanity of the age as positively benighted.

The most successful seeker for right answers during this period (or nearly any other) came early: ISAAC NEWTON (1642–1727). After he had invented differential calculus, Newton's calculations showed how comets, cannonballs, and other matter visible in the universe move and react according to mathematically consistent patterns. One of these patterns was the law of gravity, which noted that any two bodies attract each other, according to their masses and the square of the distance between them. No, Newton didn't formulate this law when an apple hit him on the head. Voltaire did have an apple story from Newton's stepniece, who said that Sir Isaac *watched* an apple falling in his garden, but there's not much confirmation that then was the moment.

Newton was a notoriously stuffy fellow, who did not unbend often. Neither did he act terribly humble. If pressed to go beyond what he had published, his reply was likeliest to be a lofty, "I frame no hypotheses." The picture of public scientific authority, Newton was president of the Royal Society for the last twenty-four years of his life. The Royal Observatory at Greenwich, founded in 1675, three years after Newton delivered a paper on optics to the

Society, has been giving us GMT (Greenwich mean time —the *right* time) ever since.

Privately, though, Newton did experiments that weren't so precise. He dabbled in alchemy, hoping to manipulate the universal substance into a mysterious something even more significant than, as he put it, "ye transmutation of metals." Whatever the results, Newton kept his experiments under wraps: such knowledge, he wrote to a friend, was "not to be communicated without immense danger to the world."

PHILOSOPHICAL ORDER

The philosophical upshot of work by Newton and other EMPIRICISTS such as LOCKE and LEIBNITZ (which see), who followed in the mathematical traditions of Galileo, Descartes, and Spinoza (see THE RENAISSANCE) was a split in the idea of what was true or knowable. Their writings showed that a certain kind of truth could be obtained by mathematics and experiment with the real world rather than by speculation, argument, authority, fasting, or prayer. Thus the idea of an EMPIRICAL or SCIENTIFIC TRUTH rather than moral or legal truth was born, preparing the way for amoral characters like Captain Nemo (*20,000 Leagues Under the Sea*) and Dr. Frankenstein in fiction, and amoral inventions like cyclotrons and brain electrodes in fact.

Interestingly enough, though, eighteenth-century philosophers were able to square away the idea of this new scientific truth with the existing religion, and with the benign-neglect ethics of powdered wigging and aristocracy. Since the universe works together like such well-oiled clockwork, some religious philosophers took that as proof that there must have been a clockmaker—i.e., God. But since there's a certain amount of chaos around on earth—fires, floods, famines, earthquakes, atrocities, and so on—they thought God must have left us to our own devices, for the time being at least. The idea of God as an absentee landlord we call DEISM.

Another philosophic idea that even more readily lent itself to upward elevation of aristocratic visions, and noses, was called THE GREAT CHAIN OF BEING. Taking the belief from Plato that there really was a realm above ours, more ideal and perfect than ours, and taking the idea from Aristotle that various species down here could be classed and ranked in an order of perfection, eighteenth-century philosophers such as LEIBNITZ (LIPEnits, 1646–1716) could maintain that the universe was constructed in a gigantic caste system, with different forms of life arranged in a descending order of perfection like the links of a chain.

At the top, of course, was God, who started it all. Then there were the angels. Below the angels, as we all know, came man. Persons. And perdaughters. Below them were the beasts, below beasts were the vegetables, and at the bottom link were the rocks.

It all sounds harmless enough—like those evolutionary trees and protozoans in biology class—until two corollaries are added. We can get them from ALEXANDER POPE's *Essay on Man*, probably the most popular piece of philosophy till the days of the Reverend Norman Vincent Peale:

Corollary One:

> Order is Heav'n's first law; and this confest,
> Some are, and must be, greater than the rest,
> More rich, more wise.

Upward mobility was out. The idea was to know your place and stick to it, mainly because of Corollary Two: these places had been set by the Divinity, so no questions about it. Whatever you might think about earthquakes, floods, or your job as a chimney sweep,

All Nature is but art, unknown to thee;
All chance, direction, which thou canst not see;
All discord, harmony not understood;
All partial evil, universal good:
And, spite of pride, in erring reason's spite,
One truth is clear: whatever is, is right.

Or as Leibnitz put it in *Theodice* (1710), this must be the best of all possible worlds. Otherwise, God would have created a better one. This philosophy that all is for the best is called OPTIMISM.

How do we get from the Great Chain to the powdered wig? That's easy. After you'd read this philosophy, you knew that your upper-caste position wasn't just fun; it was natural and divinely sanctioned. If you were at the top, you'd want to look as different as possible from the beastly ones below you in the chain. So you improved nature or cultivated it. You took the basic ornaments, clothes and such, and improved them, with wigs and more such: lace, silk stockings, high heels—and that was for men. Women wore such an amazing variety of ornaments, including shaped black silk "beauty spots," that the British Parliament passed a law against using the beautician's arts in order to seduce a man into marriage.

If you were a king, like Louis XIV, you lived even more ornamentally. You built a palatial estate like Versailles, which housed a hundred and fifty thousand nobles and staff, all in their proper places. You held nine-day parties for six hundred guests. You sponsored concerts, theater, and ballet indoors and decreed that outdoor festivals and parades be as ostentatious as possible. And if this cost more taxes to the lower orders, that was all right: whatever was, was right. It was the function of underlings to support their superiors in style. Slavery, of course, prospered during this period.

ARTISTIC ORDER

Even for artists, Renaissance enthusiasm was out; order and decorum were in. A genius like BACH (which see), probably the most inventive man with a melodic variation that ever lived, was content to stay in his place as a music teacher in a Leipzig public school, with an occasional foray to play somewhere else as an organist. He stayed put, raised ten children (during two marriages), and composed hundreds of religious pieces. You can hear the stability of the period in Bach's religious music or in that of the other noted baroque composer, HANDEL (which see). There are innumerable ornamental runs up and down the scale, but underlying them is a rock-solid stability of faith, key, tempo, and melodic frame. Think of the "Hallelujah Chorus" from Handel's *Messiah* or of one of Bach's fugues—lots of movement, but one always comes back to the beginning with the last big chord at the finale.

Later on in the century, baroque music became even more ordered as composers like HAYDN and MOZART (which see) ushered in the CLASSICAL PERIOD.

There was structure everywhere in the eighteenth-century art world. You've seen the five-beat HEROIC COUPLETS that Pope wrote in; he and his contemporaries also structured their works along classical lines, imitating the odes and eclogues of Horace and Virgil, among others. In drama, the idea of order was entrenched to the point where critics could fault Shakespeare for not being structured enough. On the stage in France, two classically controlled playwrights, CORNEILLE and RACINE (which see), were in. In England, there was Dr. Johnson, of course, and the fashionable COMEDY OF MANNERS, where the artifice of life and art was the thing, and the playwright's aim was to make his scenes as cleverly artificial as the actors' mannerisms. Realism on stage was a century away.

In real life, manners were the outward show of thoughts,

at least according to LORD CHESTERFIELD, the most
famous advisor in that area up until Emily Post. Not that
Chesterfield intended to be famous in that regard—his letters
were written to give advice to his son. But when they were
published after his death, the readers of the day snapped
them up as an updated Castiglione's *Courtier* (or *The Prince,*
too, in spots). Manners for Chesterfield included reserve in
conversation, modesty of learning, avoidance of talk about
religion, kindness to servants and tradesmen, good posture,
and choice of good-mannered women for mistresses, so that
one's decorum might be polished even while one was otherwise engaged. These latter two precepts earn Dr. Johnson's
celebrated verdict of the *Letters* as teaching "the morals
of a whore and the manners of a dancing master," but
Voltaire thought them the "best book on education ever
written." And although the *Letters* didn't make Chesterfield's son much of an achiever, they did help make his
name a synonym for a gentleman's behavior, sofa, and
cigarette.

Underneath the icing and the wigs of the upper strata,
however, things weren't all that well ordered. The age had
its critics. There was HOGARTH (HOEgarth, 1697–1764),
the English artist who made engravings in storyboard
sequence, like today's comic strips. His *The Rake's Progress,*
The Harlot's Progress, and *Marriage à la Mode* were as
popular as they were descriptive, detailed, and slightly
grotesque. They gave explicit instruction how a man or
woman or both could progress through sin and infidelity
to insanity, venereal disease, and death. Naturally people
looked at the first few pictures in each set as carefully as
they studied the moralizing last ones.

Another satirist of the vices of the age was JONATHAN
SWIFT (1667–1745), whose humor ran to the scatological.
In GULLIVER'S TRAVELS, for example, Gulliver puts out
a fire in the Lilliputian queen's palace with—well, just look
up scatological, and you'll understand with what.

Though there are more messy moments in the *Travels*, the book's satire is explicitly ordered in good eighteenth-century fashion. The voyage to the island of the tiny Lilli-putians satirizes human pettiness. The trip to the land of the giant Brobdingnagians satirizes human grossness. The visit to the flying island of Laputa lampoons the excesses of the day's scientists, and the trip to the land of the Houyhnhnms (say it like "whinny"—they were talking horses) derides human meanness with its apelike Yahoos. By the end of the fourth voyage Gulliver has become so misanthropic that he sees his wife as an "odious animal" and insists on eating alone. You can see why the children's versions usually include only the first voyage, and that heavily edited.

The number one satirist of the age, though, was VOL-TAIRE (volTARE, the pen name of François Marie Arouet, 1694–1778). He wrote plays, novels, poems, histories, and a dictionary—not of French but of philosophy. He also wrote reams and reams against the Catholic Church establishment, signing innumerable letters with "écrasez l'infame" ("crush the infamous thing") and pamphleteering with a productivity unsurpassed even during the days of the New Left's less refined equivalent, "Off the pigs." Most of his career was spent in exile, out of the reach of Catholic French authorities.

Not that Voltaire was all *that* antiestablishment. He liked order almost as much as the next eighteenth-century man. Even religion was all right in its place. "I want my lawyer, my tailor, and my wife to believe in God," says one of his characters, "so I shall be less robbed and less deceived."

But the intolerance of the Catholic Church was getting out of control in parts of France. In one town, they tortured a Protestant man to death on suspicion that he had killed his son to prevent his turning Catholic. In another a sixteen-year-old boy who, under torture, confessed to vandalizing crucifixes was publicly beheaded and burned in the name of Our Savior before cheering crowds.

So Voltaire understandably had no illusions about the purity of establishments or their philosophies. His best-known work, CANDIDE, proceeded to lampoon the Church rulers and the philosophy of the Great Chain of Being as far out of existence as one book could. Leibnitz, the philosopher of optimism, is turned into DR. PANGLOSS, who insists that all is for the best as he and his pupils, the lovers CANDIDE and CUNEGONDE, are robbed, raped, hanged, flogged, kidnaped, and otherwise abused by fortune and the clergy as they try to find happiness and each other. Why won't Pangloss admit that he's wrong? Well, he says at the end, when the lovers have been reunited, he can't recant because he's a philosopher. To admit that he was wrong would be an unprofessional thing to do. And besides, he maintains, there's a happy ending of sorts to all their troubles, even though Cunégonde's turned ugly and they have to work every day on their farm. . . .

Candide also gets in a few good shots against ROUSSEAU's doctrine of the NOBLE SAVAGE (which see). The savages Candide runs into try to eat him, and their women cohabit with monkeys. And talking of human nature, Candide asks his friend Martin, who has seen the world: "Do you think that men have always massacred each other, as they do today? Have they always been liars, cheats, traitors, brigands, weak, flighty, cowardly, envious, gluttonous, drunken, grasping, and vicious, bloody, backbiting, debauched, fanatical, hypocritical, and silly?"

"Do you think," Martin replies, "that sparrow hawks have always eaten the pigeons they came across?"

The solution to living in this imperfect world of ours? Work without complaining—or philosophizing. Cultivate your garden. Candide and friends do, settling down on a modest little farm; at last they don't have to worry where the next disaster's coming from. Of course, gardening full-time won't work if you live in the city, though you see the garden's a metaphor, philosophically speaking, for your life. . . .

The other thing you should know about *Candide* (which had a long run on Broadway not long ago) is that it's very much like RASSELAS, Samuel Johnson's tale about a prince who searches for happiness. Alike in more ways than one. Voltaire is said to have written *Candide* in bed, during four days of July, 1758, and published it in February, 1759 (the Church banned it the same month). Johnson wrote *Rasselas* during the evenings of one week in January, 1759, because he needed quick money to pay for his mother's funeral. Both works are imitations of *Arabian Nights* tales, but, understandably, Voltaire's story is funnier.

The philosophy of cultivating gardens was at least partly agreeable to that other philosopher of influence, JEAN JACQUES ROUSSEAU (rooSO, 1712–78). Only difference was, he wanted everybody to do it—the real back-to-the-land, natural-man number. Voltaire didn't fall for this romanticizing of the savage state: replying to a copy of *The Origin of Inequality* that Rousseau had sent him, Voltaire said, "No one has ever used so much intelligence to persuade us to be stupid."

ARISTOCRACY DISORDERED

But Rousseau didn't discourage easily. He wrote an opera and an operetta, two romantic novels, articles for the *Encyclopedia,* and numerous essays published later as *The Confessions.* The second of his novels, *Émile,* was about a child who was raised the natural way. Rousseau had numerous influential theories on child rearing, along with three mistresses and five illegitimate children, all of whom he abandoned to a foundling hospital.

Despite his lack of exemplary behavior, Rousseau's ideas of the good natural life soon had people like Marie

Antoinette commissioning new-built country vacation cottages and dressing like milkmaids when they were on holiday. And speaking of Marie Antoinette, by the way, Rousseau also should be remembered for that story "of a great princess, who, on being informed that the country people had no bread, replied, 'Let them eat cake.'" Not that Rousseau had Marie Antoinette in mind then—he wrote the lines in 1768, two years before she arrived in France. But since they weren't published until the 1780s in *The Confessions,* when the people read "princess" they knew who to blame.

Even more influential than Rousseau's novels or his confessions, though, were the ideas in *The Social Contract.* In that work, Rousseau maintained that the only rightful authority was the general will and described the way to freedom for society. Liberty, equality, fraternity, democracy —all these good things were in people, Rousseau argued, if they would only get in touch with their natural instincts and act, now.

Well, by the late eighteenth century the aristocrats in France had gotten overstuffed and the people had gotten desperate. They didn't need much persuading that action was needed. Aristocrats had to go. Sixteen years after Rousseau's death, the now wigless heads of the aristocracy were tumbling into baskets underneath the guillotine. The governors of the new state prepared a constitution with words and ideas taken directly from *The Social Contract,* and even devised a new calendar, naming the months after their "natural" functions—like "budding" and "reaping." The era of aristocratic order and the powdered wig was coming to an end.

Oh, yes, Rousseau, far-sighted man of fashion that he was, helped accelerate the trend away from baroque ornament by wearing a fur hat.

The Other Baroque Names You Should Know

COMEDY

MOLIÈRE (moleYAIR, 1622–73). In France, Molière's been lionized as the French Shakespeare, even though his tragedies were flops when Molière played in them, largely due to the nervous hiccup that continually interrupted his delivery of lines. When he played in his own comedies, though, Molière's hiccup helped. The court of Louis XIV loved his satires of the age's many foibles. They applauded *The Misanthrope* and *The Miser* as satires of hypocrisy and sour spirits; *The School for Husbands* and *The School for Women* as satires of flirtation and infidelity; *The Bourgeois Gentleman* and *The Affected Young Ladies* as satires of social climbing and social conventions. *Tartuffe,* Molière's most famous comedy, satirizes even more. Tartuffe's a con artist masquerading as a pious churchman, who nearly succeeds in bilking a gullible rich husband out of wife and property until the husband hides under the table . . .

English versions of Molière's COMEDIES OF MANNERS include Congreve's *The Way of the World* (1700), Goldsmith's *She Stoops to Conquer* (1773), Sheridan's *The School for Scandal* (1777), and on up to OSCAR WILDE and NOEL COWARD (which see).

ART

You know about Hogarth already. That leaves only these three: BERNINI (Baroque), WATTEAU (Rococo), DAVID (Neoclassic).

GIOVANNI LORENZO BERNINI (berNEEnee, 1598–1680), an Italian, was fantastic with fountains (spouting mermen, etc.) and did paintings and architecture, but the thing to remember him for is his sculpture. He took Michelangelo's (see THE RENAISSANCE) basic heroic human forms and made them more sensual, more slender—almost as though he'd been looking at BOTTICELLI (also which see). The result is a style that was imitated by other sculptors for nearly a century and called Berninesque by specialists. Just plain baroque is good enough for the layman, however. Look for graceful figures in slightly contorted poses, with details that are just slightly startling. In *Apollo and Daphne,* notice how the leaves and branches are beginning to sprout from Daphne's extremities as she tries to run from Apollo's clutches. In *The Ecstasy of St. Theresa,* notice how the little angel is smiling almost like a cupid, as he holds his arrow like a spear about to be plunged into the good lady's heart. And compare Bernini's *David* with Michelangelo's if you want an idea of how baroque art added the ornament of drama to classic Renaissance sculpture. Michelangelo's *David* is standing still, waiting with a determined look on his heroic (the statue is eighteen feet tall) features. Bernini's is more slender and smaller (life size), but instead of gazing forcefully from a serene posture, he's twisted like a hammerthrower about to let fly with his sling, and even grimacing with the effort.

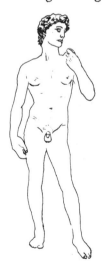

A bit too enthusiastic for the British version of the baroque, but of course neither David wore a powdered wig or silk stockings.

JEAN ANTOINE WATTEAU (wahTOE or vahTOE, 1684–1721). The delicate, almost IMPRESSIONISTIC (which see) brush strokes Watteau used made the subjects of his paintings—mostly pastoral scenes among the aristocracy—seem tiny and almost fragile, as though they could disappear with a puff of wind at any moment. They move through a haze of shimmering color and light, as though they're too graceful to be real and know it but don't care, since they're having such a good time—almost precisely the attitude of the later French aristocracy.

Watteau painted these confectionary delights while he knew he was dying of consumption. For him, the state of things was as ephemeral as it looked, so the manners of the moment took on even more importance. Perhaps those Watteau painted felt the same way, agreeing with Louis XV's political assessment: "After me, the deluge."

Threat of revolution notwithstanding, during the rest of the eighteenth century ornamentation just for the fun of it —tastefully, though—became a style called ROCOCO, after the French words for rocks and shells. Swirls and twirls were added to everything from chair legs to ceiling plaster, and there was gilt and gloss over nearly all the rest. The tradition survives today in some picture frames and wedding cakes, and of course in Valentine's Day cards.

DAVID (dahVEED, 1748–1825). When David's *Oath of the Horatii* appeared in 1785, it helped end the ornamental age and bring on a cleaner NEOCLASSIC look. The Horatii, three dedicated Roman sons about to go off to battle, are portrayed with their father as they swear an oath on their swords, all standing hard and firm and looking like Grecian marble. So does the architecture in the background, which is of course without rococo frills. *The Oath,* with its military crispness, supposedly helped inspire some of the hard actions taken by the French on Bastille Day and after.

MUSIC

Bach, Handel (early)	Haydn, Mozart (late)

Eighteenth-century music moved from that soaring, titanic quality of the Bach fugue or the Handel oratorio, which you might compare with Michelangelo, to the controlled sonata form, quartet, and symphony of Haydn and Mozart, which might be compared with Watteau or David. Though more instruments were added to the orchestra, the music still sounds lighter and more controlled, even when it's more powerful.

What made the change? The addition of a new form: the SONATA FORM. The early part of the century didn't have it. What they had was the POLYPHONIC FORM, or FUGUE. To understand the difference, think of a round, the kind of song in which you start in with the melody and then a few bars later someone else begins with the same melody, and then someone else, and so on. That's many voices (poly-phonic) singing the one melodic line at the same time. The multiple voices make for interest and variety,

especially in the fugue, where while one voice (or part on
the organ) has the melody, another may be countering with
an answering melody, and then vice versa.

When you're doing short pieces, such as the fifty-three
that comprise Handel's famous oratorio *Messiah,* polyphonic
variations can be exquisite, especially if the composer has
varied them with block harmony (chords) as Handel did
often in that work. But if the same one-melody piece is continued for an extended period, variations and answering
melodies all seeming to happen at once and interminably, the
result can be confusing, or tiresome.

At least that's what the popular taste of the eighteenth
century thought when the SONATA FORM came along and
gave them something different to turn to. The new style
presented two musical themes instead of one. This might
sound more complicated instead of more controlled, but not
so. The sonata form presents these melodic themes *one at a
time,* connected by a bridge or transitional passage and
followed by a short closing passage called a *codetta.* The
first time through this little cycle, which is often repeated,
is called the *exposition.* Next comes the *development* stage,
in which different parts of either theme are varied in which-
ever way suits the composer—put into different keys, with
different harmonics or different tempos, as his muse dictates.
But after *development* comes *recapitulation:* the return to
the two themes as we first heard them in the *exposition,*
more or less, but with enough variation to avoid monotony
and enough *piano* (softness) or *forte* (strength) to give a
sense of an ending when the codetta is reached. In the
event that this ending doesn't seem final enough, a *coda,*
or closing passage, may be added.

The resultant form produced a nice sense of order and
yet variety, moving some to think it would be timeless
enough to be called CLASSICAL. And so it was. The sonata
form was used, naturally, for SONATAS, which were written
for solo instrument plus keyboard or for keyboard alone,

in three or four movements. The form was also used for TRIOS and QUARTETS (pieces written for three or four instruments), for CONCERTOS (one sonata form for each of three movements, written for solo instrument plus orchestral accompaniment), and for SYMPHONIES. The symphony divides into four movements, three of them in sonata form. The third movement for Haydn and Mozart symphonies was written in triple meter (like a waltz) and called a MINUET, because the French used to dance to its earlier versions. Minuets moved in stately moderate fashion. After BEETHOVEN (which see) sped up the pace with a more vigorous third movement called a *scherzo*, however, the minuet in the symphony went out of fashion.

So there you have the basic forms of what's loosely termed "classical" music, as they were during the BAROQUE period of Bach and Handel and the CLASSICAL period of Haydn and Mozart.

A few words about each is enough biography:

HANDEL (HANDl, 1685–1759) was German but wrote Italian-style operas (forty all told) in England, and produced them there with some success until Londoners tired of Italian passions and patronized Gay's satire *The Beggar's Opera* (later *The Threepenny Opera*) instead. Between various bankruptcies and attempts at operatic comebacks, Handel turned to ORATORIOS, religious epics for soloists, chorus, and orchestra. He wrote twenty-three of these including the immortal MESSIAH, which he completed in twenty-three days when, he said, "I did think I did see all Heaven before me, and the great God himself." Mass performances of *Messiah* were a tradition after Handel's death, and even now people still gather at Christmas and Easter to hear it performed in thousands of localities. In New York, one can even attend the annual *"Messiah* Sing Along" the week before Christmas, which draws thousands every year.

JOHANN SEBASTIAN BACH (BOCKH, 1685–1750) also wrote oratorios, and about three hundred cantatas (portions of oratorios), two hundred of which survive, along with assorted fugues, and other instrumental works—enough to fill forty-six thick volumes of his manuscripts. Though not the entrepreneur that Handel was, Bach was also prolific in another way: twenty-one children, ten of whom survived, and four of whom became musicians of importance. One son you might remember is Karl Philipp Emanuel, who pioneered in establishing the Sonata Form that made his father's fugues temporarily obsolete. Since about 1830, however, the works of Johann Sebastian have been back in the public eye, and today he's more frequently performed than, well, anyone.

FRANZ JOSEPH HAYDN (HIGHdn, 1732–1809) is known as the first master of the Sonata Form and the symphony, of which he wrote more than a hundred. He also wrote operas, masses, piano sonatas, overtures, and various lesser pieces, most of which were to entertain the Esterhazy family, whom he served for thirty years wearing servant's livery and sitting at the officers' dinner table. The last nineteen years were more prosperous. During that time he wrote his Symphony no. 104 (*London,* the last of twelve he did on commission in England), considered by some to be his best. Haydn was certainly pleased with the performance, as he wrote in his diary: "The hall was filled with a picked audience. The whole company was delighted, and so was I. I took in this evening 4000 gulden [about $30,000]. One can make as much as this only in England."

His music is as buoyant and cheerful as he was. Haydn's subordinate musicians at the Esterhazy estate called him "Papa" because of his fairminded settling of their squabbles —a nickname that's been carried on to describe his paternal influence in developing the symphony, sonata, and string quartet. "Papa" also suggests the kindly wit that fills his music, as in Symphony no. 94, the *Surprise* symphony, where the slow, quiet second movement is suddenly interrupted with a loud chord for the full orchestra, supposedly to wake the sleepers in the audience.

WOLFGANG AMADEUS MOZART (MOEtsart, 1756–91) didn't end in Haydn's affluence and his music has more melancholy. Though he composed over six hundred works, sacred and secular, vocal and instrumental, and served as royal composer to the emperor of Austria, he lived in poverty and was buried in an unmarked grave. A child prodigy, he was playing his own compositions in French salons when he was eight years old and composed and conducted his first opera when he was thirteen. The early exposure may have made Mozart a bit blasé about meeting his performance deadlines; he didn't write a line of the overture to his opera *Don Giovanni*, for example, until the day of the premiere, getting the completed parts to the orchestra still dripping with ink and so late that they had to be performed at sight (without rehearsal). Still, the work was hailed as a masterpiece—which didn't surprise Mozart; he'd finished it long before, he maintained, in his head. Of Mozart's twenty-four operas, *The Marriage of Figaro* (which insults the idea of aristocratic order), *Don Giovanni*, and *The Magic Flute* are among those still frequently performed, along with many of Mozart's twenty-five string quartets, forty-eight symphonies, twenty-seven piano concertos . . .

Two other baroque composers worth knowing about came before Bach and Handel and were well known enough for both Bach and Handel to be influenced by their melodies.

In England, there was HENRY PURCELL (PURsul, 1659–95), the organist at Westminster Abbey who produced an ode or anthem for every public event in his position as the king's composer. One opera of his is still regarded highly: *Dido and Aeneas*, from which "Dido's Lament" may be familiar to many. He also did incidental music for Shakespeare's *A Midsummer Night's Dream* and *The Tempest*.

In Italy, Venice to be exact, there was VIVALDI (ve-VAHLdee, 1678–1741), the priest turned violin virtuoso who established the CONCERTO form by gradually whittling down the part for a leading small group within the orchestra until it became a leading solo instrument. Bach used to copy the Vivaldi concertos, transcribing them for different instruments.

Four of Vivaldi's most popular concertos, then and now, are a group called the *Four Seasons*. Since these works try to portray the different seasons of the year rather than just create a melodic line, they're called PROGRAM MUSIC—a form that the nineteenth century adored.

What Not to Bother With

OPERA

Though opera, with its excesses of passion, gobs of ornament, and casts of hundreds, lavishly costumed, has been called the most baroque of entertainments, operas of the baroque century aren't around much any more. Why not? The more recent ones are better written, that's why, and operas are perishing expensive to produce. Besides Handel, Haydn, and Mozart, there are two other opera names you might want to know, though, just for their historical importance. For length, there's ALESSANDRO SCARLATTI (skarLAHTtee, 1659–1725), who wrote 115 operas, invented the OVERTURE before the singing started, and produced a famous son, DOMENICO SCARLATTI (1683–1757), whose compositions for the harpsichord are still frequently performed.

For strength, there's CHRISTOPH GLUCK (rhymes with BOOK, 1714–87), who tightened the dramatic structure of his operas to make the songs have at least something to do with the plot. Things had gotten so disorganized before that, that performances were sometimes little more than excuses for songs, occasionally degenerating into singing duels between the principals. With one of Handel's productions in 1727, the duel turned into a donnybrook among the cast, spectators, and orchestra, complete with the smashing of stage scenery while the two leading ladies tore at each other's hair.

FRENCH DRAMA

CORNEILLE (korNAYyuh, 1606–84) and RACINE (rah-SEEN, 1639–99). Their names are usually trotted out when the three DRAMATIC UNITIES are discussed: unity of time (the action of the play is no more than twenty-four hours); place (only one); and action (no subplots, no comic relief). These were thought to be essential to tragic intensity. And in France, the title role in Racine's tragedy *Phèdre* is aspired to by actresses the way English actors wish for Hamlet or Lear. But the plays are the things, and you won't see them played here too often, especially not in their original French rhymed couplets.

LITERATURE

JOHN MILTON (1608–74) is ranked number three by English departments coast to coast, right up there with Chaucer and Shakespeare. Only thing is, reading him can be stupefying (unless you read him aloud) and talking about him with enthusiasm can draw you the same sort of looks smokers reserve for health enthusiasts.

Milton, you see, is hard to understand. He knew more classical myth and history than the average ancient Athenian, and more Judeo-Christian lore than the average Pharisee. It all shows up in his work, making wearying trips to the footnotes inevitable, unless you simply want to give up and skip most of his allusions. Another thing that makes Milton hard is that he uses what's called PERIODIC STRUCTURE. You have to read half a page or so, waiting till the end when he gives you the key elements of the long, long sentence, before you have any idea what he's talking about.

The third strike against a popularized Milton is that there's more argument than action and definitely a dearth of racy passages. His great works are poetical versions of biblical events: *Paradise Lost*, about the creation and Eden, *Paradise Regained*, about Christ's temptation, and *Samson Agonistes*, about the blind hero against the Philistines, a self-image Milton certainly entertained (see ARNOLD).

Like Bach and Handel, Milton went blind from too much close reading. After that happened, he used to write by dictation, frequently at 4:00 A.M. What came out of those pre-dawn sessions were the only lines of poetry since the Bible to put words in the mouth of God, Satan, and the rest and make them believable—at least to those who've pictured the supernatural as a realm for philosophers.

DANIEL DEFOE (dehFOE, 1660–1731) wrote *Moll Flanders,* about an enterprising wench who used her body and wit to go from Newgate jail to relative prosperity and centuries later to unsung immortality as the model heroine for much of today's romantic fiction. Defoe also did *Robinson Crusoe,* now a children's classic about survival on a desert island, where Crusoe has the help of a native named Friday, giving rise to today's gal/guy Friday want ads and the popular expression "Thank God it's Friday."

JOHN DRYDEN (1631–1700). Lots of poetry, criticism, plays, and satire in couplets, rhymed, instead of Miltonic unrhymed blank verse. But dry, very dry.

The rest of SWIFT, unless you like bad poetry and hate religion, with one exception: "A Modest Proposal." That's an often-emulated satire of conditions in Ireland, proposing that the Irish economy be bolstered by selling Irish infants for food.

The rest of POPE, except for *The Rape of the Lock,* the mock-heroic poem about the lord who trimmed off one of Arabella Fermor's curls as a trophy while she was playing ombre (a card game like bridge). The light metrics and luxuriant imagery make *The Rape* the verse equivalent to rococo painting, and one gets a bit of the underlying humor from this couplet, spoken by the woman wronged herself:

> "Oh, hadst thou, Cruel! been content to seize
> Hairs less in sight, or any Hairs but these!"

JOSEPH ADDISON (1672-1719), a crony of Swift and Pope, wrote essays, poems, political and literary periodicals (*The Tatler* and *The Spectator*), and one successful tragedy (*Cato*). These days he's only remembered because of his balanced prose style, which Johnson advised writers to study day and night, and which Benjamin Franklin said he learned to write from imitating.

RICHARDSON (*Pamela, Clarissa*); FIELDING (*Shamela, Tom Jones*); and STERNE (*Sentimental Journey, Tristram Shandy*). If one doesn't count Defoe, and many don't, these are the first English novelists and novels. The novels are fat, complicated, and with the exception of *Tom Jones,* the one you may have seen Susannah York filmed in, too archaic in language for most outside the academies.

PHILOSOPHY

The full theories of these philosophers may be important to other philosophers, but they're not to you. All that's likely to surface in conversation or everyday print are these few catch phrases from each:

THOMAS HOBBES (HOBBS, 1588-1679). A grim Royalist philosopher, he advocated man's giving up his natural rights to the control of the "Leviathan" (his word for the state) in a social contract, because the lawless alternative is unattractive. As Hobbes put it in *Leviathan,* "Life in the state of nature is solitary, poor, nasty, brutish, and short." Rousseau didn't agree, of course.

GEORGE BERKELEY (BURRklee, or BARKlee to the British, 1685-1753). Referred to as a subjective idealist, since he thought that things existed only if they were perceived, and that the world, therefore, was an idea in the mind of God. If you don't follow that argument, you're not alone. Samuel Johnson didn't either. When asked how he could refute the belief that everything is an idea, he kicked a large stone and said, "I refute it THUS!" Of course Berkeley could maintain that the stone and the sore toe were a perception of Johnson's mind. . . . Anyway, apart from fueling debates on whether there's any noise when a tree falls in an empty forest, Berkeley's theory of existence = perception doesn't crop up much any more.

JOHN LOCKE (LOCK, 1632–1704) said that the mind is a blank page, or *tabula rasa,* when you're born; your thoughts therefore depend on what your environment does to you (that's called sensation) and on what you do with those sensations (your reflections). Certainly more sophisticated an idea than "you are what you eat," the *tabula rasa* concept has been grist for the mills of egalitarians (one *tabula rasa* is obviously as good as another) and behaviorist defense lawyers (The ghetto made him do it, your honor!) ever since.

SCIENCE

If you simply memorize NEWTON's three laws of motion from his *Principia Mathematica,* you'll be far ahead of the game.

First Law: the law of inertia. "A body at rest continues in its state of rest, and a body in motion continues in a straight line, unless compelled to change by forces impressed upon it."

Quote this one when you're trying to get someone out of bed in the morning.

Second Law: the law of acceleration. "The change in motion is directly proportional to the force that is applied."

Quote this one when you're trying to get someone out of bed in the morning, quickly.

Third Law: the law of reaction. "To every action there is always opposed an equal and opposite reaction."

Quote this one when someone's trying to get *you* out of bed in the morning.

HISTORY

The age's history doesn't matter, but you might like to know its foremost historian, Englishman EDWARD GIBBON

(1737–1794). Abroad at age twenty-six, out one night amid the Roman ruins he got an idea. Twenty-three years and seven lofty prose volumes later, he completed *The Decline and Fall of the Roman Empire,* in time to be read by those Britishers who were losing a sizable portion of their empire in North America. Gibbon gives credit for Rome's fall not only to the greed of the emperors but also to the spread of Christianity. This appraisal earned Gibbon fame as a free-thinker, though it didn't endear him to many in the religious establishment.

ECONOMICS

In 1776 in England, ADAM SMITH (1723–90) published *The Wealth of Nations,* the book that called England "a nation of shopkeepers." It also advocated an unregulated (*laissez-faire*) free-market economy, and maintained that the real wealth of any nation was its people; i.e., its labor force. Not long after that in America and France, the people initiated a share-the-wealth policy, and the ROMANTIC era began.

V

THE NINETEENTH CENTURY

The One Nineteenth-century Idea
You Need to Know

For most of us, the nineteenth century means *late* nineteenth century: old-fashioned clothes and old favorite stories: high-button shoes, capes, and *Sherlock Holmes;* pinafores and *Alice in Wonderland;* top hats, long nightshirts, and *Peter Pan* (though *Pan* came in 1904). And some dimly recalled romantic novels with all bicycles and earnest conversations under parasols.

Still, there's more of the nineteenth century floating around these days than just childhood memories of Victoriana; more even than tall old mansions and antique oak furniture. The nineteenth century, a great time for earnest conversation and serious thought, produced a batch of serious Big Ideas that keep coming up in today's conversations, editorials, and reviews, not to mention galleries and stages.

The one of these big ideas that's best to know is the one that more or less spun off the rest: ROMANTICISM, especially since it's making a comeback these days in everything from music and fiction to backpacking and natural foods.

Romanticism includes a whole flock of characters, from long-haired musicians and fire-breathing radicals to sturdy foresters and woodland spirits wild. They all had one thing in common:

A Passion for Passion

ROMANTICISM'S EIGHTEENTH-CENTURY BEGINNINGS

You remember the Great Chain of Being? (See THE BAROQUE ERA if you don't.) Well, the Romantics acted as if they had a yen to go *down* the chain instead of up. As early as GOETHE (GEUteh, 1749–1832) in the 1770s there was a movement in German theater to get away from aristocratic restraint and powdered-wig decorum and to let the emotions hang out in what they called STURM UND DRANG (storm and stress). Lots of moans and wails, emotional tempests and whirlwinds, just like the plainer folks down in the less aristocratic social orders.

Also, as we said last chapter, Rousseau moved people further down the chain, getting women out of their corsets and into milkmaid's costumes—and even into breastfeeding. Taking the hangout route another step, one might say, down to animal nature.

And interpreting Bishop Berkeley's thought that "Nature is the language of God," we could go yet another step, down into the worship of what Longfellow later called "the forest primeval," and what WORDSWORTH (which see) later called "rocks and stones and trees."

PASSION FOR THE PEOPLE:
REVOLUTIONARY POLITICS

After those children of nature, the American colonists, managed to beat the British (1781) and the sons of liberty in France managed to behead Louis XVI (1793), the romantic idea began to catch on, though first, in France, it wore neoclassic clothes. Rococo ornaments were thrown out of the salons, and, following the influence of David, who was now a political and artistic power, people began to redecorate salons and themselves in the Greco-Roman style. Ladies turned to stolas, many filmy as nightgowns and worn to leave one breast bare. Men saved the togas for when they were posing for statues; for everyday wear they simply tossed out the silk stockings and knee breeches of the aristocracy and donned the long trousers of the working class.

And the decorous, controlled wit of the past century was out, too—just as unfashionable as the powdered wig. One couldn't speak with polished epigrams and restraint, after all, when one was storming a Bastille or cursing one of the aristocrats who was being carted away to the guillotine. And if one was the aristocrat in the tumbrel, one couldn't either— even if one felt up to it, the mobs wouldn't let a restrained word in edgewise. There was simply too much passion.

Things got even more intense when ROBESPIERRE (robesPYAIR, 1758–94), *de facto* prime minister of revolutionary France, got carried away with guillotining enemies of the Republic and started in on his fellow assemblymen. They guillotined him instead, after shooting him, which ended Robespierre's Reign of Terror at about five thousand executions.

PASSION FOR THE POET: BACK TO NATURE

During the early days of the Revolution (1791–92), a young Englishman named WILLIAM WORDSWORTH (1770–1850) was in France having a passionate revolutionary fling at democratic politics and a passionate affair with a French surgeon's daughter. The love affair ended with the birth of an illegitimate daughter and with the last of Wordsworth's money—he had to leave for England.

After sad farewells, guilt, and a nervous breakdown of sorts, Wordsworth settled in the Lake Country of his boyhood (northwest of London and northeast of Wales), and began writing poetry and recalling the days of his youth to pull himself together. Ah, Nature, he mused, never did betray the heart that loved her. He thought of daffodils, and the land, the environs of the common people—farm people, that is— their languages, their songs, the old folk ballads . . .

And came up with a formula for poetry: lyrical ballads about nature and common folks, in the plain simple language of the common man. Especially the common man who's somehow an outsider. A refreshing change from heroic couplets and lofty aristocratic diction, not to mention good for the soul. To sum it up, said Wordsworth, all good "poetry is the spontaneous overflow of powerful feelings." *Sturm und Drang* was in, and in English.

MORE POETS, MORE PASSIONS

While meditating in the Lake Country, Wordsworth teamed up with another poet named SAMUEL TAYLOR COLERIDGE (1772–1834) who was a less clean-cut figure (addicted to opium) but nonetheless interested in new poetry. They decided to collaborate on a new volume of poetry to illustrate the new ideas. Coleridge's contribution was to the spooky side of nature: the supernatural. He wrote "The Rime of the Ancient Mariner," who was cursed for shooting a natural albatross, "Christabel," who was bewitched by a lesbian forest spirit, and "Kubla Khan," about a visionary songstress who wove enchanting verses, a stately pleasure-dome with caves of ice and a yen for the muse's mystical "milk of paradise." All done up in haunting rhyme and metrics.

Put them together, as Wordsworth and Coleridge put

themselves together in *Lyrical Ballads* (1798), and romantic art was really on the move. Out of the mold and into the woods, with Wordsworth in the daytime and Coleridge after dark.

The next few decades produced more romantic writers on both sides of the Atlantic, and on both the light and dark sides of the romantic spectrum. Among the "LIGHT" RO-MANTICS to remember were:

PERCY BYSSHE SHELLEY (1792–1822), who, when he wasn't writing passionate odes to the West Wind ("I fall upon the thorns of life! I bleed!") wrote about atheism, wicked aristocrats, and the need to help the common people. He also proclaimed poets, since they set the moral visions of a people, as "the unacknowledged legislators of the world." He had to write his poetic legislation in Italy, though; England wasn't ready for his liberated lifestyle.

SIR WALTER SCOTT (1771–1832), who put romanticism back into the days of medieval ROMANCE (which see), with lances and tourneys and jousts and eternal passions for ladies fair—good nostalgia for Britain and good role-models for chivalrous Southern gentlemen in the U.S.A.

And of course JOHN KEATS (1795–1821), who wrote odes to a Nightingale, to eternal lovers painted on a Grecian Urn, and to Autumn, the season of mists and mellow fruitful-ness, while he was dying of consumption. His poems, in-cidentally, are considered the best-structured of the Romantics', and are written less about nature than about human nature—the mind. Fascination with one's own mental workings, a quality shared by most of the romantics in varying degrees, is called ROMANTIC EGOISM.

On the other side of the Atlantic, Emerson (which see) lionized Nature as the source of poetry, calling for hymns to "the familiar and the common," "the meal in the firkin, the milk in the pan." His disciple, THOREAU (which see), even lived outdoors by Walden Pond for two years. Of course neither of them called this living in Peasant style, since there weren't any peasants in America.

Among the DARK ROMANTICS were:

MARY WOLLSTONECRAFT SHELLEY (1797–1851), Percy's second wife, who wrote the classic horror novel about how it wasn't nice for Dr. Frankenstein to fool Mother Nature.

George Gordon, LORD BYRON (1788–1824), who wrote well-turned eighteenth-century-style verses, but about an archromantic type that came to be called the BYRONIC HERO—unrepentantly sinful, dashing, moody, making his own morals amid dark and stormy passions. Playing the role himself, Byron attracted women by the hundreds. He slept with some, married or not, and with men, and also with his half-sister Augusta Leigh. This last affair ended his marriage, and his time in England, in 1816. Byronically unrepentant, though, he counted two hundred other affairs during 1817–18.

The BRONTE (BRONtee) sisters, who gave us precursors of today's Gothic novels with *Jane Eyre* (Charlotte: 1847) about a young governess and a Byronic Mr. Rochester, and *Wuthering Heights* (Emily: 1947) about the more Byronic, even ghoulish Heathcliff.

American NATHANIEL HAWTHORNE (1804–1864), who wrote of the early New England Puritans and their repressed sexuality, depicting passions from adultery (*The Scarlet Letter*) to outdoor witchcraft ceremonies ("Young Goodman Brown").

PASSION ON CANVAS: ROMANTIC ART

Of course romantic writers were not alone to glorify nature and the common man. In France, David began talking less about classical restraint and more about "electrifying the soul" (as well as about not painting for aristocratic patrons any more). Other French artists began making electrifying oils of common folk in wild moments of natural passion. The

Raft of the "Medusa" (1819) by GÉRICAULT (zhayreé KOE), one of the most famous, shows huddled masses on a raft after a shipwreck, tempest-tossed, yearning toward a rescuing sail on the far horizon. The painting was in memory of those few who survived the real *Medusa*'s shipwreck off the coast of Africa. Since those in authority were to blame (the government-owned *Medusa* lacked lifeboats and emergency rations) for the horror of the raft's voyage (149 set sail on the raft; fewer than 20 remained when it was found, and some of those were dead), Géricault's painting was a political statement as well.

Eleven years later, France had another revolution, commemorated by the other famous romantic painting, DELACROIX's (dellaKRWAH) *Liberty Leading the People* (1830).

A leftist counterpart to America's limping fife, drum, and flag trio of 1776ers, this one has a bare-bosomed Miss Liberty, tricolor French flag in one hand and bayoneted rifle in the other, urging the people onward to storm the barricades. Tinged with a romantic glow of sunlight and a haze of cannon smoke, of course.

Other romantic artists, glorifying Nature, painted—what else?—landscapes. Forests, lakes, mountains, and big storm clouds, but all *sans* aristocratic picnics and aristocrats. Nature was even more romantic painted at sunset, and still more so when that most romantic of all symbols came up—the moon.

ROMANTIC MUSIC: PASSION IN FASHION

BALLET got into the nature spirit in Paris (1832) with LA SYLPHIDE, the first of the romantic ballets, about a passionate Scottish bridegroom who deserts his bride to run off to the woods with a bewitching forest sprite. A few years later came GISELLE (1841), about a peasant girl and another haunting forest spirit in Germany—a whole *corps de ballet* of them, in fact. These are the Wilis, ghosts of women who have died of a broken heart, who have the power at night to make a man dance to his death. Made for bad interpersonal relations, but splendid dancing, and a favorite today.

In OPERA, where romantic passion had been the stock in trade since the seventeenth century, things couldn't get any more passionate. They did get a bit splashier with the decor, though (see GRAND OPERA), and we do start seeing more commoners as nineteenth-century heroes and heroines. KARL MARIA VON WEBER (VAYber, 1786–1826) wrote Der Freischütz about a peasant hunter who bargains with the devil to win the fair maiden in a shooting contest—a theme from German folk legend. And of course there's ROSSINI's (1792–1868) BARBER OF SEVILLE, BIZET's (beeZAY, 1838–75) CARMEN, a working-class beauty also from Se-

ville, and WAGNER, whose heroes and heroines come bel-
lowing out of Norse mythology. More of him later.

But the most romantic of the now-familiar nineteenth-century
operas has to be WILLIAM TELL, Rossini's last (1829) and
some would say, best. We all know it's a story with a com-
mon-man hero, the local peasant archer who defeats the
proud tyrant Gessler after shooting an apple off his son's head.
For a romantic overture (played before the opera begins)
there's a musical version of a landscape called "The Storm,"
complete with twittering birds, thunder, and howling winds.
And the finale of the overture is so romantic a burst of super-
heroism that the twentieth century borrowed it for an opera
in another form about a masked man with a noble savage at
his side. ("Return with us now, to those thrilling days of
yesteryear . . . A fiery horse with the speed of light, a cloud
of dust, and a hearty 'Hi, ho, SILVER!'")

Not for nothing did they call *The Lone Ranger* and its ilk
"Horse Opera."

In ORCHESTRAL MUSIC, the classical period was ending
as BEETHOVEN (which see) wrote symphonies to the hero
(no. 3), the pastoral (no. 6), and the brotherhood of man (no.
9), and a sonata to moonlight. Poems from romantics like
Goethe and Heine were done up into orchestral numbers
(*Lieder*) by SCHUBERT, SCHUMANN, and BRAHMS, who
also did German folksongs and Hungarian dances. CHOPIN
wrote mazurkas, Polish folk dances, as well as polonaises, more
Polish folk dances, for the piano. LISZT wrote Hungarian
Rhapsodies, gypsy folk melodies, and his protégé GRIEG used
folk themes from Norway. TCHAIKOVSKY wrote a Russian
hymn and a folk dance into the *1812 Overture*, along with
The Marseillaise, the French national anthem from the Revolution. ANTONÍN DVORÁK orchestrated Slavonic dances and
wrote Negro spirituals and Bohemian folk dances into his
New World Symphony.

And if that wasn't peasant music enough, JOHANN

STRAUSS, JR., made all Europe whirl to an obscure Alpine country dance called "the waltz."

Musical forms changed in ways other than just folkways, however, especially at the hands of Chopin, who departed from classical sonata form with dreamy piano preludes, études, and nocturnes, and sprightly impromptus and scherzos. Capricious capriccios and soaring rhapsodies were more romantic forms for the musical outpouring of powerful feelings.

And concert styles began to favor the romantic performer— the virtuoso superstar who could hold audiences spellbound. The crowds loved it when Paganini, violinist supreme, wound up a performance with a razor blade in his bowing hand, slicing the strings one by one as he played the last few notes, to finish the piece on one string alone. And when Franz Liszt sat down at the piano, sporting shoulder-length hair and a coatful of glittering medals, the ladies threw their jewels onto the stage, battled over his gloves and even his cigar butts, and of course swooned. Sometimes, if the swooning lady was in the front row, Liszt would carry her up onto the stage with him and hold her draped over his left arm while he finished the composition one-handed.

UNPLEASANT PASSIONS: NATURALISM

Naturally, not everyone was in the mood for swooning ladies and wild applause. A German philosopher, ARTHUR SCHO-PENHAUER (ARtoor SHOWpunhower, 1788–1860), wrote that human and natural wills are always in conflict, producing perpetual pain in this worst of all possible worlds. For this he's justifiably known as the father of philosophical PESSI-MISM, though he did say that we can use science and art to forget our bleak reality—temporarily.

Nineteenth-century writers, some of them, agreed but didn't want to use their art to let people escape. These naturalists wanted to show the full horrors that go on in a world where there are too few happy endings, thus taking the romance out of romanticism.

BALZAC's works (BAHLzak, 1799–1850), especially *The Human Comedy*, showed a law-of-the-jungle struggle for money between the debt-ridden aristocracy and the money-hungry bourgeoisie.

HERMAN MELVILLE (which see) wrote of doomed sea-going heroes Captain Ahab, Benito Cereno, and Billy Budd, all done in by natural evils too big for any man to conquer.

Less adventuresome but just as relentless was FLAUBERT's (floeBAIRE, 1821–80) *Madame Bovary*, an attack on happy endings. Emma Bovary, the bored wife of a country doctor, looks for romantic excitement and finds instead boring adultery with one cad after another, debts, and suicide.

OUR ANIMAL PASSIONS: EVOLUTION

The idea of the happy ending didn't get much help from nineteenth-century scientists, either. The *deus ex machina*, the benevolent force that made everything come out all right, didn't seem to be around when investigators looked at the land systematically.

The most famous of these men of science, CHARLES DARWIN (1809–82), voyaged in 1831 to exotic locales on *The Beagle*, gathering data on local fauna. What he noticed was that one species of animal could have different characteristics in one locale than it did in another. Why? Because the change was an advantage to its survival in that locale, he reasoned years later, thus coming up with the THEORY OF EVOLUTION.

The theory explains that random mutations of birth which help a species win the competition for food and shelter and mates in a given environment will give the mutated versions of that species an advantage. They'll get more food, more mates, and eventually drive out the unmutated versions of the species. Natural selection weeds out the less fit, while the strong survive, reproduce, and survive again until a better mutation comes along. No happy ending because of virtue or a benevolent deity; just chance mutation, and strength, and reproductive power.

After *The Origin of Species* (1859), "survival of the fittest" became a household phrase, and a battleground for theologians vs. intelligentsia. At the same time, discoveries in geology were proving that the earth was millions of years older than the Bible said it was, even if one allowed for seven days of creation and several hundreds of years between each "begat" after Adam. Astronomers were proving that space was a far, far bigger place than we'd imagined, and that the earth was by comparison far smaller—and man smaller still. By the time Darwin came out with the *Descent of Man* (1871), in which he specifically wrote of man's evolving from the apes, many were ready to believe that humans were only another creature evolved in intelligence from very lowbrow ancestors, even down to primeval slime. Not terribly inspirational material for moonlight sonatas.

MORE PROPER PASSIONS: VICTORIAN WRITERS

English literature, relatively secure amid burgeoning British industrialization, political reform bills, and the growth of the Empire, resisted the naturalist's trend to belittling man in a godless universe. DICKENS (which see), to be sure, showed great quantities of suffering among the common people, but he wasn't naturalistic—his people have too much good humor, and right gains at least a partial victory in his novels, even for the likes of Ebenezer Scrooge. TENNYSON (which see) proclaimed that although nature was "red in tooth and claw," he was still sure of immortality, and for a good romantic reason:

> A warmth within the breast would melt
> The freezing reason's colder part,
> And like a man in wrath the heart
> Stood up and answered, "I have felt."

Englishman MATTHEW ARNOLD (1822–88) also saw a romantic way out for a world "swept with confused alarms of struggle and flight": "Ah, love, let us be true / To one another!"

Some British writers preferred to laugh the whole naturalistic business off—for which they're remembered fondly and read frequently, especially to children. Going off to fight fearsome naturalistic beasts looked lots easier if you were reading EDWARD LEAR's "They went to sea in a sieve" (to the land where the Jumblies live), or LEWIS CARROLL's "Jabberwocky" ("Beware the Jabberwock, my son! / The jaws that bite, the claws that catch!"). The evolutionary struggle for survival was much easier to take along the primal seashore of Carroll's "The Walrus and the Carpenter":

> "Now, if you're ready, Oysters dear,
>   We can begin to feed."

> "But not on us!" the Oysters cried,
>   Turning a little blue.
> "After such kindness, that would be
>   A dismal thing to do!"
> "The night is fine," the Walrus said,
>   "Do you admire the view?"

And if one didn't ever, ever want to grow up and face this rapacious animal cruelty, there was James Barrie's Nevernever land, with Peter and Wendy and Tinker Bell, where one could fly away from pirates and crocodiles—if one could only figure out which was the second star to the right and keep straight on till morning.

In Russia, which was still serf-bound, in prerevolutionary despair, writers chose less frivolous and more Important subjects. Crime and punishment, for example, or war and peace. Both DOSTOEVSKI and TOLSTOI (which see) were able to transmit social horrors, like Dickens, but with much stronger religious overtones. Interestingly enough, both

Dostoevski and Tolstoi are hard to find in Russian bookstores
these days.

MORE ROMANTIC POLITICS:
PLAYING THE PEASANT

Of course none of the romantic poets wanted to go back
to the land as a *real* peasant. They just wanted to enjoy the
things they thought a peasant could enjoy if he had their
leisured sensibilities. Still, some romantic poets had a fling
at peasantry. Wordsworth, Coleridge, and a poet named
SOUTHEY had visions of an egalitarian society on the banks
of the Susquehanna in Pennsylvania which they called
"Pantisocracy," meaning equal rule by all. Coleridge even
married one of the ladies who was going, the sister of
Southey's fiancée, so that he could join up. But the project
collapsed (as did the marriage). Another poets' utopia that
did get started, "Brook Farm" in West Roxbury, Massachusetts, included Nathaniel Hawthorne, but it lasted only six
years. Work, poetry, and egalitarianism didn't seem to mix.

PASSION FOR THE PEOPLE II:
MORE REVOLUTIONARY POLITICS

Enter KARL MARX (1818–1883), German political philosopher. Of course egalitarianism didn't work now, he said, but
the common man was destined to rule eventually. His *Com-
munist Manifesto* (1847) helped him get expelled from
Prussia two years after he published it, so he settled in
London's Soho, mining the library for economic data that
would support his theory of workers' revolution.

The theory had four points, easy to follow in one easy
sentence. (1) Ideals, politics, and religion are all man-made,
so don't look for divine help in the (2) class struggle, in
which the rich get richer off the sweat of the working class,
(3) who can stand only so much of this unfair treatment
and will eventually rebel, so (4) why not have the violent
revolution now and get it over with? "Workers have nothing

to lose but their chains. They have a world to win." Sooner
or later after that revolutionary day, the workers will be
the dictators; everyone will own everything and nobody will
own anything. No social classes, no religion—except for this
DIALECTICAL MATERIALISM. And sooner or later, no
dictatorship, when the race has evolved to the point where
the species isn't greedy and property-hungry, like the petty
bourgeoisie.

Well, the workers' paradise idea didn't catch on in London,
or anywhere until the next century, but two other philosophical schools did try to get on with the job of solving the
problems of the masses. Both of them were anti-idealism.
UTILITARIANISM, in England, developed the axiom that
a right action is one which produces "the greatest good for
the greatest number"—of people, naturally. And in America
PRAGMATISM was boiled down, in the public mind,
to "if it works, do it." The philosophies caught on, since
there wasn't time for leisurely debate. Empires were being
built.

IMPERIALISM:
PASSION FOR THE RULING CLASS

Which brings us to another spin-off of the romantic view.
IMPERIALISM may sound like just plain old aristocracy,
at first, of course, but don't be deceived. Imperialism has
lots in common with the romantic idea of passion and individualism (think of Coleridge's Ancient Mariner, "Alone,
alone, all, all alone, / Alone on a wide, wide sea!"), which
combine to produce the superhero who can make laws for
others. Armed with his superior will, he can lead an army
into another country and say "This land is our land" and
make the locals believe it.

NAPOLEON BONAPARTE (1769–1821) was the first to
try imperialism in the nineteenth century; in fact, the Little
Corporal had been at it from 1796, when he conquered
northern Italy. By 1799 he was First Consul of France, and by

1804 he was emperor of what eventually included most of Europe.

But then he lost. As every schoolboy military strategist knows, Napoleon's best move was to use a citizens' army instead of only mercenaries, and his worst was to attack Russia and get stranded there in the winter. Also against Napoleon was the fact that he was trying to conquer (he preferred to say "liberate") European nations who didn't want to turn French and didn't see Frenchmen as being any better than themselves.

After Waterloo (1815), imperialists tended to operate more as businessmen than as military types, and on other continents, where Europeans were seen as something more advanced. The industrialized nations had goods to trade with, and guns to regulate the trade. Pretty soon a shrewd businessman could be regulating the affairs of his company and the town around it, and then the next town, and then the whole country—as the British did in India, and the British, French, Germans, Belgians, and Portuguese did in Africa.

Their rationale for ruling another race wasn't anything as crude as the Spanish conquistadores' bullying rule over Latin Americans. Knowing about Darwin helped give a new and different justification: since the white man considered himself higher up on the evolutionary ladder, it was the "White Man's Burden," as KIPLING put it, to rule. A nifty variation on the old "Great Chain of Being" notion of inequality, but there were other ideologies equally popular. Europeans were bringing true religion to the notives; they were stamping out cannibalism and human sacrifice; they were administering justice and medicine; they were teaching the natives useful trades . . .

Art and philosophy also gave imperialists aid and comfort. From Goethe's FAUST (1832) they could take the moral that striving and conquest were the chief end of man—as Faust finds out and so wins his bet with the devil. They could read the same thing in Charlotte Brontë's *Jane Eyre* ("We are born to strive and endure, Mr. Rochester—you as well as I. Do so.") and in Longfellow ("Let us then be up and doing . . .").

Those with guilty consciences could read NIETZSCHE (which see) and think of themselves as quasi-Byronic "supermen" who, above the laws of the common herd, could make their own standards of right and wrong.

And if they went to the opera or the concert hall, they could see the works of a contemporary superman, RICHARD WAGNER (REEKart VAHGner, 1813–83), a sometime pal of Nietzsche's who saw opera as the embodiment of all the arts (the *Gesamtkunstwerk*) and himself as the master of the opera. For producing what amounted to the best of every other art form, he felt entitled to sleep with whomever he liked, break promises, demand money from strangers, welsh on debts, wear only silk, insult at will, sulk, rage, and talk endlessly as the spirit moved him, and otherwise generally disregard the codes of lesser mortals. And so he did.

But his operas (see OPERA) are still performed.

THE PUT-DOWN OF PASSION: AWAY FROM IT ALL

Naturally not everyone could cope with imperial heroes or Wagnerian passions day in and day out. Toward the end of the century, the great themes began to seem ponderous, and asking the great questions began to seem pretentious. Especially in Paris, many artists tired of inspiring portraits and even of scenes that were frighteningly realistic. The IMPRESSIONISTS (which see) turned to painting light instead, disregarding (or pretending to) what the light fell on. Other painters, EXPRESSIONISTS, distorted shapes and textures to emphasize the emotions instead of the image. SYMBOLIST poets emphasized their moods by producing symbols instead of stories or ideas.

In music DEBUSSY (which see) wrote the equivalent of symbolism or impressionism: drifting melodic fragments that refused to make the usual progress to an old-fashioned tonic chord.

In drama, IBSEN (which see) tired of bourgeois complacency and struck back with "message drama": rebellious wives, syphilitic offspring, disenchanted doctors. Antiromantic, yes, but fulfilling the function of Shelley's poet as the legislator of moral law. Like Shelley, Ibsen also had to write outside his native country.

Some writers and artists, though, couldn't have cared less about reforming society. In fact, they decided, an artist shouldn't bother with anything except Art. Forget nature, man, politics, and especially moral earnestness. Decadence was the in thing. All art was for art's sake, not the public's. The world was going to hell, or not, and there was no sense trying to do anything about it. So OSCAR WILDE went back to comedy of manners (*Lady Windermere's Fan*, 1892; *The Importance of Being Earnest*, 1895). BEARDSLEY did amusing etchings, often erotic; SWINBURNE (which see) wrote odes to death; PATER (1839–94), who had the temperament of an evangelist, nevertheless wrote about stoicism and living for the moment; and nearly everyone read FITZGERALD's deliciously melancholy translation of *The Rubáiyát of Omar Khayyám* (1859), which recommends, as an antidote for thinking, wine, in large quantities.

AND FARTHER AWAY

PAUL GAUGUIN (goGANH, 1848–1903) went them all one better; he abandoned the brokerage business in 1883 to spend his time painting, and then abandoned his family and everything else to escape to Tahiti. He stayed native there from 1891 till the end, and kept painting, sending back to Paris brilliantly colored canvases of native girls, birds, and trees, done in a style that's a blend of oriental, Egyptian, Renaissance, and primitive. He also sent back his opinion of the society he had left: "Civilization," he said, "is what makes you sick."

Not long after that, a doctor in Vienna came to the same conclusion and published *Civilization and Its Discontents*. But that was in the twentieth century.

The Nineteenth-century Names You Should Know

MUSIC

Nineteenth-century music is almost as popular today as it was then. The odds are that any current "Who's Who" of musical names, any "balanced" concert program, or any day's broadcast on a "classical" music station will list more than 50 percent of its composers from the nineteenth century. Today's most popular pianist, Arthur Rubinstein, specializes in music of the romantics. Our orchestras use instruments —trumpets, trombones, tuba, timpani, snare drum, bass drum, cymbals, triangle, harp, English horn, bass clarinet, and contra bassoon—that the nineteenth century brought onto the concert stage. For ceremonial romance, we use mid-nineteenth-century music to begin (Mendelssohn's "Wedding March," 1844), and when the ceremony's over we march out to Wagner (from *Lohengrin:* 1848). Some contemporary composers are even beginning to write seriously in the romantic style.

And of course musicians in today's orchestras still dress in those nineteenth-century white-tie-and-tails costumes.

The popularity's understandable enough, what with the dearth of emotional oomph in modern poetry, art, and avant-garde music. But it does add up to a lot of names to know. . . .

At the top of the list, both chronologically and in musical stature, is LUDWIG VAN BEETHOVEN (BAYtoe ven, 1770–1827), one-time student of Mozart and Haydn. He started as a late-blooming child prodigy when his father, an alcoholic singer, pushed him into a musical career in hopes of growing fat on the profits. Soon young Beethoven was managing the family finances, an experience that made him canny businessman enough to become the first patronless but prosperous fulltime composer. Haydn called him the "Great Mogul."

Besides money, Beethoven's music has also earned him favorable comparisons with Shakespeare, with Michelangelo, and—by one prominent twentieth-century composer and conductor—with God. He has the breadth and positive spirit of Shakespeare, the statuesque solidity and structuring of Michelangelo (and the temperament), and that "rightness" which makes his works sound as though they'd been, as the saying goes, written in Heaven.

An independent musician of such genius can afford to be a bit eccentric, and Beethoven was that too, not only in his dour expression and rumpled long hair. He was known to crack the legs of the flimsy eighteenth-century spinets with his vigorous attack when he performed in concert. And once he held up a performance because one of the "pigs"—as he called them there to their faces—in his aristocratic audience talked while he was playing.

He was eccentric in musical form too, substituting the more colorful scherzo for the third-movement minuets in his early piano and violin sonatas and string quartets and later in his symphonies. He used more wind instruments in the orchestra than his audiences had been accustomed to, and at the end, as everyone knows, he switched movements around and brought in the human voice for the chorus of the Ninth Symphony. This innovation wasn't all inspiration. Contrary to believers in the Muse, Beethoven revised and rewrote constantly. A look at his notebooks shows how painful a process he went through to get that effect of a melody lined in Heaven.

For this individualism, and for his heroic and solitary battle with his deafness, Beethoven's known as the last classicist and the first romantic in music.

What's best to know of his works? Well, he thought that his best was the *Missa solemnis,* the Mass in D, which he wrote (in total deafness) in five parts as though it were an extra-long symphony. He's also revered for his *Emperor* piano concerto and his Violin Concerto in D Major.

But he's more frequently revered for his symphonies. Among the nine, the most frequently performed are: no. 3, the *Eroica,* which he supposedly dedicated to Napoleon but took back, tearing up the dedication page, when he learned that Napoleon had made himself emperor; no. 5, whose four-note depiction of "fate knocking at the door" became the Allies' "V for victory" 130 years later, and whose third movement sweeps directly into the fourth without a pause; no. 6, *Pastoral,* which has five movements instead of the usual four; and of course, the *Choral* Symphony, no. 9.

Which brings us to the nineteenth century's greatest moment of romantic grandeur: Vienna, May 7, 1824, when after two rehearsals the Ninth Symphony had its premiere. Beethoven was on stage, back to the audience, absorbed in the score of this work that had taken him from 1817 to complete, and was so difficult that the chorus and soloists begged him to lower the high notes (he refused, of course). When the performance was over, the applause was so tumultuous that the local police were put on alert, but Beethoven didn't even notice the ending—he was still immersed in the score. Then one of the soloists gently turned him around to face the cheers. The realization of just how totally deaf Beethoven was hit the audience like an electric shock, and they responded with new outbursts of feeling, wave upon wave, until as his biographer writes, "it seemed as if it would never end."

Three years later, the man who had written "strength is the morality of the man who stands out from the rest, and it is mine," died. If we can believe the legend, he died during a storm in the night, awake, shaking his fist at a thunderbolt. Twenty thousand mourners were in the Vienna streets for his funeral.

FRANZ SCHUBERT's (SHOObert, 1797–1828) Ninth

Symphony in C Major has been compared with Beethoven's Ninth for its breadth and passion, but the rest of his works take a different direction. He's remembered for his songs, poems from German poets such as Goethe, Schiller (who wrote the "Ode to Joy" in Beethoven's Ninth), and Heine, which he set to music and called *Lieder* (LEEder). Musicians still wonder what Schubert could have done if he'd had fifty-seven years, like Beethoven, instead of only thirty-one. Schubert's Eighth, or *Unfinished,* symphony, abandoned after only two movements, may have been one of those he dreamed of when, dying of typhoid fever, he complained that new ideas were still coming to him.

Don't confuse Schubert with ROBERT SCHUMANN (1810–56) who, like Schubert, wrote *Lieder* for voice and piano, but whose other works, like his *Manfred* Overture, inspired by Byron's hero, are not performed so often.

FELIX MENDELSSOHN (1809–47) could play Beethoven's nine symphonies on the piano from memory when he was still in his teens, and he could also compose: the *Midsummer Night's Dream* Overture was done at age seventeen—though the famous "Wedding March" wasn't added until he was thirty-five. Today he's noted for holding romantic, graceful melodies under logical classical control in such works as the *Italian* and *Scotch* symphonies, and the oratorios *St. Paul* and *Elijah.* To him we also owe the organizational pattern of today's concert programs, which he developed as a director in Leipzig.

For romantic piano, one name to know is FRÉDÉRIC CHOPIN (SHOWpan, 1810–49). We've already talked of his lyric departures from the classical form (with polonaises, nocturnes, etc.). Another departure was his use of grace notes (played lightly immediately before another note), trills (quick alternations between two notes), arpeggios (chords played one note at a time, in quick succession, up or down), and other performer's embellishments. He fit the romantic mold in his personal life, too, burning with Polish nationalism but living exiled in France with revolutionary novelist Aurore Dudevant (who wore men's clothes in public and wrote under the name of George Sand), and with a goblet of Polish earth as a keepsake.

FRANZ LISZT (LIST, 1811–86), the concert-stage piano superstar, is remembered primarily for his "tone poems" or "program music" written to illustrate something else, like his *Orpheus, Il Penseroso, Hamlet*, "Liebestraum," and his symphony after Goethe's *Faust,* which gives one movement each to Faust, Gretchen, and Mephistopheles. The work of his that's best known today (besides the Hungarian Rhapsodies) is *Les Préludes*, meant to illustrate what happens during life, our "preludes to the unknown song whose first solemn note is tolled by death," as he put it. Liszt is also known for his friendship with Wagner (see OPERA) and for the achievements of his daughter Cosima, who was Wagner's mistress (until her husband divorced her), then his wife, and finally, when he died, ruler of the still-productive Wagner Festival Theater in Bayreuth.

Somewhere near the top of the ranks for romantic flamboyance has to be HECTOR BERLIOZ (BERleeooze, 1803–69), the fiery Frenchman who at age twenty-four saw Harriet Smithson playing Ophelia and Juliet with a Shakespeare company in Paris, fell madly in love, was rejected without a meeting, and then turned her into the *idée fixe* theme of the still-famous *Symphonie fantastique,* a musical description of wild dreams that come when a rejected lover tries suicide with opium. The romantic ending is that Berlioz printed his own sad story in the program notes; Miss Smithson, now down on her luck, read them at a concert performance two years later, met Berlioz for the first time that night, and married him the next year. Unromantically enough, she turned out to be a shrew and an alcoholic.

Berlioz's other dream was to hear ten thousand trumpets from a mountaintop, but that one didn't materialize. The age wasn't quite *that* romantic.

JOHANNES BRAHMS (1833–97) wasn't that romantic either. He never married, blaming his inability to honor a woman with a permanent union on the childhood years he spent playing the piano in Hamburg bordellos. Critics dubbed his First Symphony "the Beethoven Tenth," because of his solid use of classical sonata form and theme and variations. In comparison with Beethoven, of course, Brahms looks more romantic, with his haunting lyricism and folk themes, but in comparison with the other musical titan of his time, Wagner, Brahms looks very classical indeed. Today, like the other two "Bs," Bach and Beethoven, Brahms has works in everyone's repertoire: symphonies (four), piano concertos (two), a violin concerto, solo piano and chamber music . . . and of course the famous lullaby.

Last of the romantics with heavyweight popularity is PETER ILYICH TCHAIKOVSKY (chyeKOFski, 1840–93). A romantic sentimentalist, Tchaikovsky was thought of as a veritable weeping machine by some. He did cry a lot, often out of fear and shame at his homosexuality; his last symphony he named the *Pathétique.* Yet his *1812 Overture,* especially when done outdoors with the real cannons and fireworks, brings hundreds of audiences cheering lustily to their feet every year. His opera *Eugene Onegin* has been compared with CHEKHOV (which see) for its quiet and realistic ending. His *Romeo and Juliet* Overture, and his ballets, *Swan Lake, Sleeping Beauty,* and the *Nutcracker,* enchant audiences everywhere.

Nonetheless, Tchaikovsky was a trifle neurotic, as could be seen when he regularly conducted an orchestra holding his chin with his left hand, convinced that otherwise his head would fall from his shoulders.

Other romantic names that come up often are two nationalists we've already mentioned, Dvořák and Grieg, from Bohemia and Norway, and two we haven't: MUSORGSKI (1835–81) and RIMSKY-KORSAKOV (1844–1908), both Russians. mooSORGskee's brought out every Halloween with his *Night on Bald Mountain,* other times with *Pictures at an Exhibition* (orchestrated by Ravel years after Musorgski wrote it for piano), and year-round in Russia with *Boris Godunov,* an opera about a Macbeth-style czar who murders to gain the throne and then falls, tormented by guilt. RIMskee-KORsuhkof comes out after dark too, with that symphonic suite that fairly reeks with romantic atmosphere, *Scheherazade.*

The last of our nineteenth-century composers, CLAUDE DEBUSSY (dehbyooSEE, 1862–1918), was romantic enough in his personal life—passionately attached to four women and innumerable cats—but his music was something very different. Around 1890 he began weekly cafe chats with fellow Parisians MANET and RENOIR, the IMPRESSIONIST artists (which see) and MALLARMÉ, the SYMBOLIST poet. Both groups were into subjective responses—the artist's emotional impressions—rather than trying to show the subject as a camera, or an "objective" reporter, would see it. Stylistically, impressionism and symbolism emphasized individual parts—shimmers of light in the paintings, symbols in the poems—rather than any "whole" subject or story narrative.

Why not the same for music? Debussy had always been fascinated with unorthodox harmonics, which put the emphasis on individual notes rather than on a melodic movement to a tonic-chord conclusion. In 1893 he wrote Quartet in G Minor, and the next year completed "Prelude to the Afternoon of a Faun" from a Mallarmé poem, and from these shimmering, momentary melodies, IMPRESSIONIST music was born. The best-known impressionist piece, Debussy's third movement of the *Suite bergamasque,* is called "Clair de lune."

OPERA

The first names to know about nineteenth-century opera are the kinds of opera that developed, in Paris mostly, during the period.

GRAND OPERA was the predecessor of Cecil B. DeMille

movies. Loaded with everything: lush scenery, ballet numbers, flashy solos, thunderous choruses, and melodramatic "rescue plots." Verdi's AÏDA (which see) is a good example. So is *William Tell,* which, since it's by an Italian, emphasizing beautiful songs, is also a good example of the "bel canto" school of opera.

COMIC OPERA was grand opera on a more sensible budget, with smaller casts and less scenery and without the soaring loftiness of serious opera. The singers could talk on occasion (instead of using the *recitative* or "song-speech" of grand opera). From the nineteenth century Verdi's *Falstaff* is one of the best known, with Mozart's *The Marriage of Figaro* (eighteenth century), Wagner's *Die Meistersinger,* and Rossini's *The Barber of Seville* also often heard from.

LYRIC OPERA mixes moods: serious one moment and humorous the next, but without talking. Gounod's *Faust,* Saint-Saëns' *Samson et Dalila,* and Bizet's *Carmen* are the three most performed.

And the one everybody knows from Gilbert and Sullivan is the LIGHT OPERA, or OPERETTA. Played for laughs, but with grace and with lots of verve. Besides G&S's *H.M.S. Pinafore, Pirates of Penzance, Mikado,* and so on, there's *Die Fledermaus,* "The Bat," by Johann Strauss, Jr. (1825–1899, not to be confused with Richard Strauss, 1864–1949), and Jacques Offenbach's (1819–80) *Orpheus in the Underworld.* This last may not sound like comedy material, but Offenbach made it a comedy of manners of sorts, satirizing the foolishness of French society with a shepherd who'd rather just tend to his music and not get involved.

Discounting PUCCINI (whom we'll come to in the twentieth century) the two big names to know in nineteenth-century opera are WAGNER and VERDI.

We've already talked of what a one-of-a-kind boor Wagner was personally, but his WAGNERIAN OPERAS, also one of a kind, are regarded more highly. They're different, and not just because their women wear winged helmets and steel breastplates. Wagnerian singers sing louder, of necessity, because the Wagnerian orchestra is bigger and more important. The pieces blend together without a pause, because Wagner was fanatical about unity and didn't want any one song or performer emphasized more than another. The characters each have leitmotifs, melodic themes that Debussy dubbed "calling cards" (a technique borrowed from the *idée fixe* theme of "Her" in Berlioz's *Symphonie fantastique*).

Sitting through one of the four operas that comprise the *Ring Cycle*, Wagner's most famous work, can be a nerve-jangling experience, not only because they're long, and about the death of the gods (Norse gods) who refuse to give up their magic ring of immortality. Wagner uses a musical technique with his harmonics, refusing to return to his tonic chord, and yet continuously tantalizing with almost-tonic dominant chords, all the way through the opera until the big orchestral finale. Then, in the *Götterdämmerung*, the last of the *Ring* operas, Brünnhilde rides into Siegfried's funeral pyre, Valhalla burns, the Rhine gold goes back to the Rhine Maidens, and all is resolved.

Other works: *Tristan und Isolde*, written before the *Ring* cycle was complete, is a *Romeo and Juliet* of Celtic myth, except that instead of poisoning herself Isolde simply dies, after the wounded Tristan has expired in her arms. *Parsifal*, Wagner's last, is about the questing grail knight who searches for a sacred spear. Both share the "unified" songless structure of the *Ring*, and the other technical innovations, along with the religious mysticism. *Die Meistersinger von Nürnberg*, written just after *Tristan*, is more lighthearted, in the comic opera style. *Tannhäuser* and *Lohengrin*, earlier works, still place more emphasis on the orchestra than was common. An air from *Lohengrin* is heard at the end of many weddings, though some refuse to allow Wagner's pagan melodies into a church. *The Flying Dutchman*, Wagner's third opera and the earliest that's still performed, was probably inspired by a fly-by-night boat trip to France, when Wagner had to escape creditors from the three cities he'd lived in before.

Mecca for Wagnerians is Bayreuth (byeROIT), the Bavarian town northeast of Nürnberg where Wagner established a theater to perform only Wagnerian operas. That happens every summer, a quasi-religious rite for many who thrill to the psychological depths of the music and the continuing themes of renunciation and redemption in the tales. Wagner's own views on religion and race, that the Aryans had descended from the gods and that the Israelites were former cannibals, made him popular with the twentieth century's least popular Germans.

The Italian equivalent of Wagner's German nationalism comes in GIUSEPPE VERDI (VAIRdee, 1818–1901). The most often-performed opera composer and some say the best, Verdi broke away from the "bel canto" school with his *Macbeth,* for which he wanted a Lady Macbeth whose voice was as ugly as her looks. No pretty songs, just pity and terror, especially during the sleepwalking scene. After that, among others, came *Rigoletto* (1851), about a jester who murders his daughter by mistake; *Il Trovatore* (1852), in which one brother beheads another; and *La Traviata* (1853), taken from the younger Dumas's *The Lady of the Camellias,* about a loose woman who gives up her young nobleman lover to preserve his reputation and then dies of consumption. Passion, Italian style.

These three years of composing were enough to keep plenty of opera companies in performances, but there was more to come. In 1871 Verdi staged the grandest of grand operas, *Aïda,* another *Romeo and Juliet* tale but set in Egypt, where the Egyptians are warring against the Ethiopians. Aïda, the daughter of the Ethiopian general, is in love with the Egyptian leader, a tenor. Like R&J, the lovers end in a tomb, only this one's a pyramid. Great scenery, especially after the battle when they march in the throngs of prisoners,

and when—budget, stage, and stagehands' union permitting—
the camels and elephants come in.

Verdi's greatest tragic opera is *Otello* (after Shakespeare's
play), which he wrote when he was seventy-three years old.
At age seventy-nine, he did *Falstaff,* also after Shakespeare,
one of the best of the comic operas. Years between, he amused
himself in retirement on his farm, living the simple life he
considered appropriate for a small-town lad of humble origins
whose name translates into English as "Joe Green."

ART

The first of the nineteenth-century artists to know is generally
the first on a list of English poets too: WILLIAM BLAKE
(1757–1827). A mystic, Blake did the engravings for his
lyrical poems, the best known of which are *Songs of Innocence* ("Little Lamb, who made thee?" etc.) and *Songs
of Experience* ("Tyger! Tyger! burning bright . . ."). His
artistic style is more romantically flamboyant than the verses,
as seen in his oft-reproduced portrait of God, long hair askew,
leaning over with his huge set of compasses to scribe out the
earth. Blake's philosophy was romantic too, as in his oft-

quoted maxim from *The Marriage of Heaven and Hell:* "The road of excess leads to the palace of wisdom."

FRANCISCO GOYA (1746–1828) wasn't romantic, but his two most famous paintings are flamboyantly realistic, almost surreal in their harsh lights and distorted postures. *The Third of May, 1808,* shows Napoleon's soldiers gunning down, at point-blank range, Spanish civilians against a wall in Madrid. *Saturn Devouring His Children* shows a wide-eyed Cronus (see THE ANCIENT WORLD) taking the second or third bite out of a man's top half, while he's tearing the bottom half into smaller portions with his hands.

Passing over *The Raft of the "Medusa"* and others we mentioned earlier, we come to the center of the art world, Paris, in the second half of the century. There ÉDOUARD MANET (mahNAY, 1832–83) got into the idea of painting light instead of subject matter and began what his 1867 catalogue later called "his impression" of subjects. Critics soon labeled the style IMPRESSIONISM.

Manet started with a subject that few were ready for in 1863, though, no matter what the light was doing: his *Luncheon on the Grass* showed two ordinarily clothed men reclining in a park with a nude woman, who looked at the viewer as though she did that sort of thing often. The light on her is harsh, as was the audience's reaction, even in Paris.

The light on Manet's masterpiece, *Bar at the Folies-Bergère,* is more glittering, shimmering over the wine bottles, the fruit, the crystal chandelier, the crowd reflected in the mirrored wall, and the barmaid, with a uniform lack of emphasis. The girl has no personality and there's no story being told—only surfaces for the light to fragment itself upon.

CLAUDE MONET (moNAY, 1840–1926) did the same sort of thing with the front of Rouen Cathedral, and with water lilies, getting rid of outlines and shapes altogether and leaving only shimmering shades. He also did a painting of a sunrise at sea, "Une impression," that solidified the impressionist movement's title.

GEORGES SEURAT (sirRAH, 1859–91) broke the shimmers down even further, leaving only little points of color to give a mosaic-like blend, figures floating serenely, all part of the same haze. "Pointillism" wasn't the name Seurat called it—he used "divisionism," which doesn't leave any white background showing—but the name stuck anyway. His most famous work, *Sunday Afternoon on the Grand Jatte*, is about nine feet by ten feet and understandably took Seurat two years to finish, dot by dot.

The most attractive of the impressionists' work, if you like pleasantness and charm, is by AUGUSTE RENOIR (reNWAHR, 1841–1919). His French cafes and sun-drenched landscapes look like the most agreeable places and people one could ever hope to find, and at their freshest, brightest moments, too. Getting to Renoir country these days, though, is expensive: *Le Pont des Arts, Paris*, one of Renoir's landscapes, sold in 1968 for $1.55 million.

EDGAR DEGAS (deGAH, 1834–1917) liked to get the impressionist effect of divided light colors by using pastels and to position his scenes at angles which showed a lot of open floor space, as though the viewer were sitting on a ladder or looking at a Japanese print. He also liked the idea of the momentary scene, the figures caught in motion. Ballerinas were his favorite subjects.

A painter with less pleasant, though more striking, visions was VINCENT VAN GOGH (van GO, though some say van GOKH, 1853–90). He's the one who layered thick, swirling brush strokes on the canvas, squeezed dots and streaks straight from the tube, and painted the colors he felt rather than those which he called "locally true." Painting feelings rather than what's seen is called EXPRESSIONISM. *The Starry Night*, his masterpiece, brings the chaos of a whole universe down into a swirling, exploding night sky above a little village, showing how untranquil he felt even on a clear night. Psychologists are fond of analyzing his self-portraits, which get more distorted as he got more self-destructive—he's also the one who

cut off his ear and later ended his life, having not sold a
single one of his paintings. In 1970, one of them was auctioned
for $1.3 million.

Getting further away from the reality of the photograph
was PAUL CÉZANNE (sayZAHN, 1839–1906), who reduced
his subjects almost to their geometric shapes and painted
them as if they were seen from more than one angle at the
same time, and even from more than one distance. Warm
colors, reds and browns, would be used to bring a subject
"closer" to the surface of the painting, and cooler blues and
greens to make it recede. For this ABSTRACTION of geometric forms and color principles from natural settings,
Cézanne's known as the father of modern art.

Only one nineteenth-century sculptor to know: RODIN
(roeDANH, 1840–1917). His massive, towering figures were
what he hoped was the sculptural equivalent of the later
MICHELANGELO (which see) in grandeur and expres-
sionistic distortions, and in the fact that some of them
looked unfinished. The most famous Rodin in the pop world
is the often-lampooned *The Thinker,* sculpted as a figure
sitting by the gates of hell, contemplating the suffering going
on inside. The most famous in the art world is *Balzac,* a
statue of the naturalistic *Human Comedy* novelist that

towers (ten feet) over the world's mortals like a gargantuan
hawk. Underneath the statue's floor-length dressing gown
was a fully sculpted body that Rodin had formed first,
though few in the 1898 crowd who saw it at the unveiling
would accept the unromanticized view as even partially real.

LITERATURE

Two novelists one *ought* to know are JANE AUSTEN (1775–
1817) and expatriate American HENRY JAMES (1843–1916).
Why? To know civilized sensitivity and irony. Or *Sense and
Sensibility,* as she put it (1811), or *The Better Sort,* as he
put it (1903), or *Pride and Prejudice,* as she put it . . .

Highbrow lit. "Gentle Jane" is noted for her portraits of
English country life at the end of the eighteenth century,
when aristocracy was still an occupation, marriages meant
money and estates for life, and one was somehow obligated
to cultivate oneself to a degree worthy of such a noble position. Jane herself never married, partly for reasons of health
and perhaps because there weren't males to be had in Europe
who were as worthy as the Mr. Rights who finally wed her
heroines. Though we can't be sure, she may have had a
blighted love affair.

Henry James, brother of philosopher-psychologist William
James, lived abroad (London) from age thirty-three and
wrote novels that made him the model of cultivated intellect
for Americans back home: one of those persons "on whom,"
as he put it, "nothing is lost." One of his persistent themes
is how the Old World civilizes and corrupts at the same time,
making life difficult if not impossible for fresh Americans
like Daisy Miller, or Isabel Archer (in *Portrait of a Lady*).
James himself was civilized to the point of being bothersome
away from his desk, as is clear from a story about him told
by novelist Edith Wharton. We pick up her narrative after
James, riding in a motorcar, has gone on for two-hundred-
word sentences in an effort to ask directions of a man on
the street:

"Oh, please," I interrupted, feeling myself utterly unable to sit through another parenthesis, "do ask him where the Kings Road is."

"Ah—? The King's Road? Just so! Quite right! Can you, as a matter of fact, my good man, tell us where, in relation to our present position, the King's Road exactly *is*?"

"Ye're in it," said the aged face at the window.

As one might guess, James's involved syntax can be maddening, though if one's to become one of those persons on whom nothing is lost, one really ought to take the time . . .

A more homespun view of Europe came back to Americans from correspondent SAMUEL CLEMENS, better known as MARK TWAIN (1835–1910), in *The Innocents Abroad* (1869). Twain hated the romanticism of Sir Walter Scott for corrupting the South with unrealistic ideals, but all the same his stories of boyhood along the Mississippi, *Tom Sawyer* and *Huckleberry Finn,* have becomes ideals in themselves, making millions of boys long for romantic adventure, or at least for a raft to float downstream on. Twain's later pieces of bitter satire add to some biographers' case that he was a split personality (Twain—get it?). There's no status in knowing him, though: just a kind of down-home smugness, as in "Foreigners always spell better than they pronounce" (*Innocents Abroad*), or "There warn't anybody at the church, except maybe a hog or two, for there warn't any lock on the door, and hogs likes a puncheon floor in summertime because it's cool. If you notice, most folks don't go to church only when they've got to; but a hog is different" (*Huckleberry Finn*).

TOLSTOI, Count Leo (TULstoy: 1828–1910) and DO-STOEVSKI, Fëdor (dostuYEVski: 1821–81). Both Russian, both religious, both on "one-of-these-days-I'll-get-around-to" lists, because they both wrote long novels with lots of long and easily forgettable Russian names. Dostoevski's tales move along at a more frenetic clip, possibly because he was a compulsive gambler, writing for quick cash, who as a boy lost his father in a brutal murder, and who, after his first novel, was arrested as a revolutionary, put before a firing squad, released at the last minute, and sent to five years' hard labor in Siberia.

Dostoevski's *Crime and Punishment* tells of a poverty-stricken intellectual who thinks he's a superman above the law (see NIETZSCHE) and can therefore get away with ax-murdering a miserly old woman. He's straightened out by a religious redemption involving a prostitute who really does have a heart of gold, while he's serving years of hard labor in, naturally, Siberia. In *The Brothers Karamazov,* Dostoevski's other most famous, there's also murder (of Father Karamazov) and redemption, including the oft-quoted "Legend of the Grand Inquisitor," where Christ comes back to earth and is jailed by the Inquisition. Along with Dostoevski's *Notes from the Underground,* these two novels have been admired by twentieth-century EXISTENTIALISTS (which see).

Tolstoi had a less traumatic existence as a gentleman farmer on his family's Russian estate, but his WAR AND PEACE, the 1500-page novel with everything, is still number one in a *genre* with thousands of new contenders every year. The war is Napoleon's 1812 campaign into Russia, and the peace is what everyone else, from princes and princesses to serfs, is looking for. By the time the book ends, some have found it, as have many of the book's readers.

Anna Karenina, about a woman who finds love away from a beast of a husband and is driven to suicide, and *The Death of Ivan Ilyich,* about a successful judge who isn't, are also often mentioned in existential conversations. People don't talk much about the other works, or about Tolstoyism, the nonviolent version of Christianity Tolstoi developed into an organized religion.

DRAMA

HENRIK IBSEN (IBsen, 1828–1906) has been called a "dramatist of ideas" for the women's lib in *A Doll's House* (the housewife leaves her male chauvinist husband), the freethinking in *The Master Builder* (who vows to stop building churches), and the unflinching honesty in *An Enemy of the People* (the doctor reveals that the town's new health spa has polluted water). Ibsen's also been called a dramatist of REALISM, because of the way his characters are driven by forces beyond their control—as in *Ghosts,* where the main character suffers from inherited syphilis, or in *Hedda Gabler,* his most famous, where the heroine's frustrations drive her to meddling and then suicide.

In most of Ibsen's plays, the real villain is social convention, those complacent lies that cover up what's been rotting too long. For this he's also been called a "Message" dramatist—someone who's telling society what it Needs to Know. Serious business, even though Ibsen's plots really are like this one-sentence summary by Somerset Maugham: "A number of people are living in a closed or stuffy room, then someone comes (from the mountains or over the sea) and flings the window open; everyone gets a cold in the head and the curtain falls."

But whatever one says about Ibsen, he's still staged, and his honesty's as refreshing in his plays as in his last words: on his deathbed, when his wife tried to tell him he was getting better, he replied, "On the contrary."

The French IMPRESSIONIST movement didn't extend to drama but the style of Russian dramatist ANTON CHEKHOV (CHEkof, 1860–1904) comes close to it, even though he thought he was writing REALISM. His plays have no angels or villains, and barely any messages—only people, little individuals bumbling around in their own little worlds, in love with the wrong lovers and not even able to talk with each other very well.

The twentieth century has adored Chekhov. His unheroic heroes have turned into today's alienated antiheroes, and his dispassionate passion—he was a medical doctor among the Russian poor, who was himself dying of tuberculosis—has become today's tragicomedy. *The Cherry Orchard,* his play about impoverished aristocrats whose orchard's being turned into a housing development, is performed especially often. Interpretations sometimes lean to Chekhov's, who said he was writing a comedy, even with some farce in it; other times they lean to the more poignant presentation of the play's first director at the Moscow Art Theater, the man of The Method, Constantin Stanislavsky.

What Not to Bother With

MORE LITERATURE

HERMAN MELVILLE's (MELvil, 1819–91) MOBY DICK is one of the great American novels that nobody reads. Melville wrote it after he'd succeeded with travelogues and adventure yarns about sailors and South Sea cannibals and wanted to do Something Meaningful. With a prose that's part Biblical, part Shakespearean, and part sailor, *Moby*'s chock full of seaman's lore and encyclopedic *minutiae* about whales, which makes it less than popular today. For the adventure, though, you should see the movie with Gregory Peck, or the seventies counterpart where the great white whale's a great white shark and the mad Captain Ahab's a shark hunter named Quint. If somebody quotes you *Moby*'s first line, "Call me Ishmael," respond quickly with "But call me."

RALPH WALDO EMERSON (1803–82) made his living as a lecturer. Father of the American romantic movement called Transcendentalism, which he began after he'd been to England and met Wordsworth, Emerson was also the first to call for Americans to stop imitating English writers and get into "self-reliance." But that was long ago, and nobody wants to hear lectures from anybody these days, much less read Emerson's.

HENRY DAVID THOREAU (THORoh or thuROH, 1817–1862), a protégé of Emerson's in Concord, Massachusetts, was revived in the sixties for his essay on civil disobedience, written after he spent a night in jail rather than pay a local poll tax because he opposed the U.S. Mexican war involvement. He's also remembered for taking to the woods (Walden Pond) at the edge of town, where he could "front only the essential facts of life." That meant watching Nature, for two years. He did, however, go into Concord regularly for meals at his mother's.

CHARLES DICKENS, or "Boz," as he first penned himself (1812–70), had an enormous following for his novels of harrowing social injustice, sentiment, and whimsey, all three of which are found in great quantities in any one work. Each week crowds waited for the next installment of his latest serialized novel, so eagerly that in New York in 1841, the dock was packed with Dickens fans when the English ship came in with the magazine, *Master Humphrey's Clock,* that contained some concluding chapters of *The Old Curiosity Shop.* As the ship docked, through the winter air came the crowd's anxious shouts to those on board: "Is little Nell dead? Is she dead?" (She was—an event that made grown men weep.)

Today the films of *Great Expectations* and *David Copperfield* are perennial late-show favorites, and *Oliver Twist* did very well as a Broadway musical–movie not long ago. And of course everybody knows about Ebenezer Scrooge in *A Christmas Carol,* and Fagin, the children's Napoleon of crime from *Oliver Twist.* Often, too, allusions to the first and last lines of *A Tale of Two Cities* pop up. "It was the best of times, it was the worst of times" (the French Revolution), and "It is a far, far better thing that I do, than I have ever done. . ." (taking the last ride to the guillotine, after his wastrel's life, to die in place of the hero).

But Dickens, like other nineteenth-century authors, many of whom were paid by the word, tended to run on a bit. Nowadays his books aren't talked about much outside the academic world, where they have time for him.

GEORGE ELIOT was the pen name of Mary Ann Evans (1819–80), who shocked Victorian England by living unmarried twenty-four years with another writer, George Henry Lewes. Her *Silas Marner* is the novel high-schoolers all over America once loved to hate. *Middlemarch,* her best, is the closest English novelists come to Tolstoi, though, so if you've some time on your hands and have finished *War and Peace* and *Anna Karenina* . . .

Between bouts of dipsomania and necrophilia, EDGAR ALLAN POE (1908–49) produced the first detective mysteries and Southern Gothic horror stories. Everybody's read "The Raven" and "The Gold Bug," but aside from noting his influence on the SYMBOLIST poets and other decadents (which see) nobody takes Poe seriously, any more than they did last century when he showed up for a West Point morning inspection stark naked. Best title of Poe's for romantic atmosphere: *Tales of the Grotesque and Arabesque* (1840). Best asessment, by James Russell Lowell, in "A Fable for Critics" (1848): "There comes Poe, with his Raven, like Barnaby Rudge, / Three-fifths of him genius and two-fifths sheer fudge."

ALFRED, LORD TENNYSON (1809–92), is scoffed at for his Victorian earnestness about: progress via industrialism ("Let the great world spin forever down the ringing grooves of change"); miilitary honor ("Theirs not to reason why, theirs but to do and die"); and sentiment ("I hold it true, whate'er befall; / I feel it, when I sorrow most; / 'Tis better to have loved and lost / Than never to have loved at all"). Lines like these made him the poet laureate of England for forty-two years, but they're camp today. More respectable for an unabashed romantic wallow in Arthurian legend (see THE MEDIEVAL MYSTIQUE) is Tennyson's *Idylls of the King*, which contains Galahad's immortal "My strength is as the strength of ten, / because my heart is pure." You might suggest him as the poetic equivalent to TCHAIKOVSKY (which see) if you run into an enthusiast.

Except for Flaubert and Balzac, already mentioned, the other nineteenth-century French writers are by now just names and familiar titles. Three of the names everyone knows are ALEXANDRE DUMAS (Dumas *père*), who wrote the swashbuckling *The Three Musketeers* and *The Count of Monte Cristo*; his son, ALEXANDRE DUMAS (Dumas *fils*), who did *La Dame aux Camélias* (see VERDI); and EDMOND ROSTAND, who did *Cyrano de Bergerac*, about the cruelties of fate in the days before plastic surgery.

Less familiar are BAUDELAIRE (bohDLAIR), 1821–67), MALLARMÉ (mahlarMAY, 1842–98), VERLAINE (verr-LANE, 1844–96), and SWINBURNE (1837–1909), names dropped when conversations turn to decadence in life, SYM-BOLISM in poetry, and IMPRESSIONISM in art or music. All but Swinburne (whom one British reviewer called "swine-born") were French, and none were often sober. They did, however, also influence another generation of poets, the IMAGISTS (see THE TWENTIETH CENTURY).

PHILOSOPHY

IMMANUEL KANT (KAHNT, 1724–1804) is chronologically closer to the end of the eighteenth century, but he was interested enough in romantic themes to make him more at home in the next. He was pro the American and French revolutions, anti dogmatism and skepticism, and set as one of his basic premises that we want to be treated as "persons" rather than "things"—all good romantic notions, as was his idea that a good action had to be done with a "good will."

Kant's *Critique of Pure Reason* is referred to now and again by college students as a pinnacle of intellectual achievement (as in, "What are you tryin' to write there—another *Critique of Pure Reason?*"). And his "Categorical Imperative," the notion that our actions ought to be based on principles that we would want everyone, categorically, to follow, survives as the moral question, "What if everybody did that?" Those who walk their dogs on city streets should therefore take notice of their immorality.

FRIEDRICH NIETZSCHE (NEEcheh, 1844–1900) championed the Superman in theory, but turned away from its nearest living relative, Wagner, after a friendship of five years. He's known for saying that God is dead (in *Also Sprach Zarathustra*), for condemning Christianity as a slave religion, for championing Dionysian frenzy as a life-enhancer equal to Apollonian order (see THE ANCIENT WORLD), and for castigating the "herd mentality" that exalts mediocre values for safety's sake. His ideal Superman, he said, should be above good and evil, answerable only to the Will to Power, one of the "aristocratic races, the magnificent *blond beast*, avidly rampant for spoil and victory." Just before his last eleven years, during which he was totally insane from a brain infection, Nietzsche wrote, "My time has not yet come; some are born posthumously." These days he's remembered as the Nazi's philosopher.

ARCHITECTURE

Except for Victorian architecture, which went wild with gables and gingerbread, there wasn't much developed. The word was "revival": architectural nostalgia for Greece, Rome, and Gothic England. Columns, towers, and turrets with lots of rooms for lots of Victorian youngsters. Servants' quarters too, of course: all the way upstairs for sleeping, and the kitchen under the first floor for the staff's meals and hobnobbing, as every *Upstairs, Downstairs* fan knows. For something different, we have to wait till the geometric abstractions of artists hit the architectural drawing boards, in THE TWENTIETH CENTURY.

VI

THE TWENTIETH CENTURY

The One Twentieth-century Idea You Need to Know

What's Really Right to know during the most recent years is really anybody's guess. When we're faced with a new crop of thirty thousand different books every year, plus untold magazines, newspaper reviews, and articles, and TV, theater, film, and so on, we're up against the same deluge of information we talked about in the foreword of this book. It's difficult to see any firm trends at all, much less pick out the things that are sure to be most significant.

If we just back up, though, and concentrate on the earlier part of this century, we can get a better perspective and feel a bit more secure about what's going to last. We can see one idea that links up the most important things from those early decades. And we can even make the cautious assertion that this one idea is still kicking around a bit here in the seventies:

New Rules Is Few Rules, or
Primitive Is Futuristic

Breaking out of the establishment's civilized rulebook wasn't all that new an idea, actually. Artists had been rule-breakers since the Renaissance, and primitivism—a return to pre-civilized simplicity—was just the logical extension of romanticism's slide down the Great Chain of Being (which see). The directions for this twentieth-century idea were set when Cézanne started going abstract in his paintings and when Gauguin went native.

But where the movement went after that was enough to keep the cultural world further off balance than it had been since Attila the Hun.

A good high point to begin with is Paris, May 29, 1913, the evening SERGEI DIAGHILEV's (DYAgihlyef, 1872–1929) BALLET RUSSE premiered *The Rite of Spring*. It looked as if a great night was in the offing. The great VASLAV NIJINSKY, who had wowed all Paris with the new dashing Russian dance leaps and whirls, was choreographer. And the *Rite*'s Russian composer, IGOR STRAVINSKY (strahVIN-skee, 1882–1971) had given Parisians two hits in the past two years: *The Firebird* and *Petrushka*.

But then came *The Rite*, a ballet about a virgin who dances herself to death in an ancient Russian ritual sacrifice. When the curtain went up, the audience went into hysterics. One part of the crowd hurled insults at the orchestra and the dancers, while another, called the Apaches, screamed that the work was a masterpiece and that the audience were swine. No one could hear the orchestra amid the bedlam, not even the performers. As Stravinsky tells it, Nijinsky had to stand on a chair in the wings, calling out instructions to the dancers "like a coxswain," while Diaghilev had the electrician switching the houselights on and off, hoping to quiet the crowd. It didn't work. Neither did bringing in the police. The night's performance had to be scuttled.

It wasn't the dance of death that stirred everyone up—the performance never got that far, and besides, there'd been dances of death happily received ever since *Giselle*. What did it was the music. Stravinsky scored the ballet with driving, irregular rhythms—using two or more different meters for different instruments, both alternately and at the same time, and will dissonant chords that the whole orchestra pounded again and again. The effect was a primitive violence in the music that moved the audience to an equally primitive response.

When *The Rite* hit Boston, the Boston *Herald* struck back:

> Who wrote this fiendish Rite of Spring,
> What right had he to write the thing,
> Against our helpless ears to fling
> Its crash, clash, cling, clang, bing, bang, bing?

However, the artistic community wasn't intimidated. Following a growing tradition begun by Flaubert, who said that hatred of the bourgeois was the beginning of wisdom, and Baudelaire, who said that an artist "must shock the bourgeois," and even Matthew Arnold, the Victorian poet and critic who called the uncultured public "The Philistines," the artists knew who the chosen people were and where the battle lay. If primitive passion stirred everyone up, that just indicated that they were on the right track.

One of Stravinsky's friends in Paris was a Spanish artist who helped the Diaghilev ballet with scenery and costumes:

PABLO PICASSO (peaKAHso, 1881–1973). Picasso knew a bit about the primitive himself, having studied the geometric planes and distortions of African masks and other folk art from the bush country—material designed to speak directly to the primitive consciousness, either to portray evil spirits or frighten them away.

Already adept at virtually every style of painting at age twenty-six, Picasso decided to use some of the primitive distortions in his own material, especially the distortions that twisted parts of the subject around as if they were seen from different angles. Nose at the profile, for example, while the face was seen from the front. Or eyes dislocated, or torso turned around too far to be real. Taking a lead from Cézanne, Picasso painted parts of his subjects and backdrops at different angles, producing paintings that appeared to some as though the original painting had been crumpled up, or torn up, and the result painted again.

Shocking, the press responded. The new style was called CUBISM, because the multiple angles of vision appeared to break the work into only geometric forms, especially cubes. And the *New York Times,* when the cubists hit New York in 1913, wrote that these artists were "making insanity pay."

Again, though, the movement went on undismayed. It grew from the ANALYTIC phase, which painted a subject from so many viewpoints that they could scarcely be recognized as anything more than lines and planes and cubes, to SYN-THETIC CUBISM, which used only a few viewpoints and brighter colors.

Put this style together with expressionist art, the painting of the feeling rather than the subject, and passion, both primitive and civilized, can be stirred up in yet a new way, as it was by the mural Picasso painted in memory of a Spanish town, Guernica, that had been bombed during the Spanish Civil War. Next to the *Guernica, The Raft of the "Medusa"* looked almost mild.

SCIENTIFIC PROOF OF THE PRIMITIVE

As if the arts weren't already giving enough primitivism to a world where many schools still refused to teach the theory of evolution, a Vienna doctor named SIGMUND FREUD (FROYD, 1856–1939) began convincing many that there were primitives not just in the avant-garde museums or ballet orchestras, but inside us all.

What was even more distressing was to learn that these primitive passions came out at night to get their wishes in dreams, that they demanded horrible things, like killing and sleeping with parents, and that they wouldn't go away. Despite will power, fasting, and prayer, the inner savage (the ID) was still waiting its turn. If left unsettled, the inner conflicts it stirred up could cause one to betray himself with embarrassing "Freudian slips" of the tongue, or any of the other self-defeating mistakes and accidents Freud listed in *Psychopathology of Everyday Life*. Worse, the conflicts could develop into compulsive behavior and even madness.

What's more, Freud was showing how the patterns of our

inner savagery had worked their way not just into our inner actions but our public performances, too. Plays were seen as acting out our primitive conflicts between the unconscious and the conscious, as in *Oedipus Rex*, where the hero kills Father and marries Mother even though he's deliberately trying not to. Homes and rooms were seen as womb-symbols to which adults could retreat, not just for shelter but to imagine they weren't yet born. Eating, drinking, and smoking weren't just for food and taste; they were also for oral gratification, a yen for more breastfeeding. We brandished cigars and raised buildings and statues tall to mimic erect phalluses. We collected because our toilet training hadn't made us comfortable about letting go.

And when we were good, we were good because of a primal conscience called a SUPEREGO, the remnant fears and pains from parental beatings that could hit us again with guilt. Our individual superegos kept our personal aggressive instincts in check; in public, we held ourselves to the straight and narrow with an invented deity who served as a cultural superego. "Love thy neighbor as thyself," said the cultural superego, a commandment, Freud said in his conclusion to *Civilization and Its Discontents,* that "is impossible to fulfill; such an enormous inflation of love can only lower its value, not get rid of the difficulty."

If that weren't depressing news enough, in *Beyond the Pleasure Principle* we learned about another unpleasant unconscious desire: the death wish. We didn't want just to get back to the womb; we wanted to get back to *before* the womb. Not just darkness; oblivion. The big sleep.

Even if one didn't believe it all, it was enough to make a body self-conscious. Enough to make even a century self-conscious. Even Freud. Once when he addressed a group of his colleagues, he put a cigar in his mouth and was aware of their looks. "Gentlemen, please remember," he said, "that this is also a cigar."

Anyone who knows about *Auntie Mame*, where children at

a progressive school slither nude along the floor like fish
"spreading the sperm" so they won't grow up to be "repressed,"
knows what lengths people went to, trying to escape the
curse of lost LIBIDO. The real world, especially America,
took the doctrines very seriously.

THE SOPHISTICATED PRIMITIVE

The new psychology gave the literary world what every
writer dreams about: new conflicts and new symbols. Car-
toonists gleefully made their villains with longer noses to
capitalize on youngsters' Oedipal dislike of their daddies.
Dramatists like O'NEILL (which see) somberly wrote tragedies of Oedipal and Electral triangles, apemen who worked
below deck, and about "Nature—makin' thin's grow—bigger
'n' bigger."

Even an ultraliterary poet like T. S. ELIOT (which see)
went to primitive fertility myth for the structure of *The
Waste Land,* a ritual quest for spiritual water that fails.

Novelists JAMES JOYCE and WILLIAM FAULKNER
(both of which see) began writing less external action and
more internal monologue, stream-of-consciousness associations,
sequences of ideas connected by memory and feeling, not
reason, in the manner of a patient's ramblings on a psycho-
analyst's couch. Since innermost thoughts were more "real"
than external actions, it was enough to give a day-in-the-life
treatment of a character in which, externally, nothing happened. And so the plotless novel was born. Another rule
biting the dust to let loose more primitive passion.

Was it pleasant? No, but as Mack The Knife, in Brecht's
expressionist *Threepenny Opera* (an uncomic remake of Gay's
The Beggar's Opera) says, Art's not supposed to be pleasant.

Audiences found expressionist music even less entertaining
than the New fiction or Poetry. The leader in that field was
ARNOLD SCHOENBERG (SHURNbergh, 1874–1951). The
principle was easy to understand: the more freedom one had,
the more emotions could be expressed. So why not total

freedom? Forget a musical key, where one note was the bottom of a scale (as in *do*) and seven others, *re, me, fa,* and so on, each a whole or half step apart according to whether the key was major or minor, were used more than the remaining available tones. Use all twelve notes—all the keys on the piano, black and white. There'd be no sense of scale, no key, no *do*, no tonic chord (based on *do*) to come home to. But there was freedom.

And Schoenberg did develop rules, of sorts. In what were called "tone rows," the composer would use each of the twelve notes in a sequence. No one note of the twelve could be used more than once in a single tone row. One instrument of the orchestra could be playing one tone row and move on to another while another instrument could pick up where the first had begun—more or less like a baroque fugue or round, but without the key.

"Serial music," a variation of Schoenberg's system, added rules for rhythm, harmony, tempo, and dynamics, making the possibilities for free expression almost (there are about half a billion variations possible just for twelve-note sequences) limitless.

Schoenberg began atonal compositions in 1909 and worked out the tone-row system by 1924. Very few audiences since have come to like it, but many composers are still fascinated with what might be done with all this freedom. Meanwhile the orchestras are still playing the music of the nineteenth century.

MORE SCIENTIFIC SUPPORT: FOR FEWER RULES

So. The arts were now without fixed form. Art wasn't representational. Music had no key or stable meter. Drama was like dreams. Literature was like ramblings (see also FREE VERSE). All the nineteenth-century rugs had been pulled out from under. Primitive structures were gone, and now primitive passion could go off in all directions.

But what about science? What about those ringing grooves

of change, that scientific progress that would evolve us into super beings?

Well, we were learning more, and we were learning that more is less certainty. As ALBERT EINSTEIN (1879–1955) put it, we were like a man trying to understand the mechanism of a closed watch that he could never open.

One thing Einstein did tell us about what was inside the watch, though, is that only one thing is constant: the speed of light. Everything else—time, space, velocity, mass, and energy—is jumbled. The value of one is relative to the value of the other.

For example, as your velocity increases, so does your mass (you weigh more), but your aging decreases. Time runs more slowly for moving things than for those that are stationary. And if you could travel at the speed of light, time in relation to what was behind you would stop altogether: if you were looking at a clock, or a street scene back there, nothing would move. The hands of the clock, the cars, and the people would be frozen, because the light from the moments after you last saw them wouldn't be able to catch up with you.

Velocity would change the color of the things you saw, too. Things you moved away from at high speeds would look reddish, and those you moved toward would look bluish. (Astronomers now use the "red shift" in the light from stars to tell how rapidly they are moving away from us.)

Most bewildering of all, space itself, said Einstein, is curved. If you kept moving forward in a straight line, you would eventually come back to where you began.

As Einstein calculated it, nothing was stable (except the speed of light). And unsettlingly enough, Einstein's theories weren't just bewildering mathematical equations: they checked out when astronomers and physicists tested them. Relativity was real.

THE FEW-RULES PHILOSOPHY

Where did that leave us? Intellectually unsettled, as had

two world wars and the experimental proof of another Einstein theory: that the amount of energy in a given body is equal to its mass times the speed of light squared. A lot of energy indeed. A few pounds would be enough to blow up an entire city. And in 1945, they were.

Faced with disquieting notions about what had happened to the Japanese, not the least of which was that the same thing might happen to them, a number of American intellectuals were visibly impressed in 1946, when an article in *Life* magazine described a relatively new European philosophy called EXISTENTIALISM.

Not that existentialism did much to cheer them up. Its tone was set by two essays of nineteenth-century philosopher SØREN KIERKEGAARD (KIRkegor, 1813–55): "Fear and Trembling" and "The Sickness unto Death."

The dilemma of a man, said Kierkegaard, is comparable to the Old Testament story of Abraham and the Angel. The Angel tells Abraham to sacrifice his son, which would be fine if Abraham were certain that the Angel was really an angel and that he himself was really Abraham. But he's not. And he can't be certain. Yet he still has to choose.

The universe, said French philosopher JEAN PAUL SARTRE (SARtr, 1905–) presents the same sort of dilemma. Nothing is stable or certain, except death. The universe is like a void, without a meaning of its own. So is every man's life. Unsettling, as Sartre had pointed out in *Nausea* (1938).

During his years in the French Resistance, Sartre had learned how to cope with this sort of hostile environment: one makes choices. The only meaning to one's life is the meaning that one chooses to give it. Heredity and environment aren't the essential qualities of an individual; he's what he chooses to be. Existence (what he chooses and does) precedes (is more important than) Essence (what he was to begin with).

Since the 1946 *Life* article, a number of existentialist terms have become a part of the language. You can remember many of them by thinking of the letter A, for Abraham and the

Angel. A look at the basic emptiness of the universe prod
angst, or *anxiety.* The essential isolation of each person,
cause of the responsibility to choose, by ourselves, to be
whatever we are, makes us like strangers: *alienation.* Since
the world has no meaning, it's *absurd,* and since we die, our
lives are *absurd,* too. A fictional character who must function
alone in this absurd human condition is an *antihero.* If he, or
a real person, can manage to keep choosing and stick by his
choices, he's become *authentic.*

It wasn't much—this facing up to perpetual nausea and
doubt until death ended it all. But at least there was the
certainty of believing this was the best we could hope for.

It didn't have to be all *that* gloomy, either. Knowing there
wouldn't be a second time around could help us appreciate
the first trip. As American poet WALLACE STEVENS (1879–
1955) put it in "Sunday Morning," a poem about a woman
who's not in church, "Death is the mother of beauty."

Others dramatized the existential dilemma in different
ways. ALBERT CAMUS (kaMOO, 1913–60), who was
absurdly killed in an automobile accident, wrote of Sisyphus,
who rolls his huge rock uphill, thoroughly involved in the
process, and then, at the top, watches it roll back down again.
At that moment he makes his existentialist choice: he chooses
to go back after the rock and roll it up again. That makes him
engagé, as Sartre put it, or as Camus said, happy. Camus
also did novels and short stories, among them *The Stranger,*
The Plague, and *The Fall,* exploring the possibilities of guilt
and innocence in a universe where there aren't any rules.

Onstage, one dramatist, LUIGI PIRANDELLO (1867–
1936), used the world's lack of directions to create the mind-
boggling *Right You Are If You Think So* and *Six Characters*
in Search of an Author. Other dramatists went even further,
into the totally meaningless environment, and created
THEATER OF THE ABSURD where things happen at
random. Samuel Beckett's *Waiting for Godot* doesn't go quite
that far. Godot is the divinity who never comes, though the

two lead characters are still waiting for His instructions. Science—parodied as the works of "Fartov and Belcher"— gives no help. The one character who doesn't have to choose, the slave, is named Lucky. But he gets beaten by his imbecilic master. The play was called "a tragicomedy."

Probably the best existential vignette, though, wasn't on stage: the real-life deathbed scene of GERTRUDE STEIN (1874–1946). As her companion, Alice B. Toklas, recorded it, Stein said, "What is the answer?" When Toklas was silent, Stein uttered her last words: "In that case, what is the question?"

ANOTHER PRIMITIVE RESPONSE?

With the heavyweight artists and intellectuals hitting their audiences with one bewildering Truth after another, a re-action was predictable. On the level of the marketplace, of course, the reaction had occurred from the very beginning: popular audiences simply ignored the serious artist and went to the movies, or read the comics, or bought a detective novel, and had their portraits painted by artists who would make them look better, not stranger. All of which did nothing to decrease the serious thinker's sense of alienation.

The new philosophy, too, received a large share of apathy from the general public. Especially in America, the existential-ist movement was associated with "Beat-generation Atheists" (though there were, and still are, religious existentialists), be-cause of its emphasis on one's utter freedom of choice. An-other strike against public acclaim for this new philosophy came after Sartre "converted" to Marxism and began urging "engagé" involvement in the class struggle. Existentialism was now associated with "New Left Radicals," which made it less than attractive to millions.

But in the sixties, reaction began in earnest, even at the serious levels. Since then we've had drugs, serious rock, hair, tribal happenings, nude therapy, oriental mind-expansion, body language, psychic healing, out-of-the-body travels, and

religious revival, nationwide. Not to mention witchcraft, reincarnation, exorcism, animal anthropology, and talking to
plants.

Doubtless the iconoclasts of the early half of this century
would call ours a primitive return to superstition, a need for
that quasi-parental certainty.

But then, if past directions in politics are followed, and
we bomb ourselves back into the Stone Age, we may have no
choice. Primitivism may be the wave of the future, whether
we like it or not.

Where could primitivism, and we, go if that happened?
Well, we've seen some examples—from the poverty and bad
manners of those intentional primitives, the Greek cynics,
through medieval monasticism and Rousseau's noble savages.
If we worked at it, maybe we could get back to an Edenic
state or to a Golden Age like the one in Greek myth.

Still, there's really no foretelling. If there's a Deity, He or
She knows, but we don't. We'll have to let the future take care
of itself.

But at least we've come to the idea and problems of the
present now.

We've caught up.

Twentieth-century Names You Should Know

LITERATURE

IMAGISM and FREE VERSE are two of the literary theories
of the century you ought to know about. The IMAGISTS
wanted "hard, dry" images instead of romantic emotions or
soft symbols, but another way to remember imagism is to
think of the portrait of Gertrude Stein that Picasso painted in
1905, when he was just getting into CUBISM. In that portrait,
he painted Stein as though she were seen from several angles
at the same time: the nose almost a profile shot that doesn't

quite correspond with the angle of one half of the face, that doesn't quite correspond with the other half, or with the eye of the other half. Ugly? Not according to the theory. It showed more and was therefore more real than a single-point-of-view presentation.

If we would come at the image we wanted to write about from several angles, wrote Gertrude Stein, we could get the same kind of clarity, the same kind of reality. Of course it would be necessary to repeat, each time we wrote a new view. As in "A Rose is a rose is a rose is a rose."

And of course that made for slow reading. A quicker way to the imagist truth, said poet and critic T. S. ELIOT, is to find the "objective correlative," the one image that will convey to everyone the poet's impression of the subject matter. The classic example is EZRA POUND's two-line poem about people waiting for the trains at the Paris Métro: "The apparition of these faces in the crowd: / petals on a wet, black bough."

You'll notice that Pound's poem doesn't rhyme or have a regular meter. As with Stravinsky's music or Schoenberg's, there aren't the traditional sound structures. That's FREE VERSE. The most famous free-verse poem is the most famous twentieth-century poem: T. S. Eliot's *The Waste Land* (1922). There are rhymes and regular meters here and there, but only where the poet wants them. In the first lines, "April is the cruellest month, breeding / Lilacs out of the dead land, mixing / Memory and desire, stirring / Dull roots with spring rain," there's a pattern, but not the usual one. Later there's rhyme, but with unusual meter: "Sweet Thames, run softly till I end my song, / Sweet Thames run softly, for I speak not loud or long. / But at my back in a cold blast I hear / the rattle of the bones, and chuckle spread from ear to ear."

There's also allusion everywhere (see MARVELL in the Renaissance chapter for the one in the last two lines), which made Eliot add footnotes to the poem, and which gave scholars and critics and students no end of explaining to do.

Then in 1971 the original poem, a much longer version which Ezra Pound had cut and made comments on, surfaced and started the process of explanation again.

If Eliot is the poet for academics, the poet for the people is ROBERT FROST (1874–1963), the man John F. Kennedy invited to read at his 1961 inaugural ceremony. Lately we've learned that the kindly white-haired New England rustic was a rotter in his personal life, but as least we still have the poems. "Stopping by Woods on a Snowy Evening," "The Pasture," "Directive," "Nothing Gold Can Stay," "Choose Something Like a Star," and on and on. We also have Frost's opinion of free verse, which he said was like "playing tennis with the net down."

The poet most highly esteemed, though, is WILLIAM BUTLER YEATS (YAYTS, 1865–1939), an Irish mystic and for the twentieth century still something of a prophet figure. His belief in seances and the Irish spirit world, and his fruitless chasing after actress-revolutionary Maude Gonne detract from his dignity at first, until one realizes that Yeats wanted it that way. As he put it in one of his later poems, "I must lie down where all the ladders start, / In the foul rag-and-bone shop of the heart."

Many of the lines Yeats wrote for "The Second Coming" (1921) are still quoted these days during hard times:

> Turning and turning in the widening gyre
> The falcon cannot hear the falconer;
> Things fall apart; the center cannot hold;
> Mere anarchy is loosed upon the world,
> The blood-dimmed tide is loosed, and everywhere
> The ceremony of innocence is drowned;
> The best lack all conviction, while the worst
> Are full of passionate intensity.

A "gyre" is a spiral, widening circles that symbolize the cycles of history. Though Yeats meant to describe the 1917 Russian Revolution with the poem, it's been seen as a description of the whole century.

NOVELISTS to know? For hard-drinking macho "grace under pressure" it's ERNEST HEMINGWAY (1899–1961), who grew up in Oak Park, Illinois, took a wound in the groin in the World War I Italian campaign, went to Paris, and, according to Gertrude Stein, became a member of "the lost generation." Hemingway used that phrase as an epigraph for *The Sun Also Rises*, about Paris, groin wounds, and bull-fights, then went on to big game hunting in Africa, wartime correspondence in Spain, and deepsea fishing in the Caribbean, with novels and short stories about each *milieu*. When he couldn't write any longer he chose suicide with a shotgun in Ketchum, Idaho.

He's parodied often for his overwork of masculinity, of adjectives like "good," "wonderful," and "clear," and of short sentences. He's remembered for superthorough craftsmanship, rewriting again and again, and for his hard-playing lifestyle. His "Hemingway hero" who had a personal "code" of behavior is mentioned often in discussion of existentialism, as is his short story "A Clean, Well-lighted Place," where a waiter looks into the existential abyss of "Nada." That was in 1933, ten years before Sartre's *Being and Nothingness*.

For writing with a bit more gloss, and for a good look at roaring-twenties decadence, there's F. SCOTT KEY FITZ-GERALD's (1896–1940) *The Great Gatsby*. Gatsby's a now-wealthy Eastern bootlegger with a heart of Midwest-American pursuit of happiness. Daisy, the woman he's loved since youth, alas, is married to an old-family Easterner, who's more into the pursuit of selfishness. And so, we learn by tale's end, is Daisy.

Fitzgerald did other novels, short stories, and essays, seen more as period pieces today. In one of them, though, *The Crack Up* (essays about his nervous breakdown), there's a definition of first-rate intelligence often quoted: the ability to "hold two opposed ideas in the mind at the same time, and still retain the ability to function."

Some novelists try to imitate the Hemingway/Fitzgerald

lifestyle (at least those who like to drink do), but they don't often imitate MARCEL PROUST (PROOST, 1871–1922). Proust is *the* novelist of sensitivity and inner reflection. The most exciting event in the sixteen volumes of *Remembrance of Things Past*, about the mind's inner workings, is the memory-triggering taste of a madeleine cookie dipped into lime-flower tea. Proust wrote in bed, in a cork-lined, semidark room.

JAMES JOYCE (1882–1941) gives Irish stream-of-consciousness in the novels but is fairly straightforward in the stories. He's full of allusions, though, which makes reading him slow going. Not that he wanted to be fast going: he once said he expected his readers to put as much time into the work as he had. A favorite trick of his was coining new words (bluddle filth to mean battlefield, for example), which didn't speed up the process any. Neither did the plot: the entire action of the novel *Finnegans Wake* takes place in the minds of H. C. Earwicker, an Irish pubkeeper, his wife, and their two sons, while all four are asleep.

Easier going and more often read (in at least parts of one book) is D. H. LAWRENCE (1885–1930). Raised with a coalminer father and an educated, sensitive mother in Nottinghamshire, England, Lawrence studied his way out of the mining town and into literature, writing up the experiences in the Oedipal *Sons and Lovers*. Known for the neoromantic passion of his characters, Lawrence wrote of brawls between lovers, and earthy passions, with lots of Freudian symbols, as in the celebrated explicit lovemaking of the gamekeeper who becomes *Lady Chatterley's Lover*.

The American novelist at the top of the list is WILLIAM FAULKNER (1897–1962). He has the same sense of the blood in the earth that Lawrence has, along with the sense of the woods, the animals, the low-down, back-country Mississippians, the good ole boys by the city-hall lawn, the women who want to get out, the fading aristocrat, and even Harvard. If you tried *The Sound and the Fury* before and hated it, try again. Or look at *The Bear,* or *Light in August,* or *As I Lay Dying.* The same raw nature of Sartre's *Nausea* or Stravinsky's *The Rite of Spring,* American-style. And with a second look, it gets clearer that Faulkner meant what he said when he accepted the Nobel Prize in 1950, "It is the writer's privilege to help man endure by lifting his heart."

ART

Besides Picasso, working with Diaghilev on ballet scenery and stage design were Matisse, Braque, Utrillo, Ernst, Miró, and Rouault, all, in one way or another, in the expressionist, cubist tradition. ROUAULT (1871–1958), for example, painted figures as though parts of them were split up by thick black lines—like the stained-glass windows he had helped make as a glassmaker's apprentice. All pushing the image further away from the photograph into geometric form.

Why not, then, simply forget the image and paint the form? That was the view of Dutch painter PIET MONDRIAN (MOHNdreean, 1872–1944). Like VERMEER (see THE RENAISSANCE) he painted rectangles, but without making them look like furniture: simply different-colored straight lines at right angles on the canvas, which related to each other in size and thickness and color, and in the white or colored space they surrounded, to produce a dynamic quality (see THE GOLDEN MEAN). Packaging hasn't been the same since his *Composition in Blue, Yellow, and Black* (1936). The clean, clear look you don't see in the 1898 Sears catalogue. The "Less is more" look has influenced architecture and sculpture, too, producing geometrical shapes in three dimensions: x's, cubes, pyramids, and so on, especially the large monumental ones outdoors.

Another artist who was after Something Completely Different was JACKSON POLLOCK (1912–56). Take away shape and planning altogether and you have "Abstract Expressionism"—which meant throwing the paint at the canvas. As with a Ouija board, the artist's unconscious psyche directs what might seem to be just a random spattering, and of course he chooses which color to throw or squirt or spatter, making the painting a coherent whole. . . ."

That was the theory, anyway. Those who filmed trained monkeys doing the same thing were less impressed than those who bought the paintings.

You should also know SURREALISM and SALVADOR DALI (1904–), which present meticulously drawn photographic images, but in impossibly incongruous situations. Watches melting over a desert landscape and being eaten by insects; a human eyeball, slashed with a razor. Nightmare images.

ART DECO, extratall and erect figures, rounded to near abstraction and draped in long, angular folds of cloth, is also a name worth knowing. The style was solidified by the 1925 Paris exhibition *Des Arts Décoratifs* and has been used for everything from Rockefeller Center to automobile hood ornaments. Art Deco's had a comeback of sorts since *Bonnie and Clyde* made the thirties bigtime box-office.

In SCULPTURE, it's enough to know that BRANCUSI's (1876–1957) abstraction of *Bird in Space* looked like a plant first coming up in springtime, and the the U.S. Customs office declared it a piece of bronze rather than art, for import-duty purposes; that HENRY MOORE (1898–) cre-

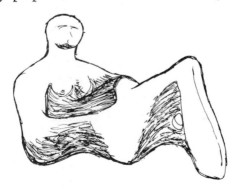

ated figures of monumental roundness; and that ALEXAN-
DER CALDER (1898–1976) invented the mobile and the
stabile, working with sheet metal to produce monuments
that also have whimsey.

ARCHITECTURE

If architects have shared the pessimism of the other arts
this century, their best buildings haven't shown it. They still
soar and glitter heroically, though the steel-and-glass-skin
rectangular design mode, brought from Mondrian and Hol-
land by MIES VAN DER ROHE (MEES fon der ROHuh,
1887–1969), has taken its lumps recently as a waste of energy and a firetrap.

The most famous twentieth-century architect, FRANK
LLOYD WRIGHT (1869–1959), built lower to the ground
and avoided the single-box look by using multiple levels and
cantilevers and by incorporating into his designs some of the
natural elements—like trees and waterfalls—that he'd seen
in Oriental gardens.

Wright's monument is the spiraling Solomon Guggenheim
Museum in New York, where one can watch the people and
the paintings too. Yeats would have loved the widening
spiral, or "gyre" shape.

You should also know the shape no one had thought of before: the geodesic dome, made out of octahedrons and tetrahedrons. The inventor, BUCKMINSTER FULLER (1895–), expects one day to dome over a city.

And if one really wants to get futuristic about it, consider the plans of the NASA architects, who envisage twenty-mile-long city-tubes in space. There'd be three cities in each tube, each covering a stripe of the inside of the tube, which would rotate so that "in" was "up" and "out" was "down" for everybody.

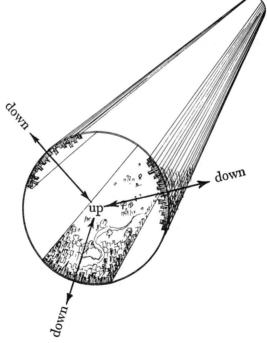

DRAMA

Three names will see you through prewar tragedy (EUGENE O'NEILL), comedy (NOËL COWARD), and whatever's in between (BERNARD SHAW).

EUGENE O'NEILL (1888–1953) packed enough suffering into the first half of his life to give him material for forty-odd tragedies during the second. Three of these, *Beyond the Horizon, Strange Interlude,* and *Anna Christie,* won Pulitzer prizes. In 1936 he won the Nobel Prize for Literature.

O'Neill plays are noted for their heavy naturalism and for evoking deep-rooted anguish as the characters come face to face with Something bigger than they are—and lose. In *The Hairy Ape,* for example, Yank is happy with his job in the ship's boiler room ("we gonna make dis ting go, get me?") until a socialite woman, dressed in white, sees him on a tour of the ship and screams in fright: "A hairy ape!" Hurt, Yank battles Fifth Avenue society (on the streets, of course), for recognition, loses, and is driven into the murderous embrace of a real-life zoo gorilla.

In *Long Day's Journey into Night,* we meet some of the demons that O'Neill had lost to during his early years: an alcoholic brother, a wealthy but miserly father, and a mother who has trouble with dope addiction. We see the family on the day Eugene (Jamie) learns that his mother's gone back to morphine, that his brother's out to destroy him with alcohol, that he has tuberculosis, and that his father wants to send him to a state farm instead of a real hospital, to save money.

NOËL COWARD's (1899–1973) comedies are considerably lighter. Lighter than air, even. Comedy of manners among wealthy British, husbands and wives usually, with lots of tuxedos and cocktail glasses and wit. *Blithe Spirit* (1942), about a first wife who won't stay dead, and *Private Lives* (1930), about a couple who won't stay divorced, are probably the most famous, but one's really a lot like another.

George BERNARD SHAW (1856–1950; he hated the "George") wrote the plays in-between, which could be classed as "social comedy." He classed some of them as *Plays Pleasant and Unpleasant* when he first collected them in 1898 (the best known of which was *Mrs. Warren's Profession* and which, because the Mrs. was a madam, didn't get a license from the London censor). In all twenty-odd of the better known which followed, there's one unpleasant fact or another the characters, and the audience, must face, because they'll both have to learn that one of their cherished beliefs is ridiculously wrong. In *Arms and the Man,* we learn that military heroism is idiocy or worse; in *Candida* that the hero ought *not* to get the woman he loves; in *Pygmalion* that education doesn't lead to happily ever after (Eliza stays away from Professor Higgins, unlike the musical version, *My Fair Lady*), and so on. But he makes us laugh while we're doing it. Critics condemn him for too many speechmaking, argumentative characters, calling the plays costumed debates. But we still see plays like *The Devil's Disciple, Caesar and Cleopatra, Man and Superman, Major Barbara,* and *Saint Joan* more often than we hear the critics.

One other name to know in drama is the name of a kind of drama: GRAND GUIGNOL (GRAHN geenYOL). Guignol was a famous nineteenth-century French puppet, who starred in short sadistic plays. Plays of the same sort acted by grownups were called Grand Guignol: lots of murders, ghosts, rapes, and suicide. The *genre* was popular enough in France to establish its own theater (called the Grand Guignol) and to be imported to England in 1908. From there it was on to the movies and prime-time TV.

BALLET

With balletomania growing by leaps and bounds every year, it's good to know a few of the poses and moves from CLASSICAL BALLET. That's the form of the dance that goes back to the court of Louis XIV, and before that in Italy (see THE RENAISSANCE). The moves can look lighter than air, but are wrenchingly difficult for a novice. Most of today's ballet companies that do classical ballet began training their dancers at age eleven, or before.

We could start with the *pirouette,* a move nearly everyone's familar with: spinning around while standing on one leg. If the complete turn is done using the other leg to help whip the body around, that's called a *fouetté.* Female dancers usually do *a fouetté en pointe:* using the blocked-toe dancing shoe to stand on the very tips of their toes. Male dancers only rarely dance on pointe, avoiding the ballerina's occupational hazard of deformed toes from so many hours of bearing the entire body weight.

The idea in classical ballet is to defy gravity: to look as though one's moves are effortless and weightless. Accordingly, two of the qualities much praised are *elevation* (height in jumping) and *ballon* (elasticity or "bounce"), and two of the steps much admired are *bourrée* (gliding with tiny steps, on pointe) and *entrechat* (jumping high and fluttering legs and feet, back and forth, before landing). Of course the dancer needs to land quietly to maintain the weightless effect.

Two classical poses also hold the effortless, floating look. The pose that looks like a figure skater gliding on one leg with the other extended behind is called an *arabesque;* unlike the skater, though, the dancer stretches the arms out front and back, parallel to the floor. The pose that looks like the familiar Renaissance statue of Mercury, one arm raised, the other out to the side, one leg supporting while the other's extended behind with the knee bent, is called an *attitude.* In other poses, a feature to look for is the *turn out,* where the hip's turned so the foot goes perpendicular to the leg. Some poses require a turn out with both legs, so that the feet are pointing in opposite directions. Not recommended for living room demonstrations if you're over thirty.

Classical ballet, though, is only half the dance scene. The other half, MODERN DANCE, is different, basically because the dancers don't pretend to float. Poses and moves are down to earth, combinations of gymnastics and spontaneous reactions and some classical figures. The dances are usually done barefoot, and never with the blocked-toe slippers. More freedom of expression.

Diaghilev's BALLET RUSSE, by being more vigorous and spontaneous, helped the modern trend begin in 1909, but the real pioneers in the field were Isadora Duncan, whose freedom of form was spiritual (some called it just showing off), and Martha Graham, whose dances are more visceral, grounded in muscular tension and oppositions. Since the Martha Graham Dance Company first began in 1925, modern dance has grown more and more popular, especially with younger audiences.

OPERA

Unlike ballet companies, which constantly produce new forms and new material, opera companies (and audiences) tend to favor the old standards from the nineteenth century. The two major composers of twentieth-century opera, in fact, are really closer to the nineteenth century than they are to us.

The more celebrated of the two is GIACOMO PUCCINI (pooCHEEnee, 1858–1924). Three of his operas are still among today's most frequently performed. LA BOHÈME (boh-WEM) is about Bohemian poets and artist types in Paris's Latin Quarter, and it's extrasentimental. Mimi, the heroine, dies of the cold winter and her lover's jealousy. When the work was first performed in Palermo (1896), the audience was applauding even after the musicians had changed to street clothes and left for home. Management had to call the orchestra back to the theater for a repeat of the finale before the crowd would leave.

TOSCA, which opened in 1900, is sheer melodrama. Heroine Tosca tries to foil Scarpia, a murderous chief of police in Napoleonic Rome, after Scarpia decrees the execution of Tosca's lover, an artist named Mario. Scarpia agrees to use blank bullets for Mario's firing squad if Tosca will let him have his way with her. Tosca consents, but after the order for blanks is given she kills Scarpia. Alas, Mario dies anyway because the villainous Scarpia had only pretended to order the blanks. Before the police can arrest her, Tosca's dived to her death from a rooftop into the Tiber.

MADAMA BUTTERFLY, about the pathetic Japanese maiden who's abandoned by her American husband, got a better reception when it came to America in 1907 than when it first opened in Italy. The music is more oriental, even impressionistic, than Puccini's others, and so is poor Madama Butterfly's tragic ending: hara-kiri.

And one other notable from the early decades: RICHARD STRAUSS (SHTROWS: 1864–1949). His *Salome* (1905) and *Der Rosenkavalier* (1911) were both Wagnerian in their use of leitmotifs (individual musical themes for each character), continuous melody, and shifting, unsettling tonality. Salome's (SALohmay) dance of the seven veils brought new levels of eroticism to the opera stage, not only in the looks of the performer but also in the suggestive music. *Der Rosenkavalier*, "The Cavalier of the Rose," is a comedy set in old Vienna, complete with drinking songs, a hero disguised as a maid, and a boy-gets-girl ending.

MUSIC

Besides Stravinsky and Schoenberg, four other serious composers from the early twentieth century are frequently heard today: Ravel, Prokofiev, Ives, and Bartók.

RAVEL (rahVELL, 1875–1937) and PROKOFIEV (proh-KOHFyef, 1891–1953) are both known for popular pieces: *Bolero* and *Peter and the Wolf*, but each did seriously innovative works as well, maintaining a sense of romantic flair and dissonance, yet moving back to classical organization. Ravel, a Parisian, was reacting to Debussy; Prokofiev, a Russian, was first reacting to Mozart and then later to the demands of Soviet politicos' taste in music.

CHARLES IVES (1874–1954) was reacting to his own fancy. He was a New York insurance executive; music was his hobby. He especially liked traditional American folk melodies, hymns, band music, and dancing songs. People didn't quite understand why he wanted to chop the melodies up and mix them together, or why the rhythms and harmonics had to be so erratic (Ives was imitating American small-town amateurs singing or playing off key, or mixed together, as different music from different bands would be heard by someone standing in a parade). Ives had to pay to have his compositions published and could rarely find anyone to perform them during the early years, but by 1947 he had won a Pulitzer Prize.

BÉLA BARTÓK (BARtok, 1881–1945), a Hungarian pianist, liked East European folk melodies and wrote with the energy and powerful dissonance of Stravinsky. He's remembered by piano students for his *Mikrokosmos*, 153 short pieces used as training exercises that get gradually harder to play as one moves closer to no. 153.

AARON COPLAND (1900–; *Billy the Kid, Appalachian Spring*) and GEORGE GERSHWIN (1898–1937; *Porgy and Bess, Rhapsody in Blue, An American in Paris*) are too familiar to need commentary but too famous not to mention.

And So, As the Sun Sinks Slowly into the Horizon . . .

Of course, there's a lot more worth knowing about the twentieth century than we've had room for here. In almost every category, we've stayed with the first few decades and virtually ignored the rest. Partly because there's not enough room, but mainly because it's too difficult to judge, we've tried to leave out those people whose achievements have come during the fifties and sixties, or those who are still working—and changing—today.

But we do get into some of the more recent happenings just a bit with SAFE, BUT TRENDY OPINIONS: a section for present-day critics in our final chapter.

VII

HOW TO SOUND
LIKE A CRITIC

What to Say When You're Up Against
Sloppy Thinking

First, let's look at the names for arguments that sound fishy. Here are a few, for what they're worth; you'll find more in the FOREIGN WORDS AND PHRASES section.

AD HOMINEM: This means you talk about the man instead of talking about his argument. Used positively, this is VIRTUE BY ASSOCIATION: "He works at the White House, so he must know what he's doing." Negatively, it's GUILT BY ASSOCIATION, or NAME-CALLING. "You're gonna believe that idiot who works at the White House?"

SWEEPING GENERALIZATION: Other less polite names for this one are STEREOTYPED THINKING, BIAS, PREJUDICE, and BIGOTRY. Everybody does it.

BLACK AND WHITE THINKING, otherwise known as INSUFFICIENT ALTERNATIVES. "Are we men or mice?" "Are we shaped by our genes or by our environment?" "We're gonna do this my/the right way or not at all." Avoid this one, or else.

POST HOC, ERGO PROPTER HOC: My cure came after (POST) I drank the snake oil; therefore (ERGO), I was cured because of (PROPTER) the snake oil. The polite name for this one is "anecdotal evidence."

IGNORING THE OBVIOUS: "I've been waiting here three hours, and by God, I won't wait a minute longer!" "I've been waiting here three hours; I guess I can last a few more minutes." You're most likely to see this in people under stress, when fewer logical connections get made. "She called me a neurotic, so I hit her." The technical name for this unreasonable gap between one statement and another is NON SEQUITUR, meaning "It does not follow." But you don't have to worry about making non sequiturs, because nobody's perfect.

On the other hand, if someone else is making the mental bumbles, remember it won't do much good to give him an on-the-spot lesson in logic. Here are a few things to say instead:

What?

You can't be serious.

Want to run that by again?

You look tired.

Foreign Words and Phrases

All right, here's the more advanced stuff. When you already know what to say and want to show off while you're saying it, here's how.

For that authoritarian air, of course, Latin is the *summum bonum.* But for that cosmopolitan *cachet,* a sprinkling of phrases *à la française* is *de rigueur.* So if you think that *Gloria Mundi* is the name of a young Italian film starlet, you'd better read this. Answers are listed after the story.

BOY MEETS GIRL

The *mise en scène*, a picnic *al fresco*, *pastorale*. Marie, dressed *à la mode*, is *au courant*, one of the beautiful people, the *beau monde*, the *bons vivants*. *Très chic*.

Enter Pierre, bursting with *joie de vivre* and *savoir faire*. His heart swoons at the sight of Marie, but alas, his work overalls, unpressed, proclaim that he is far from the status of *crème de la crème*. Marie views Pierre's attire with *ennui* at first, but when he approaches, with scorn fit for a *bête noire*, one of the *canaille*.

A bright fellow, Pierre reasons *a posteriori* that the *hauteur* of this lovely aristocrat is caused by the prejudice that goes with her lofty station; she sees him as proletarian, and therefore, *a priori*, *infra* her *dignitatem*. He will nonetheless pursue her, he resolves, not by sending her *billets-doux* or *vers libre*, but here and now, with his natural *élan vital*.

Fortunately Pierre is an accomplished *raconteur*. Soon an introduction is a *fait accompli*. With neither *faux pas* nor *gaucherie*, nor even *lapsus linguae*, he charms her with such enchanting *bagatelles* that soon it is plain that an *affaire de coeur* is developing. Then he speaks of the *recherché*, even the *outré*, which is momentarily *non grata*, but soon he has effected a *rapprochement*. He offers her his wineskin, with a kiss as the *quid pro quo*. She resists, but it is only *pro forma*. After drinking, the kiss, and more drinking, *in vino veritas*; she proposes, *sotto voce*, a *tête-à-tête in camera*.

Soon they are at her place. She gives him *carte blanche*, it appears, and soon he has ventured into *terra incognita*. Both now *au naturel*, they move with *una anima*. *Amour* is his *métier*, she says; he is the *ne plus ultra*, her *sine qua non*, a *cognoscente par excellence!*

But alas, before their idyll can progress *ad finem*, a *contretemps* in the form of the *paterfamilias*. "My husband," shrieks Marie. Both clutch for their clothes, but too late. Enter Jacques, the wealthy husband, who finds them *en déshabillé in flagrante delicto*. She stammers innocently of repairing a torn mattress and the warm weather, but Jacques sees through these *non sequiturs:* the evidence is *prima facie.* *Ex post facto,* she repents, and says that if he truly loved her, he would *ipso facto* forgive her. He will have none of this *petitio principii.* He challenges Pierre to an *affaire d'honneur,* since Pierre's act of *mala fides* has given him *casus belli.*

Clothes are donned, foils are drawn, and a duel begins that would doubtless have done injury to the untrained Pierre, when, like a *deus ex machina,* Marie's *femme de chambre* arrives. Jacques cannot risk his life, she cries; he has made her *enceinte!* At this accusation Pierre, with consideration *sang froid,* stops the duel, asking, "*Cui bono?*"

His remark proves a *bon mot.* "*Mea culpa,*" says Jacques. After a whispered conference, the unhappy, though *haut monde* couple adopt an attitude of *laissez faire* to each other's indiscretions and invite Pierre to continue on with them in a *ménage à trois.*

But Pierre wants neither *noblesse oblige* nor *amor vincit omnia.* His is an *esprit fort.* And though Marie laments *ad infinitum* and *ad nauseam,* the call of freedom sounds to Pierre *a fortiori.* "*Adieu,*" says he.

"*C'est la vie,*" says Jacques.

"I am *désolée,*" says Marie.

"She is *de trop,*" whispers the maid, tugging at Jacques's arm.

Now how many did you pronounce correctly? Tell the truth.

SOOMum BONEum: Latin for "the highest good"
kahSHAY: French for fragrance or aura
ahlah FRAHNHsez: French for French: *à la [méthode]* Française in the French way.
  dee reeGUR: F. Obligatory for good form
meezannhSANE: F. Setting or milieu (meelYUH)
al FRESkoh: Italian for in the fresh air
pahstoeRAHlay: It. The simple life out in the pastures
ahlah MOHD: F. Fashionably

oh cooRAHNH: F. Current; up-to-date

boe MONND: F. The beautiful world; high society

bohnh vee VAHNH: F. Lovers of good living

tray SHEEK: F. Very stylish

zhwah deh VEEvr: F. Zest for life; gusto

sahvwar FAIR: F. Good breeding

KREMM deh lah KREMM: F. The best people

ahNWEE: F. Tedium; boredom

bet NWAHR: F. Black beast, or other loathsome creature

cahNYEyuh: F. Dog pack; rabble

AY posTIReeOHrye: L. Predicting the cause by knowing the effect; inductive reasoning

ohTUR: F. Arrogance

ah preeOARee: L. Predicting an effect by knowing the cause; deductive reasoning

INfrah dignihTAHtem: L. Beneath her dignity (You can say "infra dig" for short)

BILLay DOOZ: F. Love letters

VAIR LEEbr: F. Free verse; poems without the usual rhyme and meter

ayLAHNH veeTAHL: F. Vital spirit; life force

rack onTURR: F. Storyteller; conversationalist

FEHTAHKohnnPLEE: F. Accomplished fact

foe PAH: F. Misstep; blunder

GOEshehREE: F. Awkwardness

LAPPsuss LINGwee: L. Slip of the tongue

bagaTELZ: F. Trifles

afFAIR duh CURR: F. Love affair

reh shair SHAY: F. Rich and strange; farfetched

ooTRAY: F. Bizarre; out of usual bounds

nonGRAYtah: L. Unwelcome

rahproshMAHNH: F. Peacemaking; friendship again

kwid proh KWOH: L. Payment; something in return

proh FORmah: L. A mere formality

innVEEnoe VAIReetahs: L. Truth from the effects of the wine

SOEtoe VOEchay: It. In an undertone

TEtah TET: F. Face-to-face meeting

inKAMerah: L. In a private room or chambers

kart BLAHNHSH: F. Freedom to do what one likes

TERah inKOGnihtah: L. Unfamiliar territory

OH nahtewREL: F. Without clothing

OOnah AHnihmah: L. A single spirit

ahMOOR: F. Love

mayTYAY: F. Calling

nee pluss ULtrah: L. The highest; the acme

SYEneekway NONN: L. A necessity

KOEnyoeSHENtay: It. One who knows; an expert

parEKsehlahns: F. Preeminent

adFEEnem: L. To a finish

KOHNHtreTAHNH: F. An embarrassing mishap

PAYterfahMILias: L. Male head of the house

ahnh dayzahbeeYAY: F. Undressed, or carelessly dressed

in flaGRANtee deeLICKtoe: F. In the act

nonSEKwihterz: L. Illogical step in reasoning; a "reason" that does not fit into the argument

PRYEma FAYshee: L. Clear at first glance

eks pohst FAKtoe: L. After the deed has been done

IPsoe FAKtoe: L. Because of that very fact

pehTISHihoh prinSIPih eye: L. Begging the question; assuming that a principal part of an argument is true, when in fact it hasn't been proven. Marie assumes that a true lover will always forgive his lover's infidelity, but she hasn't proven that.

ahFAIR dohnhNUR: F. A duel

MALLah FYdeez: L. Bad faith; opposite of BOWnah FYdeez

KAYsus BELeye: L. Act that justifies war

DEEus eks MAKihnah: L. When the marines land, or the posse arrives, or the god comes out of the machine, the trouble's over.

fam duh SHAHNHbr: F. Lady's maid

ahnh SANNHT: F. With child

sahnh FRWAH: F. Cool blood; composure

KWEE BOHnoh: L. What's the use? Or, more properly, the question the detective asks to establish motive: "Who benefits by it?"

bohnh MOE: F. Witty or adroit remark

MEEah KULLpah: L. It's my fault, blame me

oh MOHND: F. High society

lessay FAIR: F. Noninterference; unconcern; benign neglect

mayNAHZH ah TRWAH: F. Three living together

nohbless ohBLEEZH: F. Obligation of nobility to be generous to underlings

amMOR WINkit OHMneeah: L. Love conquers all

esSPREE FOR: F. Strong spirit, independent

add INfihNYEtum: L. To infinity

ad NOEzheeam: L. To the point of nausea

ah forteeOReye: L. More strongly

ahDOO: F. Good-bye

say lah VEE: F. That's life

DayZohLAY: F. Lost, lonely, forsaken

duh TROE: F. Excess; a fifth wheel; in the way

And oh, yes:

sick transit GLOHrihah MUNdye: L. Say this when you're feeling nostalgic. It means, "So passes away the glory of the world."

. . . And More Jargon for the Compleat Critic

ARTISTIC CONTROL: When an artist knows what he's doing, he has control of his performance, beginning, middle, and end. You can see how he's working each part to fit in with the others, so to make a performance that has UNITY.

SPONTANEITY: This used to come from the muse, but now it's a product of the imagination, or the unconscious. The artist "taps inner resources" to "fuel" a performance that's "fresh" and "exciting." Performances with CONTROL and SPONTANEITY are BRAVURA or, if the work is difficult, TOURS DE FORCE.

TECHNICAL FACILITY: A prerequisite for artistic control, but usually a condescending term. Unless accompanied by spontaneity, "Mere technical facility" will give you a performance that is only "Serviceable," or worse, "Perfunctory," "Uninspired," or "Drab." Without technical facility, the performance is "Incompetent."

NOSTALGIA: Art from a generation or two back; entertainment; not to be taken seriously as art.

CAMP: Nostalgia not to be taken seriously as nostalgia.

SLICK PANDERING: Commercial art done with TECHNICAL FACILITY.

CHEAP PANDERING: Commercial art done without TECHNICAL FACILITY.

HOGWASH: CHEAP PANDERING done with serious artistic pretensions. If it's SLICK PANDERING but pretentious, you can call it EYEWASH: EYEWASH can be "offensive"; HOGWASH is "profoundly offensive" to "even the most rudimentary" sensibilities or intelligence.

CLAQUE: Applause or praise that has been organized in advance, usually for pay. You should maintain that any praise for art you have deemed to be PANDERING or worse comes from "A well- or pathetically organized CLAQUE."

Safe, But Trendy Opinions to Hold On . . .

MUSIC

The three "Bs," Bach, Beethoven, and Brahms, are hopelessly linked to a fourth, "Bourgeois." The Critic can't limit his taste to these or any of the other eighteenth- and nineteenth-century composers, unless he wants people to think he buys his records at the supermarket or through the mail. So make it a point to display appreciation of the atonal arhythmias of the avant garde, some of which are still with us. No matter how much you fret inwardly at waiting for the musicians on stage to clack their horseshoes or break their vases at the spontaneously appropriate moment, hold your tongue and don't fidget. If one of the musicians happens to be female and topless, and you're female too, you may, however, respond with outrage that the males' appreciation of the music is being interfered with. Remember that four-minute silences and half-hour chords in the performance are good for you, because life itself is full of frustration. If you can endure unrelieved chaos and despair here in the concert hall, think how you've strengthened your character. Think how you'll be better prepared to communicate with spontaneity. But do not have the bad form to think of (or, worse, speak of) fables such as "The Emperor's New Clothes." Such superficial judgments indicate immature tastes unbefitting an adult critic.

ARCHITECTURE AND ART

As critic, you must ally yourself with those artists who are critics of the public rather than with those "commercial hacks" who try to please the public. Pop art and junk art are dying, but there is "plaster art" to take its place. These are life-size white statues that show us how colorless we are, following the basic rule that the artist should "mirror" the emptiness/ugliness/banality of "our" (not yours, of course; the public's) lifestyle.

In architecture, the new way to mirror banality is shown by the new Pompidou Art Center in Paris, which you may refer to as "Pipe Art." The building is all pipes, escalators, elevators, stairs, and girders on the outside, as though they never took down the scaffolding. No, NO! That's not ugly· it's a satiric comment on our banality—or, because the pipes are multicolored, a "whimsical" or "playful" comment on architectural functionalism. On the inside, the building is all open space (since the pipes, etc., are all on the outside), which makes the building itself a monument to artistic freedom, appropriate for an art center, you see?

If you still don't like "exoskeletal architecture," don't admit it. It's new. If you don't like something that's radically new, you may be linked to "the public," that culturally cowardly rabble that is always frightened of something it's never seen before. You must show courage and educate the public so that it can become "the people."

You may, of course, praise Egyptian art, Greek art, and other artifacts of finer civilizations.

DRAMA

You, the critic, are permitted to wallow happily in nostalgic revivals and other musicals. Why? Because we are looking these days for a leader, a "new voice," an Ibsen, Shaw, O'Neill, who can stage events that have some authority to them. Meantime, almost anything goes, as long as it's new and different, or old. In-between, however, won't do. Remember that you mustn't confuse trends in drama with trends in music or art. At a concert or an exhibition, one is obligated to "charge one's esthetic sensibilities" with the composer's or the artist's "creative sense of modern cacophony and chaos." But at a play, one is now obliged to find "insufferable" any dramatist who gives us "mindless cacophony and chaos." Theatrical boredom went out with theater of the absurd, and chaos went out with guerilla theater. In other words, theater is a buyer's market again.

BALLET

It's usually safe to criticize the orchestra, on grounds that the ballet companies don't have money to pay for adequate orchestral talent, size, and rehearsal time when they're luring people to see the dancers. Especially if the ballet company is touring, the orchestra's likely to be just a pickup group, unaccustomed even to working with each other, let alone with the troupe.

Criticizing the dancers, though, is another matter. Beware of the stereotypical comparisons: Russians dated but theatrically proficient; Americans too casual but interestingly gymnastic and modern; Danes charming, but too willing to take off their clothes. The dancers are too likely to prove you wrong. In fact, ballet training and ballet audiences have come far enough by now that the best way to sound like a ballet critic is to applaud.

LITERATURE

You must be on your guard here, lest you be accused of illiteracy when it comes to "serious" fiction. Something that appears to be self-centered plotless, graceless, and tasteless may be a writer's courageous, subtle encapsulation of his/her outrage/lament/celebration in the face of her/his/our own internal chaos/demonic qualities/bestiality. Telltale signs that the artist has plumbed to the real inner depths are eviscerations, micturitions, purgations, hemorrhages, defecations, ejaculations, and, of course, regurgitations.

If all or most of these deeply symbolic acts are present, you are obliged to find the work a "moving account."

POLITICAL SCIENCE

The proper tone to adopt was once that of Spengler. Only fools refused to see, or were too blind to see, that the West was in inexorable decline. Our side was therefore selfishly holding on to what we could while we could, though it was inevitable that resources would have to be shared with the rising underdeveloped nations. You the critic had the strength of character to face this bleak prospect with far-seeing equanimity.

Now the proper tone to adopt is one of optimism, but tempered with realism. Only fools refuse to see, or are too blind to see, that the West must help conserve the world's declining resources, while we unselfishly assist with new energies those nations who are as yet underdeveloped. You the critic have the strength of character to face this challenge with far-seeing equanimity.

SCIENCE

By now everyone knows that modern scientists are to blame for this heartless, sterile, existential vacuum we've programmed ourselves into. You can't kick them around for bombs and doomsday machines anymore. Insecticides and computers-gone-mad are old hat, as are frontal lobotomies and Valium. The effective critic of science must come up with a new atrocity.

Fortunately, biochemists have recently produced an issue made to order: the "Frankenstein Germ." Having determined that at bottom (molecularly speaking, that is) we are all endlessly replicating mechanisms of DNA molecules and that this tendency of the DNA molecule to duplicate itself is inexorable, a life force all its own, scientists at Stanford, Princeton, and Harvard have begun to experiment with "recombinant DNA techniques." That means that genetic material is extracted from one ·organism and inserted into another—such as a bacterium or two—to see what happens. What could be produced, naturally, are unnaturally efficient organisms that recombine in ways that we mortals don't know how to stop. Understandably, research to date has produced some town-versus-gown donnybrooks between local officials and university "biohazards" committees.

One can long for the days when conflicts between academic freedom and the law were as simple as the Scopes monkey trial. But perhaps the Frankenstein Germ is only the next inexorable step up DNA's long ladder of evolution. . . .

One Final Rule

The best way to sound like a critic is in moderation. Too many critical fulminations after a performance your friends have enjoyed may bring out the critic in each of them—after you've gone home.

INDEX

[220]

Y0-BUX-557

The MISSING POPCORN
and
Other Stories

The

Pictures by Daniel Zook

MISSING

POPCORN

and

Other Stories

By
Grandmother Lois

Rod and Staff Publishers, Inc., Crockett, Kentucky

Copyright 1975

By Rod and Staff Publishers, Inc.

Crockett, Kentucky 41413

Printed in the U.S.A.

for

John Paul

Contents

"Thy word is a lamp
unto my feet, and a light
unto my path" Psalm
119:105.

1

The Missing Popcorn

"Mama, do you know what?" Allan's voice was filled with excitement. "One of our bags of popcorn is gone. We hung three bags from a rafter in the barn, and there are only two bags there now."

"Are you sure, Allan?" Mother asked. "Maybe you made a mistake in how many you thought you had."

"No, Mama, I am sure we didn't. Papa knows how many we had. He hung them up for us. He doesn't know what happened to one of the bags, either."

"Well, that is strange," said Mama. "Maybe

the cattle or the horses knocked it down and ate it."

"They couldn't have, Mama. It was up in the loft. About the only thing that could have happened is that someone took it."

"But who would have done that, Allan? We

have good neighbors. They don't go around helping themselves to things that don't belong to
them."

"Jackie Taylor might have," Allan said. Then
his eyes got bigger still. "Mama, do you know
what? I just thought of something. He had popcorn
in his lunch in school today."

"Now, Allan," Mother said sternly. "It is
wrong to think evil of others. When you decide
that Jackie Taylor stole our popcorn just because
he had popcorn in his lunch today—that is thinking evil of him."

Allan turned and ran out to the barn again.
Before long, Papa and the boys came into the
house for dinner. They were talking about the
missing popcorn.

"They seem to suspect Jackie Taylor of taking
it," Papa told Mama.

"Yes, that was Allan's idea," Mama said, "but
I don't think they should do that, do you? I told
him that that was thinking evil of Jackie, and the
Bible says that love thinketh no evil."

"That is what I told them," Papa said. "I told
them that they should not say another word about
anyone taking the popcorn. They are only

guessing, and are thinking evil of someone when they do."

In the middle of the afternoon, Allan came running in to Mama. His eyes were big with excitement again.

"Mama, do you know what?" he asked breathlessly. "We found the popcorn. We were cleaning the loft and raking together all that loose hay that is lying around up there. There the bag was, covered up with hay."

"Really?" Mama asked in surprise.

"Yes, Papa says the wire broke. The bag just dropped down and got covered up, and we didn't notice it."

"And here you were thinking that Jackie Taylor stole it," Mama said reprovingly.

Allan looked ashamed. "I know. I shouldn't have even thought of it."

"Well, I think you should ask the Lord to help you love Jackie. If you really loved Jackie, you wouldn't be tempted to think such things about him," Mother said.

"I guess that is right," Allan agreed.

2

Afraid of Mark

"Mother, I would rather not go to school today," Ann whispered tearfully.

"Why not, dear?" Mother asked kindly.

"Oh, . . ." Ann hesitated. "I'm a little bit afraid of Mark," she admitted.

"Afraid of Mark?" Mother was surprised. "Why should you be afraid of Mark? I don't think he will hurt you."

"Maybe not hurt me," Ann said slowly, "but he might do something."

"But, why?" Mother was puzzled. "I don't understand, Ann," she said. "Why would Mark do something to you?"

"He sits right in front of me, Mother," Ann explained. "And he is always doing something. He shakes the desk, and knocks down my pencils, and bumps my arm. . . ."

"But those things happen in school, Ann. It is hard to sit perfectly still all the time, especially if your desk is a little loose and wobbles some.

"And you often bump people accidentally, or knock their pencil so it rolls off their desk. You shouldn't get upset about things like that, Ann. But you said that Mark said he was going to do something to you. Why did he say that, Ann?"

"Well, Mother, I got so tired of what he was doing all the time so I, . . ." Ann hesitated and coughed a little nervously, "so I did something to him."

"You did something to him, Ann?" Mother asked in surprise. "What did you do?"

"I—I scribbled in his book, and—and broke his pencil, and hid his—his eraser," Ann admitted tearfully.

"And do you think, Ann," Mother asked in a soft, hurt voice, "that the Lord is happy about what you did?"

Ann shook her head miserably. "But, Mother, he said that he was going to do something to me, and I'm afraid to go to school."

"Listen, dear," Mother said. "You have done wrong. That is why you are afraid. The Lord says that we should be peacemakers, and when you spoiled Mark's things, you were making trouble and not making peace.

"When we do wrong things, Ann, we must make them right. You will have to tell Mark that you are sorry, and try to fix up the things you spoiled for him."

"But, Mother, I am afraid," Ann cried.

"You must ask the Lord to help you, Ann,"

Mother told her. "Doing wrong always makes us afraid. But when we do what is right, the Lord takes the fear away. I will give you a new pencil to give to Mark, and I have a good eraser here that I think might work real well in taking the marks off his book. And of course, Ann, you will give his eraser back to him, that you hid."

"O Mother," Ann cried. "I wish I wouldn't have done it."

"That is being sorry for your sin, Ann," Mother explained. "Let us kneel down right now, and you tell the Lord how you feel about it. Ask Him to help you to remember this lesson and to be a peacemaking little girl and not a troublemaking one."

"All right, Mother," Ann said brokenly.

3

Bible Bear Story

The children laughed loudly. Little Billy blinked fast and tried not to cry. He wanted his cap, but Joe and Fred would not let him have it.

Just then Fred threw it to Joe. As it passed close to Billy, he tried to grab it; but he missed it and Joe caught it again.

"If you want your cap, why don't you catch it?" Joe asked as he threw the cap back to Fred again.

This time Billy did catch it. Fred made a grab for it and jerked it roughly out of Billy's hands. The children who were watching the boys laughed loudly.

"Boys, quit it," said John. "Let him have his cap."

"Why don't you give it to him?" Fred asked as he whirled the cap back to Joe.

"You ought to be ashamed," said John. "It is not right to pick on a little fellow."

Just then Sister Mast rang the bell in the doorway behind them. "How long has she been standing there?" Joe wondered.

"Did she see what was going on?" was the question in Fred's mind.

The children settled themselves at their desks for the story period.

"I am going to read a story taken from 2 Kings 2 today," Sister Mast said. She began to read about the Prophet Elisha.

" 'Elisha was walking along the road on the way to Bethel. As he walked along, a number of children who lived in the city came running to him and began to tease him. "Go up, thou bald head. Go up, thou bald head," they cried.

" 'Elisha stopped and talked to the children. He told them that what they were doing was sin. Then God punished the children. Two bears came out of the woods and ran after the children. The children were frightened. They ran and tried to get away from the bears. But the bears caught and tore forty-two of the children.'

"What does this story teach each of us?" Sister Mast asked when she had finished reading the story.

"It teaches us that it is wrong to tease," said John, and he looked at Joe and Fred.

Joe and Fred blushed and looked down at their desks.

"Do you think all teasing is wrong, or is it just wrong to be disrespectful of grown people?"

"I think it is all wrong," said Mary. "It is so

unkind."

"We might think we are having fun when we tease," Robert contributed. "But we are making someone else feel bad, and that cannot be right."

"Lots of teasing is really telling or acting lies," Nancy said. "If we hide someone's lunch and then act as though we don't know anything about it, we are really acting a lie."

"Most teasing is just plain being mean to someone, I think," Harold remarked.

"I believe what all of you have said is true," agreed Sister Mast. "And this story from the Bible tells us what God thinks about teasing.

"I want Joe and Fred and all the children who laughed when they were teasing little Billy to stay after school tonight. And also, there shall be no more teasing of any kind done here at school," finished Sister Mast.

4

How to Be Happy

"I wish I had something to do," pouted Nancy.

Mother looked up from her sewing. "There are surely many, many things you could do," she said. "Why don't you read?"

"I am tired of reading. I have read all the interesting books around here."

"Color in your coloring books," suggested Mother.

"I don't like to color when Merlin is around," Nancy answered crossly. "He is always breaking my colors or eating them or something."

Mother looked at the pouting face of her little

girl. "You are not very happy, are you?" she asked. "Do you know a good way to make yourself happy?"

"No," said Nancy, and she tried to look crosser than ever, but a little smile came flitting across her face.

"You are cross because you are thinking about yourself and how to please yourself," Mother told her. "If you would think about what you could do to please someone else, you would be happy."

Nancy looked doubtful. "There isn't anything I could do for someone else, either," she said. "I can't think of a thing."

"I can think of several," said Mother. "You

could play with Merlin, but he is already happy so we will let him play alone. Then you could sew on some buttons for me. Or carry in wood."

"That is Wayne's job," said Nancy.

"I know it is, but think how pleased he would be if you would help him!"

"I guess he would," Nancy said half smiling. "And surprised, too."

"Think how pleased Grandma and Grandpa would be if you would write them a letter," suggested Mother.

Nancy thought a little while. Then she began to smile. "I know what I will do. I will bring in the wood for Wayne for a surprise for him and then I will write a letter to Grandma and Grandpa." Nancy was smiling a big, happy smile.

Mother smiled, too. "See, you are happy already just from thinking about what you are going to do to please others. When you do things for others, you make others happy. But you are making yourself the happiest of all."

5

Learn It and Live It

"Marlin, you should have seen what happened on the way home from school this evening." Charles threw back his head and laughed.

"Tell me, Charles," Marlin smiled. "Did the boys have some more fun out of Fatty Mason?"

"Oh, a little," Charles said slyly. "Just a very little, Marlin," and he threw back his head and laughed again.

"I don't think it was nice at all," Ruth Ann said, opening her big brown eyes wide. "You wouldn't like it if the other children treated you like they are treating Alvin."

"Charles," Father said as he looked up from his work at the desk, "have you been teasing Alvin again?"

"No, Father, I didn't do a thing to him," Charles answered truthfully.

"Well, you be sure you don't," Father reminded him. "You know what I told you about that."

"Yes, Father, I'll remember."

Marlin was wrapped in a comforter in a big chair by the heat register. He had not been able to

go to school for two days because of a bad cold. After Father looked down at his work again, Marlin said quietly to Charles, "Tell me what happened, Charles."

"Well, you know how deep the snow is. It is

drifted around here and there in the strangest ways. Down the road at that big culvert, there is a drift that hangs out over the edge of the culvert. Some of us boys noticed this, but Fatty didn't.

"So we started playing follow the leader and walked as close to the edge as we could. When Fatty was right at the edge, one of the boys gave him a little shove and he stepped aside and right off the edge of the culvert.

"You should have seen him, Marlin. He just simply disappeared. The last we saw of him was his feet. He was the same as buried alive." Charles and Marlin laughed heartily together.

Father got up from his desk and crossed the room to where the boys were sitting.

"Boys, I am very disappointed in you," Father began sadly.

"Why, Father?" Charles asked. "We didn't do anything. I didn't push him, Father. It was one of the others."

"Maybe you didn't push Alvin, Charles, but there are several things that you did do," Father told him.

"First, you and Marlin both called Alvin a name that is not nice at all. Don't you ever do that

again, even if you are just talking to each other about him. That is very unkind.

"Then another thing that makes me feel very bad indeed is that my boys would enjoy seeing someone else being treated unkindly. I know you didn't do it yourselves, but you surely enjoyed watching someone else do it.

"The Bible tells us to abhor that which is evil. Abhor means to have a strong hatred for it. Now to make fun of someone and to treat him unkindly is wrong. It is just simply sin. And sin is evil.

"Now instead of you boys hating or abhorring this evil, I find you enjoying and liking it." Father looked at the boys sadly. "It is not enough that you don't do the teasing or play the unkind tricks. If you laugh and enjoy the wrong that someone else is doing, you are just as guilty."

Father reached for his Bible and opened it to Romans 12. "I want you boys to learn the second half of this ninth verse and learn it well. When you know it, come and say it to me."

Father read the verse to the boys, " '. . . abhor that which is evil; cleave to that which is good.' Cleave means to hold tightly to something. This verse says that we should hate the things that are wrong and should hold tightly to the things that are right. Do you understand this, boys?"

Charles nodded slowly. "I didn't know there was a verse like this before, Father."

"Neither did I," Marlin said.

"Well, I want my boys to learn it and live it,"
Father said as he went back to his desk.

6

Carol's Secret

"It's a funny thing to me. I can't understand it," Esther spoke in a puzzled voice.

"What can't you understand?" Ellen asked.

"Oh, Carol. She knows something that she will not tell me."

"Well, that is all right," Ellen responded. "You don't have to know everything Carol knows."

"Yes, I do," Esther answered, nearly in tears. "She is my best friend and I tell her everything. It isn't nice that she is keeping something from me."

"How do you know she is?"

"I saw her whispering to Evelyn, and when she

saw me coming, she stopped. Then after a while, she was off talking to Barbara, and before long I saw her with Helen. I am sure she has some secret or other that she doesn't want me to know."

"Well, really, Esther," Mother spoke from the kitchen, "if you think there is something that Carol doesn't want you to know, then you should not want to know it. If Carol is really your good friend, then there is a good reason why she is keeping something from you. You can trust her enough for that, can't you?"

"I don't know, Mother."

"And anyway, Esther," Mother continued, "if she knows something she does not want to tell you, that is her own business, and not yours. The Bible says that we should mind our own business, and not be a busybody in other people's business."

Esther sighed a sigh of discontent. "That's pretty hard to do sometimes, Mother."

"But it is the right thing to do, Esther," Mother told her. "The Lord will help you to do it if you really want Him to."

A few days later, Esther came home from school and went straight to Mother. "I found out what Carol's secret was," she told her, and held out a handful of birthday cards. "And in every card is a real pretty hankie, Mother."

"Why, Esther, isn't that nice!"

Esther nodded, but there were tears in her eyes. "It makes me so ashamed of the way I acted, Mother. I can hardly be happy about the nice hankies and cards."

"I tried to tell you, Esther, that the way you were feeling was not right," Mother reminded her.

"I know, Mother, and I see now that it wasn't. I hope I never am so nosy again."

7

Loving and Giving

"Mother, what do you think we heard in school today?" Anna Mae's eyes were big.

"I don't know." Mother smiled at Anna Mae's excitement.

"Someone moved into the old house on Tim Howard's farm!"

Mother was surprised, too. "That old house! Are you sure, Anna Mae?"

"Yes. Sister Miller told us in school today. And she said that there are some children in the family and that they are poor. She is going with the preacher's wife this evening to visit them and

invite them to come to school and to Sunday
school. I wonder so much if there might be a girl
in my grade."

"It would be very nice if there were," said
Mother. "Maybe if they are poor we could help
them with clothes and food this winter. The Lord
has been so good to us. I would love to share with
someone who needs help."

"So would I," said Anna Mae.

The next evening Anna Mae came dashing into
the house. Her eyes were sparkling with excitement. "There is a girl my age and in my grade,"
she cried.

"Do you mean in the new family that moved
into Tim Howard's place?" Mother asked. "Was
she in school today?"

"No, but she is going to come, Sister Miller
said. She said the family's name is Taylor. There
are four children in all, and one is a girl my age and
in my grade."

"What else did she say about them?" asked
Mother.

"She said that they were poor, and if anyone
has anything like food or clothes they don't
need, the Taylor family could use it."

Mother smiled a little. "Maybe I should call the minister's wife," she said thoughtfully.

After Mother had talked to Sister Weaver, she told Anna Mae that she was right. The Taylor family did need help. Mr. Taylor was sick and was not able to work.

"O Mother, what can we give them?" Anna Mae wondered.

"We will tell Father about the Taylors when he comes home and see what he thinks we should do," said Mother.

That night the family decided what they would give to the Taylors. Mother got the things together the next day. In the evening, Mother, Father, and Anna Mae drove over to the new neighbors.

Anna Mae was a little bashful, but she was very eager to see the girl her age. When she saw her, Anna Mae did not know what to think. Her name was Anna Belle; and she was small, thin, and shy.

"Anna Belle is seven," Mrs. Taylor said, "and she is in the second grade."

"I am seven, too," said Anna Mae. "I am the only girl in the second grade here. I am so glad there will be another girl my age in our school

now."

Then Anna Mae and Anna Belle smiled to each other.

"Will you be in school tomorrow?" Anna Mae asked Anna Belle.

"Yes," Anna Belle replied. "Mother said we may start school tomorrow."

"Good!" cried Anna Mae.

On the way home, Anna Mae said, "Mother, I believe my old dresses will just fit Anna Belle. She is not as tall as I am."

"I think you are right," Mother answered, "but we must pick out the nicest ones. Some of them are pretty old and worn."

"O Mother, I know what!" Anna Mae exclaimed suddenly. "We could give her those new dresses Grandmother sent to me. I grew more than she thought, and they aren't as long as they should be. Instead of letting out the hems, why don't we give them to Anna Belle? Then she will have some nice ones."

Mother looked at Anna Mae in surprise. "Are you sure you want to?" she asked. "You liked those dresses so much."

"Yes, I know I do," said Anna Mae. "But if I am going to be Anna Belle's friend, I should love her as much as I love myself, shouldn't I?"

"Yes, you should, Anna Mae," answered Mother. "Father and I are happy that our little girl is glad to share her nicest and best things, and not give just the things she does not want or need anymore."

8

When Carol Was Happy

"Mother, where are you?" Carol set her lunch box on the kitchen table. Then she noticed the dinner dishes stacked beside the sink. Something must be wrong. Maybe Mother was sick.

Carol opened the bedroom door quietly. Mother was sitting in the rocking chair, holding Baby Benny. Slowly she rocked back and forth. Benny's eyes were closed.

"Benny is sick," Mother whispered.

Carol nodded and closed the door quietly. How empty the house seemed without Mother singing and working, and without little Benny running

44

and playing and chattering to her as he always did when she came home from school.

"What shall I do?" thought Carol. Then she saw the dirty dishes again. "I could wash **the** dishes," she thought. "But how I hate to wash dishes! I've never done it unless I had to."

Then Carol thought of Mother. "Mother would really be happy," she thought. "I will just do them."

Mother was happy. But what surprised Carol the most was how happy she was. She had never thought that doing dishes could ever make her happy.

9

A Discovery

Helen and Roger were staying with their grandparents in the country. There were new sights and sounds all around them. They asked many questions and looked here and there to see new things.

They liked to watch the hens. At night they would peep into the hen house. They liked to see the row of cuddled-up hens sitting on the roost.

"Aren't they funny?" asked Roger. "They look as though their heads had been pushed into their bodies."

Helen giggled. "And see their feet curled

around the roost so tightly. I would think it would keep them awake trying so hard to keep a tight hold onto the roost so they do not fall off."

Helen saw Grandfather coming. "Grandfather," she called, "how can the hens hold onto the roost all night long without getting tired and falling off?"

"They do not have to hold on," answered Grandfather. "When they sit down, their claws shut up all by themselves. They could not fall off if they wanted to as long as they are sitting down. Only when they stand up, will their claws straighten out."

"How funny!" exclaimed Roger.

"That is the way God made them," said Grandfather. "The next time you see a hen walking, watch her feet. When she steps high, her claws close together just as they do when she sits down."

"We will," said the children.

"God made each creature differently," Grandfather explained. "Some animals lie down when they sleep. Others roost, like the chickens. Some sleep standing up. And some even sleep hanging upside down."

"God said that everything He had made was good," said Helen.

"Yes," agreed Grandfather. "And it is interesting to see how many different kinds of things God has made. He has made many more things than we could even count."

10

The Beautiful Heart

"Mother, will you buy me some pink ribbons? I want to wear pink ribbons in my hair when I wear my pink sweater. Please, Mother."

Mother looked surprised. "Where did you get such an idea, Miriam?"

"That is what Lois does," Miriam answered. "If she wears a blue dress, she wears blue ribbons. If she wears a yellow dress, she wears yellow ribbons."

"Lois does some other things that I do not want my little girl to do, too," Mother told her. "It is not safe to decide to do things just because someone else is doing them. We must be sure that what we want to do will please the Lord."

"Doesn't the Lord like pink ribbons, Mother?"

"What grieves the Lord, Miriam, is the pride that is in the heart of the person who ornaments himself just to look nice. The Christian does not do this because the Lord has asked him not to. And

that is what ribbons in the hair are for. Brightly colored barrettes, buttons, buckles, and things such as that, are for the same purpose.

"The Lord does not ask us to look beautiful on the outside, Miriam; He wants us to have beautiful hearts. A heart that is beautiful is one that loves the Lord and is obedient to all that He wants us to do. It is not proud and disobedient—that spoils the heart."

"Mother," Miriam said quietly. "I want a beautiful heart. I want you to always tell me how to have one."

11

Martha Mae's Problem

"Mother, is it true that the Hartmans are coming for dinner on Sunday?"

Mother looked down into the troubled face of Martha Mae. "Yes, it is," she answered. "I thought you would be happy, Martha Mae. Isn't Marjorie about your age?"

"Yes, she is," Martha Mae answered, "but I am not happy to have her come."

"Why, Martha Mae!" Mother exclaimed in surprise. "I thought you would be pleased."

"Well, I'm not. I never have fun when Marjorie is here. I wish she wouldn't come."

"There is something wrong when my little girl feels like this," Mother said. "Will you tell me why you do not have fun with Marjorie?"

"She is so selfish!" Martha Mae's eyes flashed as she spoke. "She will never play anything I want to play. We must always play her games and do what she wants to do."

"It sounds as though another little girl is selfish, too," Mother said gently. "Maybe Marjorie is saying to her mother, 'I never have fun at Martha Mae's house. She will never play anything I want to play. We must always play her games and do what she wants to do.' Do you think she might be saying that, Martha Mae?"

"I don't know," Martha Mae mumbled.

"I can see why two little girls would not enjoy playing together if both of them insist on having their own way," Mother continued. "No one can get along nicely that way. Father and I would be quarreling; Edwin, Carl, and Glendon would be fighting instead of getting their work done; and Laura and Anna wouldn't be able to sleep together.

"No one can always have his own way, Martha Mae. The Bible tells us that we should 'Follow

after the things which make for peace.' That means that whatever we do, we should try to do it so that everyone else is happy."

"But if Marjorie wants to color in my coloring book and I want to play with dolls, . . ." Martha Mae began.

"Why, then color in your coloring book," Mother told her. "If that is what Marjorie wants to do, then if you are trying to keep peace between you, you will do what she wants to do."

"But, . . ." Martha Mae hesitated. "I want to do what I want to do, Mother."

"That is where the trouble is, Martha Mae," Mother said gently. "It is with you. You are wanting to have your own way. You see, Martha Mae, you are the selfish one. If you were not selfish yourself, you would get along fine with Marjorie."

"Is that really true, Mother?" Martha Mae asked slowly.

"Yes, it is, Martha Mae."

Tears came to Martha Mae's eyes. "I don't want to be selfish, Mother. It is not nice to be selfish."

"No, it is not nice at all," Mother agreed. "I will tell you what we will do. When I see that you are being selfish, Martha Mae, I will remind you. I will say, 'Martha Mae, remember to follow after peace.' Do you think that will help you to remember?"

"I think it will, Mother," Martha Mae smiled slowly. "If you start right now, maybe when Marjorie comes on Sunday, I can remember all by myself."

"Good," said Mother. "We will start right now."

12

Ugly Pride

"Mama, I did better than anyone else in school today," Gloria spoke happily. "We had a spelling test and I got 100 percent, and we made health posters, and everyone voted that mine was the best, and I got my work done before anyone else so Sister Eva let me wash the blackboards. I was the best in some other things, too, that I can't think of now."

Gloria took off her wraps and hung them in the closet.

"I am glad you do your school work well," Mama answered, but there was a disturbed look on her face.

"I always get my work done first," Gloria continued. "I don't know what takes the others so long. And I usually get better grades than they do, too. I guess I am just smarter than the rest." Gloria stood by the window and drew pictures in the moisture on the glass.

"Gloria," Mama reproved her. "I don't like the way you are talking. I am glad that you do good work in school, but it is nothing but ugly pride for you to feel that you are doing better than anyone else in school. I don't believe that.

"The Lord made everyone differently. There may be others in school that are working harder and more carefully than you are. Whether the work is hard or easy for you is nothing for you to

boast about.

"We are each the way the Lord made us, and the glory or thanks for what we are or can do belongs to the Lord. You are stealing from the Lord when you try to keep the glory that is His, for yourself."

"Mama, am I?" Gloria looked startled.

"Yes, you are," Mama told her. "You should be saying, 'Thank You, Lord, for making me able to do that. I know I couldn't do it without Your help.'

"Another thing, Gloria, every gift the Lord gives us, He has given us to use for Him. If you can work fast, that is so you can get more done for Him. If you can study and understand things well, He has given you that gift for you to use in studying His Word, and learning about Him and how He wants you to live."

"Mama, I am sorry," Gloria said humbly. "I don't want to ever feel proud again."

13

"Doers of the Word"

"What was your Sunday school lesson about?"
Father asked Jimmy at the dinner table.

"It was about . . . let me see," and little
Jimmy blinked his eyes wisely and looked at
Mother.

"I know what it was about," Sharon smiled
eagerly. "May I tell you, Father?"

"No, just a minute, Sharon. Let Jimmy think a
little."

"It was about, . . . it was about, . . . oh,
now I remember. It was about Abram and Lot.
And Lot was selfish and took the best land."

"That's right, Jimmy," Sharon agreed. "And,

Father, Lot was awful selfish. All the land was really Abram's, but he divided it in two and told Lot he could have whichever part he wanted. And Lot chose the best, Father. He just let Abram have the hills and mountains, and no land to farm, hardly."

"Yes, I am glad you remembered your lesson," Father said. "Now can you remember your memory verse?"

" 'Let there be no strife, I pray thee, between me and thee,' " Sharon said. "Abram said that. He meant that he did not want to have any quarrels with Lot."

"Yes," said Father.

That afternoon Grandpa and Grandma came for a visit. Grandma was carrying a package.

"I wonder what is in that package," Jimmy whispered to Sharon. "Maybe it is something for us."

"Maybe," said Sharon. "But you must not say anything, Jimmy. That would not be nice."

Before long Grandma called Sharon and Jimmy to come to her. "I have something for you," she said, as she began to open the package.

"Coloring books!" Sharon and Jimmy

exclaimed together.

"O Grandma, may I have the one with the puppy on the front?"

"No, Jimmy, that is the one I want."

"Just a minute, children," Father said. "Have you forgotten about Abram and Lot already? The Bible says, 'Be ye doers of the word, and not hearers only.' You heard a Bible story this morning and learned some lessons from it. Now are you going to be a doer of the Word and not just a hearer?"

Jimmy looked at Sharon, and Sharon looked at Jimmy. Then Jimmy said, "You take the one you want, Sharon. I want to be like Abram."

"I'll take this one," Sharon decided, leaving the one with the puppy on the front for Jimmy. Then Sharon laughed. " 'Let there be no strife,' Jimmy, 'between me and thee.' "

"That was our verse today," Jimmy laughed as he explained to Grandma.

"That is a good one to live by," Grandma told the children.

14

"I Believe God"

"O Mother, I am so tired of lying here," Diane said tearfully. "Sometimes I think I can't lie here another minute."

"I know, dear," Mother comforted her. "But you must, and there is really nothing we can do about it."

"But I'm missing all the lovely snow and the sledding. And I am getting behind in my reader and arithmetic. And now Uncle Johns are here, and I can't even play with Fern and Herbie," and the tears that had threatened a minute before began to roll down Diane's cheeks in earnest.

"Diane, dear, please, don't cry." Mother came and sat beside the cot in the corner of the dining room. Diane had rheumatic fever and the weeks of lying in bed were getting very long and hard for her.

Everyone tried to keep her happy. Mother, Father, and the older children all read to her often. The whole family made the dining room the most interesting place for talking and doing things in order to entertain Diane. But nothing could take the place of being able to be up and well.

"We don't know why the Lord allowed this sickness in His plans for us this winter," Mother told Diane, "but we do know that He allowed it for a good reason. 'All things work together for good to them that love God,' and we do love the Lord, Diane.

"So, this sickness is for our good, some way. It is for your good and the rest of the family's good, too. We must just believe this, Diane, because the Lord said so, and we know that He always says what is true.

"So, because we know that your being sick is for our good, then we thank the Lord for it. It is a good gift sent to us from God. When we look at your sickness this way, then we can feel much better about it, can't we?

"I read something in the Book of Acts today that made me think of your sickness, Diane. The Apostle Paul was in a terrible storm on the sea, and after the storm raged for many days, everyone gave up hope of ever being saved.

"But the Lord spoke to Paul one night and told him that no one was going to lose his life. The ship would be wrecked, but everyone's life would be saved. When Paul told the sailors what God had told him, Paul said, 'Sirs, be of good cheer: for I believe God.'

"I think that verse is for us, Diane. We should be of good cheer and not be discouraged, because we believe God. We believe that your sickness is a good thing for us, from the hand of God, and we thank Him for it. That is the way Father and I feel, Diane. Can't you believe God, too, and 'be of good cheer'?" Mother smiled at Diane's tearstained face.

"I will try, Mother," Diane promised bravely.

15

The Good Report Card

"Mama, our report cards came today," Jewel called as soon as she opened the door. "Where are you, Mother? We have our report cards."

"Here I am, Jewel," Mother spoke quietly from the dining room. "Please, don't be so noisy. Raymond just dropped off to sleep."

In trooped the children—Jewel, Clara, and Millard.

"My report card is good," Jewel said confidently.

"I hope they are all good," Mother said as she took the cards from the children. "Now go change your clothes right away. Jewel, why didn't you take your boots off? You are making muddy tracks on the floor."

As Mother studied Jewel's report card a puzzled frown came over her face. A few minutes later, Jewel came in and sat down beside Mother. "My report card is good, isn't it, Mother?"

"Yes, Jewel, it is," Mother said. "But there is something I cannot understand. Here you have excellent on 'obedience,' but you do not obey here at home like you should. Like now, you haven't changed from your school clothes as I asked you to do.

"You have excellent on, 'does work well,' but you are careless with your work here at home.

Right now your room is in bad disorder.

"You have excellent on 'obeys promptly,' but I often have to ask you several times to do something.

"You have excellent on 'is dependable,' but I cannot depend on you to do many things that you know you should do, like always taking your boots off before you come into the house.

"What is wrong, Jewel? Why do you behave so well at school but so poorly at home?"

"I don't know, Mother."

"Maybe you try hard to do things well at school to please your teacher? Doesn't it matter as much to you whether or not you please your mother?"

Jewel hung her head.

"Jewel, if the Lord gave you a report card on how you behaved all this month here at home, do you think you would have a good one?"

Tears came to Jewel's eyes. She shook her head miserably.

Mother sat quietly thinking for a few minutes. Then she said, "Jewel, I think you really want to do just as well at home as you do at school, don't you, Dear? If I would make you a chart with places to mark every day on how obedient you are, how promptly you obey, how well you do your work, and how dependable you are to do the things that you know you should do without being told, it might help you to get out of these bad habits that you have at home.

"Since you have brought this good report card home from school, I know that you understand how to do these things well. Don't you want to break your bad habits here at home so that I could give you a good report card, too?"

"Yes, Mother, I do," Jewel told her earnestly. "Make me a chart and I will try hard to do just as well at home as I do at school."

"If the chart does not help you, I am sure a punishment will," Mother concluded. "But we will try the chart first and see what happens, Jewel. These bad habits must be broken."

Talking Too Much

16

"And then we went up into the loft and began to play in the hay. We jumped and jumped and jumped and rolled around in the hay.

"Then we found a pigeon's nest, and there were two little squabs in it. We nearly fell through the loft because there was a loose board, at least I did. And Henry told me to watch out—"

"Nelson, maybe you should give Wayne a turn to say something," Mother interrupted him. "He has been wanting to tell me something ever since he came in. But you don't let him."

"I was going to tell you about the new little

71

calves," Wayne began with a smile. "They had the cutest—"

"There were three of them," Nelson continued with excitement. "One black and white one, and one—"

"Nelson, you are not letting Wayne talk again," Mother reminded him. "Wayne was telling me about the calves."

"There was one black and white one, Mother, and a little red one, and one that was white with some red on it. And they tried to suck my fingers. We—"

"They sucked mine, too," Nelson put in. "And you should have seen all the pigeons—"

"Nelson," Mother spoke sternly. "You have interrupted Wayne again. Interrupting others is very rude and selfish. You want to have all the pleasure of telling me things, so you talk fast and interrupt Wayne so he can't tell me anything. Do you think this is being kind? Now sit quietly and just listen while Wayne tells me all that he wants to tell me about your visit. Then you may talk. After this, please try to remember not to interrupt, and to give others a chance to talk, too."

"I will try," Nelson said as he hung his head.

17

Morris Learns Something

"Mother, what is that verse about things always working out right?" Morris wondered.

" 'And we know that all things work together for good to them that love God,' " Mother told him. "Is that the one you mean?"

"Yes, Mother," Morris answered with a smile. "That is just what happened to me. I wanted to go along with Father to the sale this morning, awfully bad. But Father said I could not go."

Mother looked surprised. "I didn't know that you wanted to go, Morris."

"I tried to be brave about it," Morris told her.

"I knew I shouldn't fuss or beg."

"That is right, Morris," Mother told him with a pleased and happy smile.

"And, Mother, if I had gone along with Father, I would not have been here when Uncle Elmers came and brought Grandma and Grandpa. I would not have seen them at all.

"I wish they could have stayed a whole week, and not just stopped in for a couple hours. But they had to go on to that funeral, I guess.

"I would much, much, much rather have been here to see them and to play with Glen and David even if it was just for a little while. So you see, things worked out right like the verse said they would."

"Yes, they did, Morris, and they always will. That is why we should always take sweetly whatever happens and not get upset or feel bad. You be sure you don't forget that."

"I'll try not to," Morris smiled happily.

18

To Be Honest

"O Mother," Iris looked up from her bowl of cereal. "I keep forgetting to tell you that I am out of paper. I have been out for nearly a week."

"A week, Iris? Why, what have you been doing without paper for a week? How can you do your schoolwork without paper?"

"Oh, Karen and Cathy and some of the other girls have been giving me some."

"I don't like for you to be borrowing paper, Iris. You must be sure to give back to the girls what you took from them. I hope you have been keeping track of how many sheets you have been getting from each of them."

"Oh, I think I can remember," Iris said care-lessly.

But Mother was not satisfied. "How many sheets do you think you took from each of them, Iris?"

"Oh, maybe three or four," Iris answered.

"I am sure it would be more than that," Philip said. "If you took three sheet from Karen and three from Cathy, that is only six sheets for the whole week. That's about one sheet a day. You used much more than that, Iris. If you used one for each lesson, that would be three or four a day."

Iris looked uncomfortable.

"Iris, did you tell the girls you would pay them

back?" Mother wondered.

Iris nodded. "Of course, Mother. I would not ask them for paper and not pay them back."

"But then you didn't keep track of how many they were giving you. How did you think you would know how many sheets you owed them if you didn't count them?"

"I don't know, Mother," Iris answered, wiping the milk from her mouth with her hankie.

"Iris, an honest person is very careful to remember what he owes people. It is a serious thing to him that he owes someone something. The Bible tells us not to owe people anything. People who borrow have lots of troubles. They often lose their friends because of it. My mother used to say, 'He that goes a borrowing goes a sorrowing.'

"I am going to the store today, and I will get two packs of paper. The one is for you, and the other one you shall divide among all the children that you were getting paper from."

"But, Mother, I know I didn't borrow a whole pack of paper!" Iris exclaimed.

"That is all right. You must be sure that you give back to them all that you took, and more. That is the way a truly honest person will do. He will want to give back more than he owes, rather than a little bit less. Do you understand, Iris?"

Iris nodded.

"And Iris, be sure to let me know when you will be needing paper again before you use all you have. And if you ever do have to borrow, be sure to keep a careful count of what you get. Then when you pay it back, give back all that you borrowed and a little bit more. Can you remember that, Iris?"

"I will try, Mother," Iris promised.

19

A Day at Grandmothers

"It is hot today. Just like summer," Ralph sighed as he lounged on the grass in Grandmother's back yard.

"It is too hot to play or do anything," Mark agreed as he propped his chin in his hand. "I wish we had our bicycle to ride."

"That would make you hotter yet," Rachel informed him from her seat on the walk.

"I wish we could go swimming," Ralph stated. "That would cool us off."

"The water would be too cold," Rachel told him. "You know Grandmother's creek is cold until

July or August."

"Well, what can we do then?" Ralph pulled a blade of grass and began to nibble on it.

Aunt Maude came out on the porch. "Just look at all the busy people out here," she said. "Don't you know what to do with yourselves?"

"Oh, we'll think of something," Ralph said quickly. "In fact, I have an idea right now. Come on, Mark."

Mark scrambled to his feet, and Rachel stood up, too.

"Good," said Aunt Maude. "We want you to be happy and enjoy yourselves while you are here at our house. I was going to give you something to do, if you could not think of anything. It is not good to be idle and doing nothing."

"What are we going to do?" Mark wondered as he followed Ralph toward the barn.

"Oh, I thought we would go out and look around in Grandpa's shop," Ralph told him.

"You know we are not supposed to go into Grandpa's shop," Rachel objected.

"We wouldn't bother anything," Ralph replied.

Mark and Rachel followed him slowly.

"I would like to see what Grandpa is making,"

Ralph told them. "He was working on a nice table when we were here the last time."

"Well, I don't think we should go into his shop when he is not there," Rachel said firmly. "Mother said we never should, didn't she, Mark?"

Mark nodded. "Let's go down to the creek," he suggested suddenly.

"Yes, let's," Ralph agreed. "We don't have to go swimming, Rachel," he told her before Rachel could disagree.

"All right," Rachel said as she followed her brothers across the meadow.

"Now," said Ralph when they had arrived at the creek, "we can wade a little. That will cool us off."

"But, Ralph," Rachel objected, "I don't think we are supposed to."

"All right, you don't have to if you don't want to." The boys sat down and pulled off their shoes and socks. In a few minutes they were stepping into the creek.

Mark whistled. "This water is really cold!"

Ralph shivered. "It comes from the mountain behind Grandpa's house," he said.

"Maybe there is still some snow melting up

there some place," Rachel suggested.

"I wouldn't be surprised," Ralph said. "I think I heard Grandpa say there was. You just ought to feel this water, Rachel."

Rachel began to take off her shoes and stockings, and soon she joined the boys.

Everything went all right—the children thought—although the boys did get their trouser legs wet, until Ralph stepped on a slippery rock. Down he went into the water. Rachel was standing near enough that she got splashed, and so did Mark.

Before long three wet, shivering children stood in Grandma's kitchen.

"The only thing to do," Aunt Maude told them, "is to get out of these wet clothes and crawl into bed until they dry. They should be dry by dinner time.

"I think I should have given you children something to do. Not knowing what to do has only gotten you into trouble. I will think of something for you to do this afternoon, so this does not happen again. Now hurry," and Aunt Maude shooed them off to bed.

An hour or so later, Aunt Maude came into the bedroom. "Here are your clothes, boys, all dry again. Now get into them quickly because dinner is ready. Rachel is downstairs. Her dress dried more quickly than your trousers did. I think it is good that you had to stay in bed longer than Rachel did. It is my guess that Rachel did not want

to wade to begin with but just followed you boys.
Am I right?" and Aunt Maude smiled at the boys.

"I guess you are," Ralph admitted.

"Well, I have some plans for this afternoon,"
Aunt Maude continued. "I am sure that you will
enjoy the afternoon better than you did the
morning."

When dinner was finished and the dishes done,
Aunt Maude found the children waiting on the
porch swing.

"First, we are going to do a few jobs," Aunt
Maude told them. "Ralph, I want you to mow the
lawn. It has been needing it for a few days already.

"Mark, I want you to help me with some things
in the house. There is trash to empty and I need
help moving some furniture around while I clean.

"Rachel, Grandmother wants to make some
pies for supper, and she needs your help peeling
apples.

"When your jobs are finished, everyone come
here to the porch and we will decide what to do
next."

The lawn mower soon started up with a roar.
Round and round the big lawn Ralph followed the
lawn mower. The sweet smell of cut grass filled the

air.

Mark helped Aunt Maude move furniture. He carried out the trash to the fireplace to burn. He helped Aunt Maude run the sweeper over the floor. He swept the porches and the newly cut grass from the walks.

Rachel helped Grandmother make apple pies. She peeled the apples and sliced them for Grandmother. She put sugar into the pies and sprinkled a little cinnamon over them. Then she helped Grandmother make a jello salad.

"Now that is all I have for you to do," Grandmother told Rachel. "You may go now. Thank you so much for your help."

Rachel went out and sat on the swing on the porch, just as the sound of the lawn mower died down. Ralph was finished with the mowing and was putting the mower into the shed.

"Are you finished, too?" he asked when he saw Rachel sitting on the porch swing.

"I just finished," Rachel said. "I enjoyed helping Grandmother."

Ralph sat on the porch steps. "I am hot," he said, "but not as hot as I thought I would be. That is a nice lawn mower and I like to mow Grandmother's lawn."

"I am glad to hear you say that," Aunt Maude said as she came out on the porch. "It has saved me a lot of work. And Mark has been a good helper to me in the house.

"Now, because you have been such good helpers, we will eat supper tonight on the lawn at the fireplace."

"Oh, goody," cried the children.

"What do you want to do until then?" Aunt Maude asked the children.

"You tell us what to do," Rachel told Aunt Maude. "I enjoyed helping Grandmother this afternoon much more than I did getting into trouble this morning."

Aunt Maude smiled. "How about it, boys?

Which did you enjoy the most?"

"This afternoon," Ralph admitted, "but I don't understand why. I would have thought that doing what we wanted to do and wading in the creek would have been more fun than mowing the lawn."

"Doing what we think we want to do never makes us happy," Aunt Maude told the children. "I hope you have learned this and never forget it. The thing that makes us happy is doing something worthwhile and useful and doing what is right.

"When we are doing what we think we want to do, we cannot be really happy because we are being selfish. Happiness comes from doing useful things and things that are right.

"Now, if you want me to tell you what to do," Aunt Maude said, smiling happily at the children, "let me think a little. I am sure I can think of something worthwhile for you to do."

20

Wishing and Wanting

"Did a new catalog come today? Oh, goody."
Ruth picked up the big, fat book and sat down on
the window seat.

"Mama," she called, "did you see how short
the new dresses are?"

"No," said Mama. "I have not had time to look
at the catalog yet."

"They are horribly short," said Ruth.

"There will be quite a few pages in that catalog
that are not even fit to look at," said Mama. "The
spring and summer catalogs sell bathing suits,
shorts, and skimpy dresses. I am not interested in

you children even looking at the catalog until I have checked it."

"I will skip the clothes part," said Ruth, turning over a large group of pages. "May I look at the toy pictures?"

"Yes, I suppose you may."

"O Mama, here is a bicycle that would be just my size. It costs only fifty-nine dollars and ninety-eight cents. Will you get it for me, Mama?"

"That is a lot of money, Ruth," said Mama.

A few minutes later, Ruth exclaimed, "O Mama, here is a croquet set. Why don't we get a new croquet set? Ours is getting so broken up and old-looking."

Before Mama could answer, Ruth burst out, "Mama, here is a tether ball. Uncle Earls have one and so do Ben Millers. It only costs—oh, here are some horseshoes. The boys would like that, too. And here's a basketball and a basket. They could put that up on the side of the chicken house like John Martins did."

"Ruth," began Mother. But Ruth did not hear her.

"Here's a wagon that Harold would love to have, and a tricycle, too. And a tractor that has

pedals that he could ride on. I wonder if this catalog has any dolls in it. I would love to have a doll for my birthday this summer. Oh, here are some chairs and a little table. Please, Mama, get them for our playhouse. Our old things are getting so. . . ."

"Ruth!" Mama interrupted her sternly. "Do you know what you are doing?"

Ruth looked up, surprised. "No, Mama, what? I was just looking at the catalog."

"You are disobeying the Lord," Mama told her, and her voice was still stern. "God says that we should be content with such things as we have. You are wishing for this and wanting that. And the kind of things that you are wanting are not even good, useful things at all. God would not be pleased if we would spend a lot of money just for playthings."

Ruth sat thinking for a long time. "I guess it would not be right, would it, Mama? There are so many poor people who do not even have enough food and clothes."

"That is right, Ruth," said Mama. "But more than that, we should use our money to help tell others about Jesus. It would be wrong to use it just for ourselves. Our money is the Lord's money. We should use every penny of it in a way that would please Him."

21

A Wrong Made Right

Marian was very miserable. All she could think of was that she had copied an answer on her arithmetic test from Richard's paper. She had tried and tried to think of how much three times nine was, but she could not. Then, without even trying, she saw it on Richard's paper. She knew his answer was right the instant she saw it.

"I knew that it was twenty-seven," she told herself. "I am sure I would have thought of it in a minute." Then she wrote twenty-seven on her paper.

"That was cheating," a Voice spoke quietly in

Marian's heart.

Marian was miserable. "I wish I wouldn't have seen that answer," she thought. "But it is too late now. My paper is already handed in."

"No, it is not too late," the quiet Voice said. "You can still tell Sister Erb."

Marian sat staring at her book. She was a very unhappy little girl.

Just then Sister Erb spoke to her. "Is this your pencil, Marian?" she asked, as she laid the pencil she had taken from the floor on Marian's desk.

"Yes, it is," Marian said as she looked up quickly. "And Sister Erb," she faltered, "I want to change one of the answers on my arithmetic test.

I—I copied it from Richard's paper." Marian's face was flushed and miserable.

Sister Erb was very kind. She gave Marian her paper and watched while she erased the answer to number five. "I am sorry I did it," Marian said.

"I am very happy that you made the wrong thing that you did, right," Sister Erb said. "It is sin to cheat, you know."

Marian nodded. "I know it is," she said. "And I am never going to do it again."

22

The Doll in the Window

"O Mother, I saw just the dolly that I want," Jenny said excitedly. "It was in a store window in town. May I go with Father the next time he goes to town and get it with the money Grandmother gave me for my birthday? Please, Mother."

"Maybe you could, Jenny," Mother said with a smile. "You have been waiting a long time to get your doll. Grandmother has been wondering if you have found the one you want yet. She asked me about it in a letter I got today."

"You tell her that I found a lovely doll," Jenny said with excitement. "It has long hair and looks like a real little lady."

"Isn't it a baby doll?" Mother wondered. "I thought you wanted a baby doll."

"No, Mother, it is a grown-up-girl kind of doll. There are some in the catalog, I think. Let me see if I can find one that looks like the one I want."

Jenny ran upstairs and put her coat in her closet. She had been to town with her big sister who was married and lived next door. Before long Jenny brought the catalog to Mother.

"Here, Mother," she said. "This is the kind of doll that it is, only the one I saw was lots nicer than this one, I think."

Mother looked at the picture of the doll soberly. "Why, Jenny," she said, "why do you want that kind of doll? It is like a worldly girl with a short dress and fixed-up hair. Who would want such a worldly looking thing?"

"I think it would be fun to have one. There are clothes you can get and all sorts of things to dress it up."

"I am sorry that you want this kind of doll, Jenny, because you surely cannot have one," Mother said. "What is wrong to put on yourself, should not be put on a doll, either. If you would get this doll you would have to make new dresses for it of modest length just like a girl, the age the doll is supposed to be, should wear. Also you would have to fix its hair in a modest, Christian way. Would you be interested in having the doll and fixing it up like that?"

Jenny shook her head. "No, Mother, I guess not."

"You understand, don't you, Jenny, why Mother feels the way she does about getting this doll?" Mother asked.

"I am not sure," Jenny answered slowly.

"Do you understand why we would not let Jerry and John have toy guns and play they are shooting each other? And why we would not want them to be playing that they are smoking and drinking and things like that?"

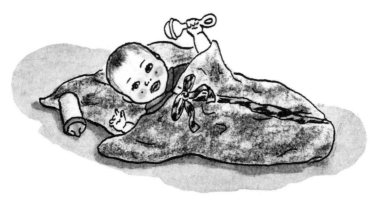

"Yes, I can see that, Mother. They should not be doing things in their play that would be wrong to really be doing."

"That is right," Mother told her. "That is the reason I would not want you to have a worldly doll and dress it up like the world, because for you to be dressing that way yourself would be wrong."

"Yes, I see that now, Mother. I guess I will keep on looking for a sweet, cuddly baby doll. I would have more fun with that, anyway."

"I am sure you would," Mother agreed.

23

The Better Way

"Melvin, come here," Mother called.

Melvin appeared in the kitchen doorway. "What did you do with Aaron's book?"

"I hid it," Melvin returned, looking at Aaron with a frown. "He looked at my book and did not put it away, so I hid his."

"Go and get it and bring it to Aaron," Mother told him. "Then I want to talk to you a little."

In a few minutes Aaron ran away with his book, and Melvin stood before Mother.

"There is something that you are doing, Melvin," Mother began kindly, "that I want to talk to you about. You are always paying someone back for what you think they have done to you.

"When your cap gets knocked off the hook, you throw someone else's cap down. When a toy of yours is broken or scratched, you scratch or hurt someone else's toy.

"Right now, you hid Aaron's book because he didn't put your book away. This is wrong. Jesus said we should not pay back. He says if someone hits us on the one cheek, we should turn the other cheek to him and let him hit that one, too. If someone takes away our coat, we should let him have our cap or jacket, or something else of ours, too.

"Jesus says if anyone needs to be punished for not treating us right, He will do the punishing. We should not do it.

"I often hear you say that you are going to do something to someone because they did it to you. Proverbs says, 'Say not, I will do so to him as he hath done to me.' Rather, the Lord says we should love those who mistreat us, or do things to us that we do not like.

"You have a very bad habit, Melvin. You have been doing exactly what the Lord says you should not do. We are going to change this.

"From now on, when someone does something to you that you do not like, you must do something nice to them. If you cannot think of anything nice to do, come and ask me what you can do. I will help you. You may go now, Melvin. But don't forget what I have said."

Melvin looked at Mother very soberly. Then he turned and slowly left the kitchen. When Mother looked outside a few minutes later, she saw Melvin sitting on the porch steps. He was thinking very deeply.

In a few minutes, Sara came around the corner of the house. She was on Melvin's bike. But she was too little to ride it right. Back and forth she wobbled.

"Sara," Melvin stood up and called to her. "Get off my bike. You will wreck it. You are too little to ride it."

"Stop me, Melvin," Sara called in a frightened voice. "I can't stop."

Melvin ran across the lawn. But before he got to Sara, she had run into a tree. She and the bike fell in a heap together.

"Oh, my head," Sara cried, holding her head.

"What did you get on my bike for?" Melvin demanded angrily. "You should have known better. Look, you broke the chain, and the handle

bars are knocked crooked. Just you wait until I get hold of your trike!''

"Melvin," Mother called warningly as she walked across the lawn to the children. "Have you forgotten already?"

"But, Mother, . . ." Melvin began.

"Do you want me to help you think of something nice you can do for Sara?" Mother asked as she stood with her arm around Sara's shoulders, while she rubbed her bumped head. "Sara is sorry for hurting your bike, I am sure. And whether she is sorry or not, we must still forgive others if we want the Lord to forgive us for the wrong things that we do.

"Now, I would suggest that you fix Sara's trike as a nice thing to do for her. If she would have had her trike to ride, she likely would not have even tried to ride on your bike.

"I think the handle bars need to be tightened, and the screw is lost so that they just turn around and around. I am sure you can find another screw that will hold them tight." Mother looked at Melvin and smiled.

"All right, Mother," Melvin said slowly. "I guess that would be a better way than hurting her trike more."

"It surely would," Mother agreed happily. "Because it is the right way and the way that pleases God."

24

A Net for Kathy

"Mother, may I go over to Morrises?" Kathy's eyes were pleading. "Please, let me go, Mother."

"You were just over yesterday," Mother hesitated.

"I know, but I like to go. Mrs. Morris is nice. Her little boy is so sweet. And I help her. I don't get in her way. She wants me to come."

It was true that Kathy was a help to Mrs. Morris. With her little boy, and now a new baby, even a little girl like Kathy could be helpful.

"Well, you may go over until I call you," Mother decided. "Try to help her, Kathy."

"Oh, thank you, Mother," Kathy cried.

After Kathy had left, Mother sat down to write a letter. She was surprised when she looked at the clock after the letter was finished.

"I must call Kathy right away," she decided as she went to the telephone. "She has been over there longer then she should have been."

In a few minutes, Kathy came running into the house. "O Mother, I had such a nice time."

"Did you help Mrs. Morris?" Mother asked.

"Yes. I dried the dishes and picked up the toys. Then I set the table for supper. I played with Barry a lot, but his mama says that helps her because it keeps him out of mischief."

"I hope you were a good girl," Mother answered.

"Oh, I was, Mother. Mrs. Morris says I am the very best little girl she ever saw. She says she never saw such a good worker as I am."

A strange look came over Mother's face. "What else did she say?" she wondered.

"Oh, she says lots of nice things about me," Kathy laughed. "That's why I like to go over there, or at least it's one of the reasons. Nobody at home here seems to like me as much as Mrs. Morris does."

"Why, Kathy," Mother said in surprise. "We all love you very dearly. I am sure we love you a whole lot more than Mrs. Morris does."

"Well, she tells me she loves me," Kathy returned. "She tells me that I am the prettiest little girl she ever saw. I'm so sweet. She wishes I was her little girl.

"My cheeks are so rosy, and my eyes sparkle, and I have the cutest little ways."

Mother looked shocked and concerned. "I hope you don't believe those things, Kathy," Mother told her.

"Of course, Mother. She says them so much; they must be true."

"No, Kathy, that does not make them true. Some people just talk a lot, and they say lots of things that aren't really true. I am not saying that Mrs. Morris has just been lying to you, but she has not been careful and entirely honest. What she has said has been a lot of flattery."

Mother opened her Bible to Proverbs. " 'A man that flattereth his neighbour spreadeth a net for his feet,' " Mother read. "That means that a person who says all sorts of nice things about us, only half meaning them, is not really our friend. What he says will get us into trouble, if we listen to him.

"This is what has happened to you. You came home thinking you are a lot of nice things you are not, and believing that Mrs. Morris loves you better than your own family, which is not true.

"What she has said has put pride into your heart, and the Lord hates pride. He tells us that if we are proud, we are in for a fall. Mrs. Morris' flattery has spread a net for your feet and you have been caught in it.

"Now run and set the table for Mother, dear. And forget what Mrs. Morris has said. That will be the very best thing you can do."

25

Larry's Feet

"I really dread to think of Larry being here," Mother told Father. "He is always getting into something that he should not be into. The children misbehave so much more when he is here."

"I really don't know what we can do about it," Father answered, "unless we could explain to the children what is wrong with Larry."

"What is wrong with Larry?" Nelson stood up from the other side of a bush beside the porch.

"Yes, what is wrong with Larry?" Gail echoed, bobbing up beside Nelson.

"I didn't know you children were playing under

the bush," Mother said in surprise.

"Come here, children, and sit on the porch steps," Father said. "I will tell you what is wrong with Larry."

The children came eagerly. They were looking

forward to Larry coming and spending a week with them. They liked to play with their cousin Larry.

"In Proverbs 6," Father began, the Lord lists seven things that He hates. One of them is, 'feet that be swift in running to mischief.' That refers to the person who is always in mischief. He goes from one naughty thing to another. It seems that he doesn't know how to behave himself and keep from doing naughty things.

"That verse describes Larry well. He is always into trouble. He has never learned or been taught by parents who love him how to behave himself.

"When Larry comes here, you children enjoy playing with him. But he does many things that he should not do. The last time he was here, he liked to scare the chickens. He would go into their pen and chase them around just to see them flutter and squawk.

"He left the water running at the barn to make a stream for the baby ducks to play in. He left out the calves, just to see where they would go. He broke a number of your toys with a hammer one day, 'just for fun' he said.

"Now Larry is coming again," Father continued. "We want to be nice and kind to him, and see that he is happy while he is here, but we are concerned because we know that he has 'feet that be swift in running to mischief.' You children will be tempted to do what he does.

"I know you are still small, but you are not too small to know that it is wrong to do what we have been told not to do. So when Larry's feet take him into mischief, Father and Mother are expecting that you children will not run along with him. We will expect that you do what you know is right to do. Do you understand this?"

Gail and Nelson nodded soberly.

"Good," said Father. "Then I know that things will go much better this time."

26

Trust and Be Happy

"Donna," Mother asked gently, "what are you worrying about now?"

Donna looked miserably at Mother.

"Tell Mother," Mother encouraged. "I doubt that it is anything that you need to worry about at all."

"Isn't it time for Father to come home?" Donna asked.

Mother looked at the clock. "No, not quite, Donna. It is cloudy this evening so that makes it seem darker and later than it is. Are you worrying about Father, dear?"

Donna nodded anxiously.

"Donna, it is not even time for Father to come home, and here you are worrying about him. Don't you know that most of what you worry about is just like that? There is really no reason at all for you to be worrying.

"I am sorry to see my sunny little girl worried so much of the time. Now I am going to tell you something, Donna, that will help you. You love the Lord, don't you, Donna?"

Donna nodded brightly.

"Do you trust the Lord?"

Again, Donna nodded.

"Do you trust Him to take care of you, of your things, and of those you love? Now think before you answer me," Mother encouraged her.

Donna thought for a few minutes. "I think I do, Mother," she answered slowly.

"Let me help you to think," Mother offered. "If you really trusted the Lord to take care of you, and of your things, and of those you love, would you ever worry about them?"

Donna looked puzzled. "I don't know, Mother."

"Do you get up worrying about whether or not I

will get breakfast for you?"

Donna shook her head. "No, Mother, because I know you will. You always do."

"Don't you worry that I might be sick and you will have to go hungry?"

Donna smiled. "No, Mother, because I know that if you are sick, someone else will get breakfast. Carol can cook."

"That is the way you should feel about the Lord, Donna," Mother explained. "You should know that He will take care of everything right, even if things don't always work out just as we want them to. You don't want Mother to be sick, but if she is, then you will still be taken care of. So you don't worry. Can't you feel that way about the

Lord?"

"I never thought about it like that before," Donna answered slowly.

"God is a loving heavenly Father, Donna. He loves you even better than Mother and Father do. You can always trust Him to do what is best for you. It says in Proverbs, 'Whoso trusteth in the Lord, happy is he.' When you go around worrying about things, you are unhappy, and it is because you are not really trusting in the Lord."

Mother looked at the clock. "Father could be here in a minute. Yes, there he is now. See, the Lord did bring him home safely."

Donna nodded with a smile.

"When I see you are worrying about something, Donna, I am going to remind you to trust the Lord, and then help you to do it. Then you will be happy as the Lord intends for you to be."

"All right," Donna smiled as she ran to meet Father.

27

The Red Box

"I wonder what is going to happen to him," Helen said half-fearfully.

"So do I," Fred agreed. "I wish he wouldn't have done it. Mother, where are you?"

"Here in the bedroom," Mother answered.

"Mother, do you know what?" Fred began eagerly.

"Cousin Ralph stole the teacher's surprise," Helen put in excitedly.

"The girls saw him," Fred added emphatically.

Mother looked surprised. "Are you sure?" she asked slowly. "But if they saw him. . . ."

"We had a treasure hunt today," Helen explained, starting at the beginning of the story. "And the treasure was in the tool shed behind the schoolhouse.

"Ralph wasn't at school today. We don't know why. But some of the children happened to see him with a red box, just like the teacher's treasure box, crawling through the fence at the back of the school ground.

"When we had the treasure hunt later on, we couldn't find the treasure. We were sure it was supposed to be in the tool shed. Finally Sister Alta came and looked and sure enough it was gone.

"When we were trying to decide what might have happened to it, some of the big girls said they saw Ralph leave the school yard, with a red box.

Sister Alta looked shocked. She wondered if the girls were sure."

"She said the treasure box was red," Fred told Mother. "Everyone was shocked that he would do it."

"But maybe it wasn't Ralph. Maybe the girls just thought it was," Mother reminded them soberly. "It's a serious thing to say something like this about someone."

"The girls were sure, Mother. Ruth and Karen both saw him. They wouldn't lie," Helen told her.

"I think I will call Aunt Marie," Mother said. "I am not going to believe that Ralph did something like that until I know that it is true." Mother went to the telephone.

"Hello," Mother answered. "Is that you, Marie? How is everyone?

"Well, that is too bad. Does it hurt him quite a bit?

"Are you keeping ice on it? I have an ice bag you could borrow if you would like to have it.

"Well, if we can do anything, just let us know." Mother turned away from the telephone, with a very serious face.

"Children, it says in Proverbs, 'He that

answereth a matter before he heareth it, it is folly and shame unto him.' That is what you have been doing. You decided and judged Ralph to have stolen before you knew the whole story. The rest of the story that you didn't know is that Ralph sprained his ankle very badly last evening and is suffering quite a bit with it. He has been on the couch with it all day and hasn't set his foot on the floor. Now, what is this talk about him being seen leaving the school yard with the teacher's treasure?"

Helen and Fred looked at Mother with their mouths open in bewilderment.

"Listen, children," Mother continued. "This is a sin that people often commit. They carelessly talk and decide this must have been or that must have happened because of what someone says they heard or saw—all without really knowing what the truth is.

"Maybe Ruth and Karen saw someone leaving the school ground with something red. But we know it wasn't Ralph. Also we do not know whether it was the treasure. We just know it was something red. Lots of things could be red.

"When we believe and decide things before we

have really heard the whole story, we are committing sin. Do you understand this, children?"

Helen and Fred nodded soberly.

"Be sure you never forget it," Mother said earnestly.

28

"A Wise Son . . ."

"A wise son maketh a glad father." Rodney read the verse that was on the wall above his big brother's desk. "What does that verse mean, Harvey?" he asked his big brother.

"That verse means that if we want to make Father happy, we should be wise."

"But what does it mean to be wise?" Rodney wondered.

Harvey thought a moment. "To be wise means always to do what we think Father wants us to do. That will make Father and Mother happy."

" 'A wise son maketh a glad father. A wise son

124

maketh a glad father.' " Rodney kept repeating the verse to himself. It was just a short one and easy to learn.

"Uncle Nelsons are here. Uncle Nelsons are here." Rodney heard Patsy call happily.

Rodney's eyes sparkled as he dashed from the room. That meant that Cousin Jerry would be here. He always enjoyed playing with Jerry.

After a few minutes of joyful greeting, Rodney turned to Mother eagerly. "May we go to the meadow to work on our dam?" he coaxed.

"Yes," she agreed. "But try to keep from getting too wet. The water is still not warm enough to get wet all over."

With a happy shout, the boys dashed away.

"We are going to have a lovely place to swim this summer," Jerry remarked.

"I know," Rodney agreed. "Father is glad we are building the dam, too. He says it will make a nice place for the calves to drink." Then a funny look came over his face. "Where are the calves?" he asked. "They are supposed to be in this field. I put them in here this morning myself. At least, I helped Harvey to put them in. But they're not here now."

The warm sunshine shone down on the boys as they worked. It shone down on Rodney's worried frown. "We better go and look for the calves," he said.

"They're all right," Jerry told him. "Let's stick at this dam. If my folks stay long enough, we can finish it this afternoon."

"I know they are supposed to be in this field," Rodney repeated. "I think I better go and see whether there is a broken place in the fence and find the calves."

"Oh, forget the calves," Jerry said impatiently. "They will be all right."

Rodney stood thinking, the worried look still on

his face. "It will only take me a few minutes to run around the fence," Rodney decided. "You keep working on the dam. I'll be right back."

Across the meadow Rodney ran. When he got to the fence, he trotted along beside it, down one side of the field, across the end, and along the fence beside the road. Then he saw the broken place. It was big enough for a calf to squeeze through. And far down the highway he saw the calves. Some of them were eating grass beside the road; others were standing in the road.

Rodney dashed for the house. "Father," he cried. "The calves are out of the meadow and way down the highway."

Harvey, Father, and Uncle Nelson came out of the house and quickly climbed into the pickup.

"If you don't need me, I better go back to Jerry," Rodney decided, while he sat on the porch steps to catch his breath. "I left him building the dam all by himself."

"Father appreciates that you came and told him about the calves being out," Mother commended him. "I hope they get them off the highway before a car hits any of them."

As Rodney stood up to start for the meadow a
thought flashed into his mind. "A wise son maketh
a glad father." With a happy smile, Rodney ran
back to the dam.

29

Blue Sky and Showers

"Richard, where is Mother?" Charles asked as he put his lunch box on the counter.

"Oh, are you home?" Richard looked up from the book he was reading. "Father and Mother just left for town. We are supposed to plant peas this evening. Go and change your clothes."

Charles was not happy about having to plant peas. It was a lovely April day. The sky was blue, and white sheepy-looking clouds were floating across it. It was a lovely day to go down to the little marsh!

Charles was sure he could find lots of frog and

toad eggs. There would probably be some raccoon tracks. The spring peepers were singing in a loud chorus, and if Charles sat still enough, they would sing while he was there, and he could probably see some of them.

Slowly, Charles unbuttoned his shirt. Slowly he untied his shoes. Slowly he unbuckled his belt. Then he stopped. He crossed to the window and opened it. The screens had not yet been put on, and Charles leaned out of the window to look at the swelling buds on the apple tree that stretched close to the window. Yes, he was right. He thought he had seen some pink. The blossoms were beginning to open.

If only he did not have to plant peas.

A few minutes later he had an idea. Quickly he dressed and ran downstairs. "Richard," he said, "I am going to the marsh for a little. I want to see something."

Richard did not look up from the book he was reading. The family could often talk to Richard and he did not hear them when he was reading a book. This was one of those times.

"The peas don't have to be planted this evening," Charles decided after he had sat for a while on a stump in the little marsh and had counted ten or twelve spring peepers that had sung around him. "Anyway, if Richard wants me, he can call me. I will stay here until he is ready to plant peas."

Charles hunted for frog eggs and found them. Then he found raccoon tracks. Some were big and some were little. "I believe a raccoon family was here," he thought. "I wish I could find a baby raccoon for a pet."

Then he heard Richard calling him. "We can plant peas tomorrow," Charles told himself. But he answered Richard and then walked slowly to the house.

"Richard," he said, "why don't we plant the peas tomorrow?"

"Why didn't you tell me when you were dressed?" Richard asked him. "We must hurry. It is going to rain."

"I did tell you when I was dressed," Charles told him. "Why don't we wait until tomorrow to plant the peas?"

"Because it is going to rain, and we can't plant anything when the ground is wet. Hurry, Charles."

The sky was dark with rain clouds and in just a minute or two it began to rain. The boys sat gloomily on the porch and watched it rain.

"Mother won't like it that the peas are not planted," Richard told Charles. "She said they should have been planted several weeks ago."

"I thought we could plant them tomorrow just as well as today," Charles told him. "That's why I went to the marsh."

" 'Boast not thyself of tomorrow; for thou knowest not what a day may bring forth.' That's a good verse for you to remember," Richard told him. "My problem was reading when I should have been working. That is just as bad. We both have been disobedient, and we will both have to take our punishment."

30

Peas for the Lord

"Mother, are my peas ready to pick?" Sharon held out a few pods for Mother to see.

"Yes, I believe they are," Mother smiled. "Mine are ready, too. I was planning to pick them in the morning."

"We planted them on the same day, and we will pick them on the same day, won't we?" Sharon laughed.

The next morning the peas were picked. "This is a whole lot of peas, isn't it?" Sharon wondered as she looked at the baskets of peas on the porch.

"It is quite a few," Mother answered. "But

when we shell them out, we won't have as many as we could use. I am thankful for what we do have, though."

Irene and Phyllis helped shell Mother's peas. Sharon worked on what had come from her own little garden.

Then the telephone rang and Mother answered it.

"I see," said Mother.

"Yes, I am sure we could help.

"We will be glad to. We will have them ready when you come."

"What will we have ready, Mother?" Irene asked when Mother came back to the porch.

"Some peas for the Howards."

"What for, Mother?" Phyllis wondered.

"When it was time to plant peas this spring, the Howards had sickness and could not get any peas planted," Mother explained. "Sister Thomas called to tell me they are having a pea shower for them now. If each family gives a part of their pea crop, the Howards will have peas, too. I think that is very nice idea."

"But, Mother, I thought we don't have enough for ourselves, even," Sharon objected. "I was glad I

had planted peas. I was going to give you mine to help you out. But if you give some of yours away, . . ." Sharon was frowning.

"The Lord will provide what we need," Mother told Sharon cheerfully. "If we don't have as many peas as we could use, He will probably give us more beans and corn than necessary. But even if He dosen't, the Lord will still provide some way."

"Well, the Lord did provide," Sharon said with a puzzled look. "Maybe if we give these away, He won't give us any more." Sharon seemed worried.

"No, Sharon, the Lord wants us to help those who are in need. The Lord blesses those who give. In Proverbs it says, 'He that hath pity upon the poor lendeth unto the Lord; and that which he hath given will he pay him again.'

"This tells us that when we give to the poor we are lending or giving to the Lord. It tells us, too, that what we have given, the Lord will give back to us again or pay us for giving in some way or other."

Sharon's eyes opened with interest. "Really, Mother?" She thought a moment. "Maybe He will give us more peas than we had before. Maybe He will give us so many peas we will have enough."

"He easily could, Sharon," Mother agreed. "But that is not why we should give. We should give because we love those in need and want to help them for Jesus' sake."

"I am going to give some of my peas, too," Sharon decided.

31

Behind the Barn

"Here, let's take this hammer," Marlin decided.

"But Father said we should never use his good hammer," Clyde protested.

"Well, where is the old one, then?" Marlin returned impatiently. "It won't matter if we bring it right back. Father just doesn't want us to lose it."

Marlin lifted the hammer from the wall. "Come on," he said as he went out the door. Clyde followed, casting a worried look toward the house.

"Now, hold these boards while I nail them

together," Marlin instructed when the boys were behind the barn.

Clyde held the boards, but he looked toward the corner of the barn at the same time.

"Hold them straight," Marlin told him. "Watch what you are doing. If we hurry we can take the hammer back in just a few minutes."

Pound. Pound. Pound.

"There, that's done. Now hold this one."

Clyde held the board, but again looked toward the corner of the barn.

Marlin looked at him impatiently. "Why don't you look at what you are doing? You are holding it crooked again. If you are so afraid that someone is going to come, why don't you hurry?"

"I feel like someone is watching us," Clyde explained uneasily.

Marlin looked around quickly. "Well, there isn't," he stated firmly. "Now hold this board. This is going to be a nice little barn when it is finished."

Pound. Pound. Pound.

"What are you boys making?" Father's voice startled the boys.

Quickly they looked one way and then another. Then Marlin looked up. There was Father standing in the opening in the barn above them.

"A barn," he answered quickly.

"Who said you could use my good hammer?" Father asked.

The boys were silent. Clyde's heart beat fast. He was frightened.

"I've been watching you boys ever since you came back here," Father told them. "You acted as though you were afraid someone was watching you. It was because you acted so strangely that I watched to see what you were going to do.

"From what I have seen, I would say that Clyde didn't want to get the hammer, but you did. Is that right, Marlin?"

Marlin nodded his head miserably.

"You thought you could use it and take it back quickly so that no one would find out what you had done. Isn't that right, Marlin?"

Marlin did not answer.

"Besides disobeying me, Marlin," Father went on, "you have been sneaking and deceitful. You did what you knew was wrong and did it in a sneaking way, hoping that no one would find it out.

"Let me tell you this, Marlin. You can never hide anything. Someone will always know. The Bible speaks of a time when the things which we do in secret will be shouted from the housetops.

" 'The eyes of the Lord are in every place, beholding the evil and the good,' " Father quoted. "Clyde could feel that someone was watching you. Yes, Someone was. God was watching you. It is far more serious that God was watching you than that I was."

Father thought a moment. "Clyde," he said, "take the hammer back to the shop, please, and Marlin, come up here to the loft to me. I must punish you so that you will learn to be an honest and dependable boy."

32

True Riches

"Do you know what I wish?" Danny looked at Mark inquiringly.

Mark shook his head.

"I wish that Father were rich and had as much money as Ronald Mason's father has. Just look at all the things he gets for Ronald. He had an old bike, but now he got a new one. He has a pony and all sorts of games and toys. Every time he goes to town, Ronald gets something new."

"I know he does. He always looks so fine when he comes to school with his fancy book bag and lunch box, and his new heavy jacket and cap. Our things are always old and patched and nearly worn out."

"Well, Samuel always wears them first and hands them down to us. That is why," Danny sighed gloomily. "They often don't even fit right."

"Maybe Father will have more money sometime," Mark suggested encouragingly. "Let's ask Mother if she thinks he will."

Danny and Mark found Mother in the bedroom.

"Mother, do you think Father will ever have any more money?" Mark asked.

"What do you mean, Mark?" Mother smiled.

"Oh, we wish Father were rich like Ronald Mason's father is. Ronald has all sorts of toys and games and fine clothes and things. He is always getting something new, and we never do. We always have to wear things that were too little for Samuel and are nearly worn out. And we have only a couple of old things to play with. We were just hoping that someday Father would get more money so that we could get new things like Ronald does."

"Boys," Mother said, "I am very happy with what money Father has. The Lord has been good to us. I know that having more money would not make me a bit happier, and I don't think it would you, either.

"The Bible says, 'Having food and raiment let us be therewith content.' And that is just the way I feel. We have all we need to eat, and we have all the clothes we need to keep us warm. These are good blessings from the Lord, and I am so thankful for them.

"Boys, I feel sorry for Ronald. Really, I do. Did you know that there has been a lot of trouble in his home? His little sister died, and his mother died. All the money that Mr. Mason had, could not keep his daughter and wife from dying. All the money and toys and nice things he gives to Ronald cannot

make Ronald as happy as you are, even though you are much poorer than he.

"And another bigger thing yet that keeps Ronald from being happy is that his father is not a Christian. Therefore, he is often unkind to Ronald and finds him a bother to have around. When Ronald goes home from school in the evening, there is no one there to talk to or play with, except the woman his father has hired to cook and clean for them.

"I feel sorry for Ronald. Neither he nor his father will ever be happy until they find the Lord and live for Him. All the money and all the things that money can buy will never bring them any happiness. 'Better is little with the fear of the Lord than great treasure and trouble therewith.' " Mother quoted to them. Her eyes were shining with the gladness of the Lord.

"I guess we must be richer than Ronald is," Danny said. "I didn't know we had so many more things than he does."

"Boys, it does not matter who has the most things," Mother told them. "All we need to be truly happy is to know the Lord and have His blessing in our home."

"And we have that, don't we, Mother?" Mark asked with satisfaction.

"Yes, praise the Lord, we have that," Mother agreed.

33

Trouble in School

"Do you know what?" Susan whispered.

Daisy gave a warning frown, and Susan quickly turned around and looked at the teacher.

Yes, the teacher was looking at her. "The second grade should study their spelling now," Sister Lois instructed them.

Susan quickly took her spelling book from her desk and opened it.

"Next week we will have a review lesson," she whispered quickly to Daisy. Then she bent her head over her spelling book. "T-o-d-a-y," she spelled. "C-r-e-a-m. F-l-a-g."

She turned her head toward Daisy again. "Our neighbors have a flag," she whispered.

"What did you say, Susan?" the teacher asked.

Susan's face turned a rosy red. The teacher was waiting for her to answer.

"I said, 'Our neighbors have a flag,' " she mumbled.

"I suppose many people of the world have a flag," Sister Lois agreed. "But you should be studying your spelling lesson now and not talking." Sister Lois spoke firmly. She kept watching Susan until Susan began working on her spelling lesson again.

The day was very warm. A fly buzzed at the window trying to get outside. Susan suddenly closed her book. She got out her notebook and opened it. There was no paper.

"May I borrow a sheet of paper?" she whispered to Daisy. She held up her empty notebook.

Daisy nodded. She took a piece of paper from her notebook and handed it to Susan.

"Thanks," Susan returned. "I wish I could sharpen my pencil." She held up her pencil for Daisy to see.

"Second grade spelling," Sister Lois said. "Susan were you talking again?"

When Susan did not answer, Sister Lois said, "Get your paper and pencils out. Your first word is *today*."

The second grade bent busily over their papers.

"Cream," Sister Lois pronounced.

"My pencil is so dull," Susan whispered to Daisy.

"Susan, come up here to this table to write your spelling words," Sister Lois instructed.

Susan's face flushed a deep red. "I wasn't looking at Daisy's paper," she said quickly.

"You were looking back," the teacher

reminded her, "instead of keeping your eyes on your own paper. Hurry, Susan."

Susan was soon settled at the table. She was too ashamed to look up. She felt like crying. She was sure that all the children were looking at her.

"I wasn't looking at Daisy's paper," she told herself tearfully. "I just told her that my pencil was dull."

"Well, you were not supposed to be talking," her heart reminded her.

"Susan," Sister Lois told her after all the spelling words had been given out, "you should work on your arithmetic now. I want you to keep working at this table for the rest of the day, as you can't seem to keep from talking when you are at your desk."

Tears burned in Susan's eyes as she went to her desk for her arithmetic book. As she fumbled for her notebook, Daisy kindly handed her several sheets of paper. Daisy had remembered that Susan's notebook was empty.

Before long, Sister Lois sat down beside Susan. "You do not seem very happy, Susan," she said kindly, in a quiet whisper.

Susan did not answer. A big tear splashed on

her arithmetic book.

"Your problem, Susan, is that you talk too much," Sister Lois told her kindly. "Not just during books, but most of the time. Talking too much always gets us into trouble. I want you to work at keeping your mouth and tongue still. Maybe this verse from Proverbs will help you. I want you to learn it, and say it to me before you go home from school this evening," Sister Lois laid a slip of paper on Susan's arithmetic book.

"Whoso keepeth his mouth and his tongue keepeth his soul from troubles," Susan read.

Was that in the Bible? Soberly Susan read it again. "I am going to learn to keep my mouth and tongue still," Susan promised herself earnestly.

34

"I Love You, Grandmother"

"Mother, I want to do something for Grandmother," Edward said. "What can I do?"

Mother thought for a moment. "There might be weeds to pull in her garden or grass to pull from around her trees. She might have wastebaskets that you could empty, too. Why don't you just run over and ask her what you could do to help her?"

"Oh, may I, Mother?" Edward asked eagerly.

"Yes, you may go right now," Mother answered with a smile.

Edward's bare feet scarcely touched the grass as he flew across the lawn to Grandmother's trailer house.

Edward peeped through the screen door. "Where are you, Grandmother? May I come in? I came to help you, Grandmother."

"Yes, Edward, you may come in," Grandmother called quietly from the couch. "How did you know that I needed help?" Grandmother smiled at him.

"Don't you feel well, Grandmother?" Edward asked. "Why are you lying down? Shall I call Mother?"

"No, dear. I just have a little headache. I will be all right. You don't need to call Mother."

"I came to help you, Grandmother," Edward said. "Do you have any wastebaskets I could empty?"

"You may look, Edward," Grandmother smiled. "I think you might find something."

Edward ran to look. Yes, there was an oatmeal box and a few papers in the kitchen wastebasket. He would empty that for Grandmother.

Then he saw the dishes on the sink. A cup and a saucer, a spoon, a knife, a fork, and a plate. Grandmother had not washed her breakfast dishes.

"O Grandmother, may I wash your dishes for you?" Edward asked eagerly.

"Yes, Edward," Grandmother answered, "that would be very kind of you."

Happily, Edward ran water into the sink and added a couple drops of detergent. With Grandmother's yellow and blue dishcloth, he washed the dishes carefully. Back and forth, back and forth, he rubbed. Finally he was finished.

"Now, what may I do, Grandmother? Do you have any weeds or grass to pull?"

"You may pull grass from around the trees in my yard," Grandmother told him. "And around the rocks in my flower bed border. I will be glad if you do that for me," Grandmother smiled at

Edward.

"Grandmother, I love you," Edward said suddenly. He leaned over and gave Grandmother a kiss on her cheek.

"I love you, too, Edward," Grandmother answered. "You are helping me so nicely; I believe my headache is gone."

"Really, Grandmother?" Edward's eyes sparkled. "Then I am glad that I came over to help you. I believe the Lord wanted me to come over, don't you?"

"I am sure He did, Edward," Grandmother answered with tears in her eyes. "You just be sure always to do what the Lord wants you to do."

"I will," Edward promised, as he ran to pull grass for Grandmother.

35

A Merry Face

"Mother, I think that Carrie has such a nice face," Milton said one day.

"Do you?" Mother smiled. "I think she does, too. Carrie is a happy little girl."

"But I don't like Mary's face," Milton continued.

Mother looked surprised. She knew that Mary was really a pretty little girl. Why didn't Milton like her face? Mother thought for a few minutes. Then she asked with a smile, "What about my face, Milton. Do you like it?"

"Oh, Mother," Milton said eagerly. "Your face

is the nicest face of all."

Mother laughed and patted Milton on the head gently. "I am glad you like it, Milton," she said. "Father has a nice face, too, doesn't he?"

"Yes, he has," Milton agreed emphatically.

"Let me tell you something," Mother said to Milton. "It is how we feel about people that makes their faces look nice to us. Did you know that?"

Milton shook his head.

"You always enjoy being with Carrie, don't you, Milton?"

"Oh, yes," Milton agreed. "She is the happiest little friend I have."

"And how about Mary?" Mother continued.

"Mary is always so grouchy," Milton

explained. "I don't like to play with her."

"Did you know that the Bible says, 'A merry heart maketh a cheerful countenance'?" Mother wondered. "The countenance is the face. If our hearts are happy, then our faces will be cheerful and happy. If our hearts are not happy, then our faces will not be happy, either. That is why you don't like Mary's face. It is pouty and selfish-looking so much of the time, because she is selfish and unhappy inside.

"I have seen your face look that way, too, Milton," Mother told him. "Sometimes when I ask you to go for your nap, or do a little job for me that you don't want to do, you get that pouty look on your face. I can tell that your heart is not happy by the look on your face."

Milton looked sober. "I don't want that kind of face," he told Mother.

"Then you must keep your heart happy," Mother told him. "Don't let cross or selfish thoughts come into your mind. Keep your thoughts always happy and kind, and you will always have a merry, happy face."